The Making of a Public Profession

Frances Kahn Zemans

Victor G. Rosenblum

American Bar Foundation
Chicago
1981

Library of Congress Catalog Card Number: 80-71013

ISBN 0-910058-97-0 Cloth
ISBN 0-910058-88-1 Paper

© 1981 American Bar Foundation
Chicago, Illinois

PRINTED IN U.S.A.

AMERICAN BAR FOUNDATION

THE AMERICAN BAR FOUNDATION is engaged in research on legal problems and the legal profession. Its mission is to conduct research that will enlarge the understanding and improve the functioning of law and legal institutions. The Foundation's work is supported by the American Bar Association, the American Bar Endowment, The Fellows of the American Bar Foundation, and by outside funds granted for particular research projects.

CONTENTS

LIST OF TABLES

LIST OF FIGURES

FOREWORD

In 1974 the American Bar Foundation initiated a research program on legal education and the professionalization process. Endeavoring to clarify the vital transition from lay people to lawyers, this program of study has included research on the law student, the law faculty, and the legal profession. In addition, a number of projects have dealt with institutional issues regarding the nature of legal education (e.g., law teaching materials, methods, and educational innovations). Our purpose in conducting several studies of law school education simultaneously was to achieve through a range of approaches, methods, and frames of reference a greater understanding of the impact of this "legal" institution on the professional development of lawyers. The specific study undertaken by Frances Kahn Zemans and Victor G. Rosenblum is a key element in our program, because of both its anticipated agenda and its broader promise for illuminating fundamental issues about the structure of the legal profession and the process and dynamics that shape its character.

The Making of a Public Profession has more than realized this promise. In the midst of the then current concerns about lawyer competence and criticism about the role and responsibility of law school training, the study's goal was to provide an empirically grounded assessment of the practicing profession's perspectives on legal education. Popular debates about the adequacy or inadequacy of what law school does and can do were based on assumptions about lawyers' attitudes and activities but were not systematically informed by the alumni of that process—the lawyers themselves, who constitute the practicing profession. Given the benefit of their careers, how do lawyers reflect on their individual educational experiences? Is there consensus among practitioners and, if so, on what issues? Do lawyers of different age and career stage diverge in their views? What about the graduates of national versus regional versus local law schools? These are but a few of the questions underlying the research and ultimately affecting the design and development of this project. While it was recognized from the outset that lawyers provide only one set of perceptions, their views are nonetheless educated by practice and thus offer perhaps a unique opportunity for examining the linkages between the "work" of law schools and the "work" of lawyers.

As the chapters that follow so clearly reveal, Zemans and Rosenblum achieved their goal and more. Through careful and rigorous analyses of data—whether on lawyers' background, context of practice, specialization, perceptions of prestige and success, contributions to skills and knowledge made by law schools, or skills necessary to the practice of law—these investigators provide rich information and rare insight about the role and limits of legal education. Their findings add to our knowledge about such issues as the complexity and diversity of the legal profession, the effect of law school credentials and early career opportunities on career access and mobility, and the relationship between the work of lawyers and their perceptions of both the necessary skills and the necessary role of law schools. In so doing, this work substantially contributes to our understanding of law schools as gatekeepers and socializers for the legal profession and, perhaps even more importantly, of the impact of status hierarchies within the legal profession on the form of contemporary American legal education itself.

In this study, as throughout this research program in legal education, the Foundation was ably advised by the American Bar Association's Special Committee for a Study of Legal Education. In particular, special thanks is extended to Chairman Ronald J. Foulis for encouraging the Foundation to do what it does best—pursue independent inquiry that advances fundamental knowledge about law. Similarly our thanks are extended to all other members of this committee who provided during their respective terms continued concern and counsel: Barbara W. Schwartz Bromberg, LeRoy Collins, Thomas B. Curtis, Robert McC. Figg, Jr., Ronald J. Foulis, Reginald T. Hamner, Patricia Roberts Harris, Richard W. Nahstoll, Chris L. Otorowski, Edward F. Rodriguez, Jr., Walter V. Schaefer, David C. Stoup, and Samuel D. Thurman.

Felice J. Levine
Spencer L. Kimball
Codirectors
American Bar Foundation
Research Program in Legal Education

PREFACE

The centrality of law in American society has contributed to the prominence and power of the legal profession. Yet at the same time that lawyers have enjoyed high social standing, they have been the objects of considerable criticism. As formal legal education has gained a virtual monopoly over the training of lawyers for practice, negative views of the profession have been transposed and elaborated into criticism of law schools and their approach to law and the legal system. While there has been a substantial debate between the defenders and detractors of legal education, little systematic evidence has been available to determine the contribution of law schools to the professional development of lawyers and how it compares with that of other socializing agents and experiences. The study reported here taps the views of the practicing bar as a step toward understanding the making of this public profession.

The successful completion of a research project of this magnitude is dependent upon the contributions of many people. We are indebted first of all to the more than 500 practicing attorneys in Chicago who took time from their busy schedules to thoughtfully complete a very lengthy questionnaire. We are also grateful to Henry Ryder, who recruited pretest respondents from among the Board of Managers of the Indiana State Bar Association and their Legal Education and Admissions Committee. Throughout the study we met with the American Bar Association's Special Committee for a Study of Legal Education, who engaged us in fruitful discussions over the direction of the study and the interpretation of the data.

Graduate student research assistants make enormous contributions to social science studies, and this one is no exception. In loose chronological order, this project benefited from the assistance of the following individuals. Jay Hook and Jane Tyler, then graduate students at Northwestern University, participated in the early questionnaire design, pre-testing, and data collection stages. The data were coded at a remarkable level of 99.2 percent intercoder reliability by Joseph Bessette, Neil Ciminero, Christopher Colmo, Alan Emdin, and Kenneth Holland, graduate students at the University of Chicago at the time. Joseph Bessette remained with the project to research the literature on legal education and the legal profession and to provide thoughtful assistance in a number of ways. The data analysis was made possible through the very able efforts and advice of Susan Ryzewic, a graduate student at the University of Chicago who kindly agreed to work beyond her original time commitment to see the analysis to completion. A number of indi-viduals from the Bar Foundation staff also provided essential assistance. Katherine Rosich organized the codebook, Phyllis Satkus handled the data processing, and Glenda Hargrove patiently deciphered, typed, and retyped innumerable drafts.

An earlier draft of the manuscript was read in its entirety by Spencer Kimball, Richard Lempert, and Felice Levine, each of whom did a care-ful reading and provided us with numerous suggestions for improve-ment, in some cases convincing us of the need for further analysis of the data. We are most appreciative of their time-consuming efforts and ex-tremely pleased with the resulting improvements in the text. Finally, Louise Kaegi of the Foundation's editorial staff worked to keep our meaning clear and linguistic usage correct. To all of these people we ex-tend our gratitude for their important contributions to the improvement of the final product.

The American Bar Foundation has provided an extremely hospitable and supportive atmosphere for conducting our research. Although neither of the authors was on the staff of the Foundation, we received the full benefits of colleagueship. Very special thanks are due to Felice Levine, who provided continued intellectual guidance and support throughout the life of the project, including in particular truly construc-tive criticisms of all aspects of our work from questionnaire design to sampling, to data analysis and interpretation, and finally to textual clarity. Both quantitatively and qualitatively her contributions have been remarkable and reflect an unselfish concern with the promotion of scholarship. We remain in debt to her and the others named and un-named who provided assistance to us.

Chapter 1
INTRODUCTION

The Legal Profession as Object of Study

The enormous influence that lawyers wield in both the public and the private sectors makes their professional development of particular concern in a democratic society. There is little doubt that the legal profession is both ubiquitous and extremely influential in the life of the American polity. The prominence of lawyers in public elective and appointive office, even considering in addition the lawyers holding numerous other government jobs or serving as important policy advisors, represents only a part of the political role of the bar.[1] More pervasive and potentially more important is the public impact of the bar in its generally private role as counselor and advocate of private interests.

In his already classic treatise, *The Growth of American Law* (1950), Hurst astutely notes the direct influence of lawyers on the doctrinal development of the law:

> It is hazardous to apportion creative credit among scholars, counsel, and judges, for the erection of these doctrinal bridges to decision. Judicial

1. The public role of lawyers is clear from their substantial overrepresentation among both the elected and the appointed officials who govern us. Beginning as early as participation in the Continental Congress and the signing of the Declaration of Independence, and continuing through occupancy of the top positions in the executive branch (president, vice-president, cabinet officers) and in state offices (Schlesinger, 1957, p. 28), lawyers have dominated public positions throughout our history. The national legislature presents the same picture: in 1978, 69.6 percent of U.S. senators and 52.2 percent of U.S. representatives gave their occupation as "lawyer" (*Facts on File,* 1978, p. 107c). Although the predominance of attorneys continues to decline, state legislatures still have a high proportion of lawyers relative to the population as a whole. In 1979, 20 percent of all state legislators were lawyers, ranging from none in Delaware to more than half (53 percent) in Virginia (*Occupational Profile of State Legislatures,* 1979). At the local level, as well, lawyers figure very prominently in political office and activity (Jacob, 1978, pp. 74–75).

opinions typically do not acknowledge such indebtedness. Thus the main evidence of the lineage of a formula is apt to be the fact that it is found outside the Reports before it is sanctioned in them. It would be presumptuous to claim that John Marshall could not, or would not, have developed the argument of his basic rulings without Webster's promptings. On the other hand there are plausible reasons for crediting the lawyer with a substantial role in fashioning the doctrinal tools of law. Briefs display an abounding fertility of invention; few judges are of the stamp of Marshall; at best the judge is much removed by even a few years on the bench from the currents of the times, and hence must necessarily rely on the lawyer for the concepts which will make intelligible the on-going world of affairs which suitors bring into the courtroom (p. 338).[2]

This role of lawyers reflects in part the tendency for fundamental social questions to become questions of law in this country, a trend continually recognized since Tocqueville's observation almost 150 years ago (1963, vol. 1, p. 280). Yet even such recognition that issues are likely to become the subject of judicial debate, thus involving lawyers as advocates, neglects the more general public role of the profession as it is played out in the day-to-day activities of the practicing bar. In his study of legal education for the Carnegie Foundation in 1921, Alfred Reed distinguished the practice of law as "a public function, in a sense that the practice of other professions, such as medicine, is not. Practicing lawyers do not merely render to the community a social service . . . . They are part of the governing mechanism of the state. Their functions are in a broad sense political" (p. 3).

As experts in and interpreters of the law, lawyers in private practice play a major role in the distribution of society's valuables, most particularly rights guaranteed by law. It is they who filter many of the public's demands on their government and determine when and under what circumstances public authority will be invoked; they are the primary gatekeepers to the administration of justice. Their advice typically determines how economic exchanges are arranged and whether any sanctions will be pursued for unfulfilled obligations. Decisions to attempt to secure legal rights or fulfill legal obligations are most often dependent on the advice of counsel. This advisory role is not, as some have thought, limited to the affairs of business interests and only a small proportion of the population. The ubiquity of lawyers in American life is indicated by the results of a recent national survey of the public: almost two-thirds of the adult population have consulted a lawyer at least once about a personal nonbusiness legal problem (Curran, 1977, p. 186).[3] The growth of the public sector in general, and of government regulation of larger pro-

2. For further elaboration of the influence of lawyers' arguments on the development of American constitutional law, see Freund (1949), Twiss (1942), and Vose (1958).

3. This extensive role for lawyers is almost peculiarly American. Compared with other industrialized nations the United States has the highest proportion of lawyers (Friedman, 1977, pp. 23–24). They, no doubt, encourage the translation of many issues handled by nonlawyers (e.g., real estate or insurance agents) in other countries into goods subject to the substantial influence of the legal profession.

portions of American life in particular, has contributed further to the involvement of lawyers in every aspect of our lives.[4]

Professional Power and Public Image

The power and influence exercised by lawyers has been matched by consistently high social standing. In the National Opinion Research Center's 1947 and 1963 studies of the general standing of various occupations, lawyers received prestige scores of 86 and 89, respectively, on a scale from 20 to 100.[5] This compares extremely favorably with the 93 received by physicians, the highest score given to any occupational group.

Yet despite their high standing with respect to prestige, lawyers have not enjoyed a very positive public image. Indeed they have long been viewed with a peculiar combination of awe and contempt. Although criticism of lawyers and the legal profession takes many forms, underlying much of it is a feeling that law has become curiously dissociated from justice, that lawyers look more to private gain from advocacy of the interests of their clients than to the public good—a view expressed in William Sloane Coffin, Jr.'s often-quoted attack on James D. St. Clair as a "hired gun" for Richard Nixon during the Watergate affair. This feeling is also manifested in repeated references to the tendency of lawyers to complicate and delay matters, to promote litigation, and to use their technical expertise in the law for questionable goals. Newspaper columnist Art Buchwald once stated in his inimitable fashion that "it isn't the bad lawyers who are screwing up the justice system in this country—it's the good lawyers. . . . If you have two competent lawyers on opposite sides, a trial that should take three days could easily last six months" (1978).[6]

4. Discounting the attribution of increased demand for lawyers' services to the growth of government regulations, Pashigian (1977) concludes that the performance of the economy is the more important factor. His conclusions are limited, however, by the coincidence in rapid growth in both regulations and the economy at the times (1920s and 1960s) of increased demand for lawyers.

Even if he is correct that the increased demand (i.e., payment) for lawyers that encouraged growth of the supply resulted largely from economic growth, the expansion of government regulation alone has the effect of increasing the actual and potential influence of lawyers on the public.

5. The scores are based on mean responses to a scale ranging from 20 (poor) to 100 (excellent). The consistency of prestige scores across years was not unique to lawyers. The product-moment correlation coefficient between the 1947 and 1963 scores was a rather astounding .99 (Hodge, Siegel, & Rossi, 1966, p. 326). For a complete discussion of the survey see Siegel (1971).

In addition to being stable, the prestige scores do not vary from subgroup to subgroup within the society. Indeed, comparisons indicate that "occupational prestige hierarchies are similar from country to country," reflecting "the fundamental, but gross similarities among the occupational systems of modern nations" (Hodge et al., p. 322).

6. In a similar vein, a *Wall Street Journal* editorial entitled "Dreaming the Impossible Dream" (1976) speculated on the benefits to be realized if attorneys followed the lead of doctors in some areas by striking in protest over rising malpractice premiums. The predicted "Paradise Regained" went as follows:

The normal intercourse of life would flow smoothly, unchecked by the law's and the lawyer's

There is an implication in both contemporary criticisms and some historical commentary that earlier in our history lawyers were different, that they operated according to a higher level of morality, that the law was a "noble" profession. Hurst, for example, speaks of "the profession's golden age of public leadership—the years from 1765 to1830—[during which] we find qualities of independence of judgment, and pride in the responsibility and dignity of legal counseling and the shaping of social institutions, such as were not manifested with equal vigor later on" (1950, p. 366). Some even offer explanations for the decline of old values such as civic virtue and public responsibility. Finding such values "ill-suited" and "less and less intelligible" to the successful lawyer in the changing nineteenth-century society, Schudson (1977) indicates that "the most available redefinition of the lawyer's role, in the context of a democratic market society, was that the lawyer would do the greatest good by submitting to the will of his clients, regardless of the justness of their causes" (p. 192).

Despite the strong implications and even explicit conclusions that the legal profession was once quite different and perceived to be more concerned with justice and the social good than was later the case, substantial contrary evidence exists. A negative view of lawyers is implicit in colonial attempts to get along without them (Pound, 1953; Warren, 1966) and explicit in early statutes severely restricting their activities.[7] These efforts were ultimately unsuccessful, and by the time of the American Revolution lawyers had generally attained both social status and economic success (Chroust, 1957–58; Pound, 1953). Despite these achievements, however, Perry Miller concludes that the dominant view in the revolutionary era was "that lawyers were by the very nature of their profession hypocrites, ready to defend a bad cause as well as a good one, for a fee, inherently corrupt and therefore unworthy of the title of American" (1962, p. 17). Even Charles Warren, who contends that the populace "mistook effects for cause" in its hostility to lawyers, recognizes a negative public opinion of lawyers: "Irritated by . . . excessive litigation, by the increase of suits on debts and mortgage foreclosures, and by the system of fees and court costs established by the Bar Associations, the people at large . . . attributed all their evils to the existence of lawyers in the community" (1966, pp. 214–15). Warren compiled evidence of negative public attitudes toward lawyers from letters and

---

limitless capacity to complicate and tangle things. Disputes would have to be resolved by common sense and mutual trust, rather than on the basis of who could hire the fastest gun. The wheels of commerce would turn more swiftly as people without special training in obfuscation and logic-chopping made clear and understandable agreements (p. 24).

7. See Kimball's *Historical Introduction to the Legal System, Cases and Materials* (1961, pp. 452–54) for selected sections of 1 Hening, *Statutes at Large of Virginia* 302 (1823). These acts by the Virginia Grand Assembly from 1645 to 1682 show an example of legislative attempts to abolish "mercenary attorneys" and subsequent repeals and revisions reflecting recognition that such an end was not possible. Eventually the legislature began to set fee limits and ultimately to set up licensing standards.

documents written between 1789 and 1815, a period centrally within Hurst's "golden age." Yet Warren's criticisms have a peculiarly contemporary ring, concentrating as they do on malpractice, excessive fees, promotion of litigation, and the amassing of wealth by lawyers (chapter 10). A later ante-bellum view of the legal profession presents the same picture:

> To conceal truth, to pervert evidence, to mislead and brow-beat judges, are supposed to be the great attainments of legal ambition. . . .
> The reasons for the obloquy cast upon the legal profession are numerous. At present we shall notice only two; the expense attending to a suit of law, and the delay.[8]

It may of course be, as Hurst (1950) actually contends, that this characterization of the bar reflects those among its numbers "who set the tone, and stood as models of professional success" (p. 368) and that the nineteenth century observed a change in tone from one of public leadership to technical expertise and partisan representation. Whatever changes took place, however, there is agreement throughout all this commentary that the legal profession was and is a primary actor in the polity and economy of America.

Law School and Access to the Profession

Concomitant with what Hurst perceived to be the changing tone and image of the legal profession came substantial changes in the nature of preparation for the professional role. During the colonial period when the profession had not yet reached its zenith of status or power, anyone with aspirations to practice law first sought an apprenticeship in the office of a member of the bar. At that time colleges did not offer courses in the law, and no independent law schools existed.

Although formal instruction in the law was first provided in England at the Inns of Court,[9] the first modern schooling in the common law began in 1753 with Blackstone's appointment at Oxford. By the end of the American Revolution a number of schools in the United States began establishing chairs in the law, the first being William and Mary College in 1779. University study of the law was at that time closely tied to the study of such allied disciplines as philosophy, political economy, and ethics. Those who chose this route to begin their legal careers were educated to make the direct connections between the law and the broader social order which were the basis for the models of public leadership of the bar in the late eighteenth and early nineteenth centuries.

At the same time that university-based study of the law was growing, the practicing bar began establishing independent law schools exclusive-

8. Miller (1962, p. 275) is quoting from James Jackson, "Law and Lawyers. Is the Profession of the Advocate Consistent with Perfect Integrity?" 28 *The Knickerbocker Magazine* 378–83 (November 1846).

9. The Inns of Court educational system (for English barristers) was revived with the establishment of the Council of Legal Education in 1852 (Smith, 1979, p. 5).

ly to provide preparation for the actual practice of law. The first of these, the Litchfield Law School of Connecticut, was opened in 1784. It was established and operated by a lawyer (Judge Tapping Reeve) and was concerned with the needs of practitioners. Instruction offered in schools such as Litchfield differed substantially in orientation from that received in universities from professors of law who were devoted to study rather than practice.

In 1826 these two trends merged in the establishment of a separate school of law within an established university with the founding of Harvard Law School. The merger was not an equal one—direct control over legal education had begun to move inexorably away from practitioners and toward educators, who were increasingly likely to have had minimal practice experience if any. The opening of a separate law school within the halls of such a venerable institution as Harvard reflected and at the same time augmented the enhanced status of the legal profession. While entry to the profession through apprenticeship remained the major route to the profession for some time, the trend toward the formalization of legal education had been set.[10]

The next major change in legal education was instituted in 1870 at Harvard by Christopher Columbus Langdell, who believed that law was a science whose tools were all to be found in the case law. The library was to be the laboratory of this new science, with all materials necessary to its study housed therein. The case method introduced by Langdell was eventually to become the basic method of instruction in virtually every law school in the country.

Based upon reading and analyzing appellate opinions to facilitate the development of analytic skills, Langdell's approach marked a drastic departure from the experience of the apprentice. Formal legal education was to train its students to "think like lawyers," with the nuts and bolts of practice to be gained after the completion of formal schooling. With respect to socialization to the profession, this mode of instruction and orientation to the case law was also quite distinct from the study of law grounded in philosophy, political economy, and social ethics. One could now enter the profession with neither the practical experience of apprenticeship nor the broad liberal education of the earlier university training in the law. Consistent with the nineteenth-century analytic jurisprudence of John Austin, which insisted on the separation of law from ethics, the study of law had now become technically divorced from concerns with social justice in both its theoretical formulations and its practical applications.

These developments within the law schools were of critical importance to the profession as the organized bar promoted and states increasingly

10. For a description of legal education in the nineteenth century see Hurst (1950, pp. 256–76). For a general history of American legal education see Harno (1953).

required law school attendance as a prerequisite of admission to the bar.[11] While one may agree with Boyer and Cramton that "a central historical datum is that law schools have monopolized the function of 'gatekeepers' to the profession for a relatively short time" (1974, p. 224), that monopoly is now virtually total. By 1970 only a few states even allowed admission to the bar by apprenticeship, and where allowed, that right is only very rarely exercised.[12] Thus, law schooling had become synonymous with American legal education. Although ultimate control over access to the powerful and prestigious legal profession was retained by the individual states, law school had become a nearly universal prerequisite, and as such it came to be viewed as the primary if not the only socializing agent for the development of future professionals. Thus, if law schools were shaping the profession, then criticisms of the profession and its role in society could reasonably focus on the law school and its presumed impact. And indeed such criticisms were forthcoming.

11. Requirements (including law school attendance) for admission to the bar in every state have been published annually in the *Review of Legal Education*, first published in 1926 by the Carnegie Foundation for the Advancement of Teaching (under the title *Annual Review of Legal Education*) and from 1935 on by the American Bar Association Section of Legal Education and Admissions to the Bar.

At the same time the organized bar became more involved in the accreditation of law schools. Indeed the American Bar Association (ABA) promoted law school education as the only appropriate preparation for practice and established standards for law schools many years before the states required them. In 1921 the ABA adopted the recommendations of its Section of Legal Education and Admissions to the Bar that all candidates for admission to the bar be law school graduates and that their law schools meet four criteria: require at least two years of college for admission, require three years of law school study (longer if part time), provide an adequate library, and have a "sufficient" number of full-time faculty ("Report of the Special Committee to the Section of Legal Education and Admissions to the Bar of the American Bar Association," 1921). By 1976, 36 states and the District of Columbia required that an applicant for admission to the bar be a graduate of an ABA-approved law school. Nine other states effectively limited their admissions similarly (Fossum, pp. 521–22).

The ABA has thus become the accrediting agency for law schools and has been so recognized by the U.S. Office of Education, Department of Health, Education, and Welfare (see "Nationally Recognized Accrediting Agencies and Associations," Office of Education, Department of Health, Education, and Welfare, 1976). According to a recently reported survey in the *Los Angeles Daily Journal* only five states (California, Georgia, Indiana, Mississippi, and Vermont) allow graduates of non-ABA-approved law schools to sit for the bar exam to obtain a license to practice (Dickerson, 1976). Although it seems inconsistent that Virginia and Washington allow admission to the bar without a law degree but fail to grant the same privilege to graduates of non-ABA-approved law schools (as indicated by their exclusion from the states listed above), this reflects the status of apprenticeship as a distinct route to licensure. In both of those states that mode of preparation must be registered in advance and includes working in a law office with a specifically designed program of study. If formal schooling is chosen, it must be in an ABA-approved law school.

12. California, Mississippi, Virginia, Vermont, and Washington still allow admission to the bar without any law school attendance. These represent only half the number of states that did not require attendance at law school at the beginning of the decade.

Criticisms of the Law School as Socializing Agent

While both numerous and vocal, the critics of legal education have largely concentrated their attacks on two alleged failures of law schools. First, they are faulted for being insufficiently practical in their failure to prepare their graduates for the day-to-day tasks involved in competent law practice. Second, law schools' neglect of the public functions of the profession, in both policy making and the distribution of justice, is blamed for the failure of the profession to adequately meet its social role. Each of these charges bears consideration.

Once legal education moved from law offices to law schools, questions arose over whether the capabilities necessary for the actual practice of law were receiving adequate attention. This issue became prominent after the revolution in legal education, begun under Langdell's tutelage at Harvard, dissociated legal learning from legal practice. A particularly vituperative attack was unleashed by Judge Jerome Frank (1950), who criticized Langdell for successfully spreading the myths that law is a science, that all its available materials are contained in printed books, and that what qualifies a person to teach law is "not experience . . . in using law, but experience in learning law" (p. 226). Judge Frank went on to deride Langdell's emphasis upon upper-court opinions as teaching the mere "tail end" of a case. Law students subjected to Langdell's "upper-court myth and legal rule magic" were likened to "future horticulturists studying solely cut flowers," "future architects studying merely pictures of buildings," and "prospective dog breeders who never see anything but stuffed dogs" (pp. 225, 227). Frank urged the development of law schools in which students would learn by doing as well as by reading and talking about doing (1933).[13]

Since Frank's early criticisms (1933, 1947, 1950) there has been a deluge of attacks on the ivory-tower character of legal education (e.g., Benthall-Nietzel, 1975; Llewellyn, 1935; Stern, 1972). Most of these critics have objected to the law schools' emphasis upon the theoretical aspects of law almost to the exclusion of the more practical. Of particular concern have been young attorneys who do not join firms where they can receive such training and who by default must develop their practical expertise through trial and error experimentation on their clients. "Why," asks a recent critic, "be proud that law students, who come to school for three years in order to become lawyers leave *not trained to be lawyers?*" (Church, 1975, p. 1). The literature is in fact replete with debates over the proper role of law schools in the training of lawyers for practice.[14] One response to criticism is that law schools provide, and in-

13. In an early statement of the realist position, "Why Not a Clinical Lawyer School?" (1933), Frank calls for law schools to recognize that legal rules and principles are not most important in deciding legal cases and to alter their curricula accordingly. See also Frank's "A Plea for Lawyer Schools" (1947).

14. See as examples Boden's "Is Legal Education Deserting the Bar?" (1970), a general discussion of the issue of making legal education more practical, and Vukowich's "The

deed should provide, those elements that are important to the profession but that cannot be readily gained elsewhere—hence the concentration on the theoretical at the expense of the more practical.

More recently the most vocal criticism of attorneys for being ill prepared has centered on the trial bar, with the critics often found in the judiciary. Chief Justice Burger's now famous criticism (1973) of the skills of trial attorneys was matched by former Second Circuit Court of Appeals Chief Judge Irving R. Kaufman's commissioning of the Clare Committee, which proposed prerequisites for the trial bar in that jurisdiction (1975).[15] Similar proposals (1978) have since been recommended to the Judicial Conference of the United States for admission to federal practice generally.[16] The technical incompetence to which these critics have directed their attention is only part of the problem. Law schools are additionally criticized for abstracting issues in the law out of the contexts in which they occur. In doing so they not only fail to provide skills needed to translate problems into legal issues but also neglect the roles of problem solver, counselor, and adviser which constitute much of the contemporary work of lawyers.

Criticisms of law schools for failing to inculcate an understanding of the appropriate social role of the bar dwell on the important policy-making role of lawyers as well as on their more general professional responsibility. In a now classic 1943 law review article that reflected con-

---

Lack of Practical Training in Law Schools: Criticisms, Causes and Programs for Change" (1971), a general review of the issue. The major academic response to growing criticism has been the accelerating evolution of clinical training in law school. For a discussion of this phenomenon see Grossman's "Clinical Legal Education: History and Diagnosis" (1974).

15. See Burger's "The Special Skills of Advocacy: Are Specialized Training and Certification of Advocates Essential to Our System of Justice?" (1973) and the report of the Clare Committee, commissioned by then Chief Judge Irving R. Kaufman of the U.S. Court of Appeals, Second Circuit, to recommend means to improve the quality of advocacy in the federal courts (*Final Report on Proposed Rules for Admission to Practice,* 1975). A brief summary of the controversy as a whole can be found in an article in the *Wall Street Journal* (Green, 1975). Robert L. Clare himself discusses the work of the Clare Committee in an article in the ALI-ABA CLE Review (1975).

16. In 1976 Justice Burger appointed the Committee of the Judicial Conference of the United States to Consider Standards for Admission to Practice in the Federal Courts. The Devitt Committee (informally named after the United States district judge who chaired it, Hon. Edward J. Devitt) commissioned the Federal Judicial Center to do a study of the quality of advocacy in the federal courts. For a review of the committee's work and conclusions see the *Report and Tentative Recommendations of the Committee to Consider Standards for Admission to Practice in the Federal Courts to the Judicial Conference of the United States* (1978). The principal recommendation is that "minimum uniform standards of competency for attorneys in Federal trial courts should be implemented by uniform District Court rules providing for an examination in Federal Practice subjects and four trial experiences in actual or simulated trials" (p. 9). A second recommendation provides for the establishment of attorney performance review committees by all district courts (p. 20). The Judicial Conference of the United States approved only the establishment of pilot programs to test the recommended changes ("Judicial Conference Joins Push for Trial Skills Training," 1979, p. 1466).

cern with the war in which the world was then engulfed, Lasswell and McDougal stressed the important role of lawyers in making public policy in modern America and called on law schools to provide training for that role. Conceptualizing policy making in very broad terms, they suggested "reorienting every phase of law school curricula and skill training toward the achievement of clearly defined democratic values in all the areas of social life where lawyers have or can assert responsibility" (p. 207). In calling for training geared to the political and social impact of the law, they opposed those who "insist that law schools should have no concern whatsoever with policies, goals, or values—that the only proper concern of law schools is method, science disinfected of all preference" (p. 205). Some 30 years later, Boyer and Cramton echoed those same concerns. "Current travails in the world of affairs," they say, "reinforce doubts that the law schools have fully equipped the present generation of lawyers to perform their professional tasks" (1974, p. 222).

Suggestions that law schools concern themselves with social effects of the law and orient their curricula toward encouraging future lawyers to use their specialized knowledge and skills for social good were reiterated with rising frequency and volume during the turbulent sixties. Like most other institutions law schools did not survive unscathed. Criticisms were focused particularly on the schools' failure to prepare their students for practice that was socially useful or to expose the role of law in perpetuating social inequities.[17] The statement of the chairman of the Association of American Law Schools (AALS) curriculum committee, Charles J. Meyers, serves well as an example of the concerns generated: "legal education is in a crisis and . . . fundamental changes must be made soon. It is not only that law students over the country are reaching the point of open revolt but also that law faculties themselves, particularly the younger members, share the view that legal education is too rigid, too narrow" (1968 committee report quoted in Thorne, 1973, p. 101). Law schools were criticized for failing to respond to new demands for changes in the administration of justice, in serving the legal needs of the public, and in the delivery of legal services. Law school was being given virtually unlimited credit for molding the shape of the profession.

No less virulent were criticisms of legal education for its failure to take cognizance of the interpersonal attributes requisite to effective counseling, and for its concentration on the interests of the rich and propertied. The desired interpersonal capacities are of course part of the package of "practical" skills considered important to the practice of

17. For discussions of these views of legal education see Stone (1971) and Wasserstein and Green (1970). For an attack on law schools and the legal establishment for constraining the delivery of legal services by tacitly discouraging their graduates from practicing public interest law see Nader (1970, especially p. 496). We will consider these criticisms of legal education in detail when we discuss the professional and social responsibility of lawyers in chapter 7.

law. But this criticism also reflected the call of the 1960s to use the law for social good and to train for service beyond the upper stratum of society.

These and similar criticisms dealt largely with the "hidden curriculum" of legal education, the message that comes across most clearly because it is the medium through which instruction is presented.[18] The orientation of legal schooling toward the development of analytic skills ("thinking like a lawyer"), with reliance on case materials that reflect the legal problems of that segment of the society able to afford the appeals for which written judicial opinions are rendered, has been attacked as conveying an image of the law as distinct from justice and substantive concerns. Legal education is thus charged with an institutional lack of concern with the impact of professional activities on the broader social system or, for that matter, on individual clients.[19] Perhaps most basically law schools have been criticized for presenting inherently value-laden materials as if they were or could be value free, with the result that communication about the value orientation of the law and its administration is all the more insidious.[20]

These criticisms of legal education as the basic source of or at least the major contributor to all the ills thought to plague the legal profession and its role in the social order give us cause to inquire just what the role of formal schooling is or can be among the range of experiences encountered by all professionals. What is the potential contribution of schooling to the socialization of professionals, and what is the appropri-

18. Tapp and Levine (1974) similarly recognize the importance of the hidden curriculum to legal socialization more generally. See Jackson (1966, pp. 353–55) for the development of this concept with respect to elementary education.

19. See for example Tapp and Levine (1974, p. 52) and Cahn and Cahn (1966, 1970).

20. Law schools responded to the tumult of the sixties with a number of curricular innovations, most of them involving an increased emphasis on clinical training in which legal issues could be considered in context. Francis A. Allen, former president of the Association of American Law Schools, notes a rather ironic connection between the practical and the value criticisms of legal education:

> Indeed, the efforts of the schools to instill in young lawyers an appreciation for the dimensions of the social crisis and to bring intelligence and knowledge to bear in the solution of the problems that have been spawned by it, has been pointed to by some bar spokesmen as evidence of the failure of professional education (1976, p. 52).

As Allen points out as an example, the Clare Committee questioned the value of such "esoteric" courses as urban development, law and economics, and law and psychoanalysis. The Supreme Court of the State of Indiana, concerned over the rising rate of bar examination failures, responded by specifying selected law school courses as requisite to sitting for the bar examination. In so doing they implied that the new flexibility in law school curricula had contributed to incompetent law graduates. See sections III and V of Rule 13, "Requirements for Admission to Examination," adopted December 18, 1973, and effective February 1, 1974, and subsequently amended several times, most recently December 14, 1977, effective January 1, 1978 (*Burns Indiana Statutes Annotated, Court Rules,* Book 2, 1980, pp. 251–53). The Supreme Court of South Carolina subsequently instituted similar restrictions (Rule 5A, "Qualifications for Admission," as amended 1979, in *Code of Laws of South Carolina 1976 Annotated, Court Rules,* Cumulative Supplement, 1979, pp. 163–67).

ate role of formal training in socializing future practitioners to membership in this powerful profession? To answer these questions we turned to
the practicing bar.[21]

The Views of the Practicing Bar

Although there is an overabundance of commentary about legal education and numerous proposals for change, most are based upon anec-
dotes and personal history rather than a systematic empirical foundation. Furthermore, while criticism centers on the inadequacy of preparation for the actual practice of law, little has been heard from the practicing bar as a whole. Lest we be misunderstood, the practicing bar *has*
been represented in this debate by a few extremely vocal critics. For example, at the peak of the period of student malaise, a young law professor remarked, "There is not a single lawyer I know with whom I went to
law school who feels that his legal education adequately prepared him
for the practice of law (or anything else for that matter)" (Savoy, 1970,
p. 444). Contrary to much of this public rhetoric, our survey—which is
the subject of this book—revealed that practicing lawyers are on the
whole satisfied with the legal education received in law school. Taking
four questions as a barometer, more than 70 percent of the practicing
bar express satisfaction with their own law school experiences in response to at least three of the questions.[22] Nevertheless, such figures,

21. See chapter 2 for an operational definition of *practicing bar*. See note 25 *infra* for a
discussion of different perspectives on socialization.

22. It should be noted that the responses are unrelated to the structural variables considered herein: law school attended or the nature of law practice, including both context
of practice and specialty. The actual questions on which the aggregate response was calculated and the results are as follows:

Do you wish that the goals [of the law school you attended] had been different?

> yes . . . . 25 percent
> no . . . . 75 percent
> ($N = 525$)

Given the courses you took in law school are there any areas of the curriculum which you would
eliminate or drastically shorten?

> yes . . . . 32 percent
> no . . . . 68 percent
> ($N = 515$)

Have you maintained a relationship with your law school in any of the following ways?
recommend it to potential students

> yes . . . . 57 percent
> no . . . . 43 percent
> ($N = 493$)

Given the same circumstances, would you attend the same law school that you did?

> yes . . . . 88 percent
> no . . . . 12 percent
> ($N = 544$)

See appendix 1 for a copy of the questionnaire, which displays these questions in the context within which they were asked (pt. I, pp. 3–5). For a description of the survey design
see chapter 2.

while interesting, do not tell us much about practicing lawyers' depth of feeling or their views regarding the factors that have influenced their professional lives.[23]

While educational prerequisites of certification for practice have become increasingly centered on formal schooling, legal education in the broad sense neither begins upon entry into law school nor ends upon receipt of a diploma. As criticisms over both the competence and the ethics of lawyers continue to abound,[24] law schools have become a popular target. Yet although law school is the route through which aspiring lawyers must generally pass, we have only sparse knowledge about its influence and even less about the process by which individuals become socialized to membership. In making an initial inquiry into this vast and complex area we make use of an as yet untapped resource—the practitioners themselves. Although they are indeed a rather satisfied group with respect to both the practice of law and the law school that provided their entrée, we shall see that they do not make the mistake, made by both defenders and detractors of law schools, of overestimating the role that professional schooling plays in shaping the profession.

Among the characteristics often imputed to a profession is the existence of a community, a shared identity among its members. This implies not only movement through the same rites of passage (law school and bar examination) but also similarities in the work carried out and in the knowledge shared within the group and excluded from outsiders. Indeed, this even implies shared values. Yet lawyers are an extremely diverse lot. Variability in both the practice of law and law schools has been documented at least since the Carnegie Foundation study of legal education more than a half-century ago (Reed, 1921). We will explore the variances in background, law school, nature of practice, and years at the bar in an effort both to provide an accurate picture of an urban bar

23. The first significant attempt to tap the views of the practicing bar was made by Robert Stevens and reported in the *Virginia Law Review* in 1973. In addition there continue to be alumni surveys by individual law schools. Although there are limits to which their results can be generalized, some of the findings are provocative and will be considered in conjunction with our own data.

Two additional empirical studies that focus exclusively on the practicing bar and their evaluation of legal education are both extremely limited. The first, a survey of Illinois attorneys (1,070 respondents from a stratified random sample of 1,865), had a broad data source but was limited to relating a general curricular approach (case study, case study and problem solving, or interdisciplinary) to preparation for service to clients (Dunn, 1970).

A second, more ambitious attempt to survey the views of practicing attorneys was undertaken in conjunction with a study of possible curriculum changes at the University of Kentucky College of Law (Benthall-Nietzel, 1975). Specific findings will be discussed later in conjunction with the presentation of comparable data from our survey of the Chicago bar.

24. For examples see note 11 *supra* and chapter 7, note 8.

and to determine how such experiences affect the process of socialization to the profession.

Despite an implication in the literature on the professions that the process of professionalization does not begin until one enters professional training (Carlin, 1962b, 1966; Becker, 1961), we shall see that with respect both to the development of the skills and attributes important to the practice of law and to the conception of the appropriate role of a professional, early learning remains quite important. Therefore, any evaluation of the current and potential role of formal legal education in the making of a profession must take care not to assume a tabula rasa in entering law students. Prospective lawyers bring to their formal training skills and attributes that are exceedingly important to the practice of law as well as conceptions of the legal profession and of their places therein. While some of these conceptions are reinforced, others are diminished or diverted in later socialization, during professional schooling, and through observations and perceptions of the behavior of those already granted membership in the professional community. These include on-the-job observations of other lawyers as well as perceptions of the rewards and punishments accorded lawyers by the profession and the general society.

In much that has been written about professional education, there is often an analytic divorce of the in-school from the later in-practice professional socialization. The most prominent observations of this disjunction are found in the works of two sociologists, Howard S. Becker and Jerome Carlin, concerned with socialization to the medical and legal professions respectively. Becker concludes in his study of medical students (*Boys in White,* 1961) that influences on the development of attitudes and behavior are by and large narrowly oriented toward success in the role of medical students (rather than a future role as doctors), with faculty judgments as standards of measurement. Quite compatibly, Carlin, concerned about lawyers' behavior and attitudes (*Lawyers on Their Own,* 1962b, and *Lawyers' Ethics,* 1966), stresses the central importance of the nature and context of one's practice to professional demeanor. For Becker and Carlin, formal schooling, while providing a variable for analysis, is largely a way station between personal background and later practice, with the latter largely determinative of professional self-concept and practices. In contrast, this study attempts to connect the two by locating professional schooling within the full context of socialization and reaches some conclusions about schools' actual and potential contributions to the making of professionals. The book focuses on four specific areas of inquiry: aspiration and access to the profession, credentials for the practice of law, the acquisition of skills important to the lawyering enterprise, and the professional responsibility of the bar. With respect to each we seek to determine the role of law school in the making of the legal profession. Although a developmental approach to the socialization process suggests consideration of the influences of various life stages on professional development,[25] law school experiences and their impact on the profession will constitute a central focus of the analysis. For law school maintains a virtual monopoly over formal preparation for the bar, controlling both access to and distribution within the profession. Just how its formal role in the preparation of lawyers affects the profession is the subject of this inquiry.

25. A developmental approach contrasts with the traditional view of psychologists, which focuses on early life experiences and training in the formation of personality traits. In the developmental perspective employed here, socialization is characterized as the process by which individuals learn skills, motives, knowledge, and values, and it includes one's total life experience as potential influences. Such a view does not necessarily negate the critical importance of early experiences to later behavior and attitudes. Indeed by emphasizing the developmental nature of socialization processes, this view attributes to early learning the establishment of boundaries for later socialization, providing references for later experiences. For examples of this perspective see Brim and Wheeler (1966) and Jennings and Niemi (1968, 1974). For further discussion of various disciplinary perspectives on socialization see Easton and Dennis (1969, pp. 7-15) and the *International Encyclopedia of the Social Sciences* (1968, vol. 14, pp. 534-62).

Chapter 2

DESIGNING RESEARCH ON THE PROFESSIONAL DEVELOPMENT OF LAWYERS

Research Design

The use of public opinion polls in both marketing research and election campaigns has become so common that there is now a broad general understanding that the attitudes of an entire population can be determined by surveying a representative sample. After considering a number of alternatives, we selected a mailed survey as the primary research tool for our study of the legal profession. While a mailed survey eliminates the individual probing that is the strength of personal interviews, this technique made it possible to obtain a larger sample and thus increase external validity—that is, the degree to which the conclusions can be generalized to the entire population being studied.

The basic purpose of the questionnaire was to elicit data to inform the continuing debate over the value of formal legal education as compared with other influences on the development of skills, attitudes, and values in the practice of law. The first pretest of the questionnaire was conducted with members of the Indiana Bar Association and included valuable group sessions conducted in Indianapolis. This was followed by a series of pretests on small, randomly selected samples of practicing lawyers in Chicago, some of whom met with us in small groups for further discussions. These pretests helped verify the utility and workability of the questionnaire in general and also enabled us to sharpen and make more definitive the thrust of particular questions.[1]

1. To cite an example, they enabled us to transform a number of open-ended questions into forced-choice questions that would be more easily comparable across attorneys. In addition, pretest respondents suggested new response categories, some of which were incorporated into the final draft of the questionnaire. A case in point was a question inquiring into the factors considered in choosing a law school. As a result of the pretests the following was added: "classes scheduled to allow opportunity to work full or part time

The Study Site and Sample

The data for this research were collected from August 1, 1975, to February 1, 1976. The city of Chicago was selected as the locale in which to study the practicing bar. Chicago is an appropriate site for several reasons. With the close correlation between the distribution of lawyers and economic activity throughout this country, a commercial city like Chicago has substantially more than its proportional share of attorneys. Second, as in other large cities, there is a broad diversity of practice with many specialties represented. Third, by restricting the study to one city, we eliminate geographical differences and have a sufficient number of graduates of individual law schools to allow for interschool comparisons on a number of variables. Finally, Chicago is an ideal setting because the legal profession has been examined here more than elsewhere, thus permitting comparison with other data.[2]

Despite frequent references to "practice" and "practitioners" in discussions of the legal profession and the debate over the role of legal education in professional development, nowhere in the literature are those terms precisely defined. In many instances the definitions of lawyer and legal practice have been little more than tautological: the practice of law is what lawyers do, and what lawyers do is the practice of law. Since many law school graduates and even successful bar examinees never "practice" law, "qualified to practice" could not suffice as our definition. In addition, since much of the debate has been between the academicians and the practitioners, it seemed appropriate that legal academicians be excluded from the study population. But what about judges, government staff attorneys, or attorneys who serve not as legal counsel but on the research staff of a legislator, as government examiners, as trust officers of banks, or as attorneys working for title companies? Ultimately it seemed conceptually most sound to consider as practitioners those attorneys whose *primary* role was the representation of the legal status of others.[3] This definition excludes judges and administrative officers. It includes government attorneys who actually represent the government but not government attorneys whose primary job is administrative or legislative. It includes attorneys who work for corporations in the capacity of house counsel or as part of the legal staff but not managers and officers who happen to be licensed attorneys.

For the purposes of this study, *Sullivan's Law Directory,* published

---

while attending law school" (questionnaire, pt. I, Q. 4, p. 3, appendix 1). See chapter 3, table 3.8, for a tabulation of the importance of this factor.

2. For other studies of the Chicago bar see Carlin (1962b), Laumann and Heinz (1977), and Lortie (1959).

3. In an effort to characterize the emergence of legal counsel as a social institution, Rueschemeyer (1973) cites three "core characteristics" of the attorney's role: "1) specialized knowledge of legal rules, 2) partisan advice to clients not related by kinship, and 3) representation of clients in relation both to other parties and to legal authorities" (p. 1). Our definition, while implying all three characteristics, emphasizes the third as distinguishing the "practitioner" from others trained and identified as "lawyers."

locally in Chicago, provided the most accurate listing[4] for drawing a random sample.[5] Those selected 825 practitioners who fit the established definition were sent a questionnaire along with a letter of explanation.[6] The response rate was an extremely respectable 66.4 percent: 548 attorneys. With declining response rates a current source of great consternation in survey research, the willingness of more than 65 percent of the practicing bar, a large proportion of whom bill their time on an hourly basis, to complete a long and detailed questionnaire (23 pages—see appendix 1) was most gratifying.[7]

4. See *Sullivan's Law Directory for the State of Illinois, 1974-75*. The standard source of statistical data on lawyers is the *Martindale-Hubbell Law Directory*. While many inaccuracies and biases in the listings occur in both law directories, we believe *Sullivan's Law Directory* to be more accurate. First, the updating techniques of *Sullivan's Directory* appear to be better. *Martindale-Hubbell* sends a postcard to every attorney listed asking for revisions for the new edition. If no response is received, the listing in the new edition remains the same as in the previous edition of the directory. In contrast, *Sullivan's Law Directory* sends representatives to canvass at least the downtown area, where the vast majority of Chicago attorneys are located, to check the accuracy of the listings. Outside the downtown area it requires the return of a postcard with updated information or response to a follow-up telephone call for an attorney to be included in the new edition. Second, since *Sullivan's* is the local law directory, published in Chicago for the state of Illinois only, most local attorneys are said to rely on it more heavily than on the *Martindale-Hubbell* volume covering the same geographical area. It should be noted that all law directories depend on self-reporting by lawyers and are so delimited.

5. The sample was drawn by use of a random numbers table, excluding those listed who did not fit the definition of practitioner. This technique insured that every practitioner in Chicago had an equal chance of being included in the sample.

The degree to which a random sample of sufficient size represents a population is apparent from a review of the variety of reasons why many of the original sample were not included in calculating the response rate. For the 89 original respondents who no longer practice law in Chicago, the reasons include: death, moving out of town, entering academia, retiring, going into business, generally dropping out, and even disbarment.

6. In an effort to increase sample size somewhat and to accommodate attorneys who agreed to participate but were unwilling or unable (or both) to devote the time necessary to complete the original questionnaire, we revised the questionnaire into a shorter version for the final follow-up. This yielded an additional 53 respondents.

A comparison between the respondents to the long and to the short versions of the questionnaire on 23 of the demographic and attitudinal variables reveals only one significant difference. Older attorneys were significantly more likely to respond to the shorter than to the long questionnaire, with the difference due largely to those over 55 years of age. By providing the older attorneys with an opportunity to give their views in a less time-consuming form, we were able to make the sample more representative of the population of practicing attorneys in Chicago. With age the only substantial difference between them—a variable that will be central to the general analysis—we can with confidence include the short-form respondents in the study.

7. That success is particularly noteworthy because of the coincidental timing of our questionnaire with a survey of the Illinois State Bar Association concerning certification ("Economics of Legal Services in Illinois," 1975, Qs. 22–28, pp. 131–32). That survey was mailed to every current member of the Illinois bar, including our entire sample. The sample for that survey was the lawyers' registration list compiled by the Attorney Registration and Disciplinary Commission of the Supreme Court of Illinois, which lists all attorneys who wish to keep their registration up to date even though they no longer practice, or may never have practiced, law in Illinois.

The high response rate may be attributed to several factors. On the basis of our pretests we concluded that the American Bar Foundation is perceived to be a legitimate sponsor for this kind of inquiry. Second, the study provided respondents with an opportunity to express their views in a forum that might have some impact on policy in an area of concern to many attorneys. Finally, unlike most surveys, this one was completely anonymous.[8]

A comparison between the respondents and nonrespondents provided additional assurance of the representativeness of the sample. Limited to data contained in law directories (age, college attended, and law school attended), our comparison revealed that the nonrespondents were somewhat older, somewhat more likely to have attended college in Chicago, and more likely to have attended law school in Chicago. Of the three, only the age difference is statistically significant,[9] with the other two factors influenced by age. That is, the older attorneys, both respondents and nonrespondents, were more likely to have attended college and law school in Chicago than their younger counterparts. Given the fading of memories and the changes that have taken place in law school curricula in recent years, the slight age bias in the sample toward younger attorneys may ultimately have strengthened the validity of our study and its potential implications for policy.

A more robust test of sample validity was also possible because of a concurrent study of the legal profession in Chicago based on a different sample of essentially the same population. A comparison between the two data sets on numerous variables confirmed the representativeness of our sample.[10]

8. To avoid the problem of external validity usually raised in anonymous surveys, we attached to each questionnaire a postcard with the respondent's name and asked that it be mailed separately upon completion of the questionnaire. This technique made it possible to identify nonrespondents for further attempts to secure their participation. This increased the final response rate, thus assuring a more representative sample, and also allowed us to compare respondents and nonrespondents for sample bias.

9. References to statistical significance appear throughout this book. For those unfamiliar with that concept, "statistical significance" means that the relationship discovered would not be likely to occur by chance. Social science researchers have generally adopted the convention that a relationship, to be labeled statistically significant, must be likely to occur no more than 5 percent of the time by chance alone.

Tables include a "χ^2" figure, which expresses the relationship between the variables as they have occurred as compared with the relationship that would be expected by chance. Along with the χ^2 figure will be a level of significance, expressed as a probability. For example, where $p < 0.01$, the likelihood that the existent relationship would occur by chance is less than 1 out of 100. Explanations of other statistical measures employed in the data analysis will be presented along with the interpretation of those data. Specific modes of analysis and operational definitions of the variables are also presented within the substantive context in which they are initially employed.

10. Sponsored by the American Bar Foundation (with additional funding from several other institutions), the study is under the direction of John P. Heinz and Edward O. Laumann. Early results of the initial study can be found in the 1976 (Heinz et al., p. 717) and

The validity of this sample has implications beyond our study because it was drawn from a different data source than is usually employed in research on the legal profession. The majority of studies have relied upon the American Bar Foundation's *Lawyer Statistical Reports*, most recently published in 1972.[11] These reports, in turn, are based on the only available source of national data on lawyers, the *Martindale-Hubbell Law Directory*. However, there are difficulties with using that directory as a data source; moreover, the limits of *Martindale-Hubbell* are not merely academic, for they have resulted in a skewed picture of the American bar. Although our data confirm both the continued predominance of the private practitioner and the decline of solo practice, they present a somewhat different picture of the practicing bar than has previously been reported.[12]

Figure 2.1 presents the *Lawyer Statistical Reports'* data on Chicago lawyers from 1954 to 1970, at three-year intervals. The 1975 data come from our sample of practicing Chicago attorneys. The solid lines connecting the 1970 and 1975 figures represent the dramatic changes in the distribution of lawyers in practice if both the 1970 statistical report and our sample data are correct. The broken lines represent the projections of change in the distribution of lawyers in practice from 1970 to 1975 had the trends reflected in the *Lawyer Statistical Report* data from 1963 to 1970 continued. While there is some variance in the projected and actual figures for business and government lawyers, the graph makes quite clear that the greatest discrepancies are in the percentages of firm and solo attorneys.[13] Although the difference between the figures is not

---

1977 (Laumann & Heinz, p. 155) volumes of the *American Bar Foundation Research Journal*.

The samples were compared for the following variables: age, sex, race, childhood residence, father's occupation, law school location, class standing in law school, nature of current practice, and attendance at law schools located in Chicago. The only item on which the two samples differ is class standing in law school, with face-to-face interviews, as expected, eliciting higher self-evaluations than an anonymous mailed questionnaire.

11. See *The 1971 Lawyer Statistical Report* (1972). The American Bar Foundation will publish a new Lawyer Statistical Report based on 1980 *Martindale-Hubbell* data.

12. Since the primary purpose of the *Martindale-Hubbell Law Directory* is to provide information about the availability of lawyers throughout an area, particularly for reference use by attorneys seeking a counterpart's assistance in another state, the directory is organized accordingly. For example, attorneys devoting "the greater part of [their] time to the affairs of a single client" are marked as belonging to the same group as those "retired, semi-retired or semi-active, or principally engaged in activities other than the practice of law," since none of those attorneys would presumably be in a position to assist an out-of-state attorney in a local matter. (See "Explanatory Notes and Symbols," at the front of each volume of the *Martindale-Hubbell Law Directory*.) For our purposes such categorization adds more confusion than clarity. Since we are proceeding on the assumption that the practice of law and skills employed therein, and therefore the benefit of traditional legal education, varies, we have made a conscious effort to avoid excluding attorneys whose work does not fit the standard conception of the private practitioner.

13. At the same time that a change in the distribution of lawyers in various kinds of

more than 12 percent in any single instance (11.5 percent for firm lawyers and 12 percent for solo practitioners), the differences are additive.
Thus, the 1963–70 figures predict only 9 percent more firm attorneys
than solo attorneys in 1975 (42 percent to 33 percent), but by 1975 there
are 32.5 percent more firm than solo attorneys—for the first time more

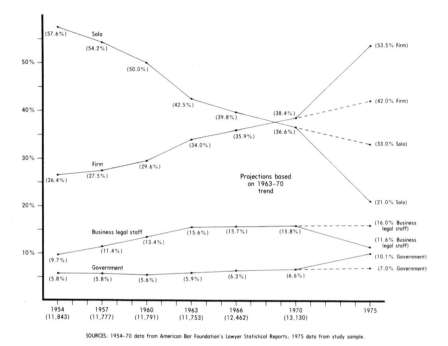

SOURCES: 1954–70 data from American Bar Foundation's Lawyer Statistical Reports; 1975 data from study sample.

Fig. 2.1. Distribution of Chicago lawyers by type of practice

practice has occurred, the demand for legal education has increased enormously. In 1965
there were 56,407 students enrolled in accredited law schools; by 1975 the figure had
jumped to 110,210. (See Fossum 1978, p. 525, for more complete figures.) Similar increases in enrollment have occurred in four of the six law schools in Chicago: DePaul, IIT-
Chicago Kent, John Marshall, and Loyola (based on figures included in correspondence
from the six Chicago law schools). These higher enrollments have had the effect of increasing the supply of lawyers. The number of successful bar examinations has correspondingly increased from 20,000 in 1971 to 30,000 in 1973 (Deitsch & Weinstein, 1976, p.
116). While significant, the growth of trained and certified lawyers should not particularly
influence the distribution of lawyers in the direction of the pattern discovered. If anything, an oversupply would be expected to swell the ranks of the solo practitioners as well
as increase the number of nonpractitioners among licensed attorneys. Furthermore, later
figures indicate that the rate of annual increase in law school enrollment has declined con-
tinuously since 1975. Excluding four law schools recently granted provisional approval
(not included in earlier figures), total enrollment in ABA-approved law schools increased by
only 0.45 percent from 1977 to 1978 (White, 1979, p. 577).

than half of all practicing attorneys are affiliated with law firms.[14] This finding is quite important for understanding the current nature of the profession.

Traditionally the lawyer was a private practitioner who worked alone. The solo practitioner was the theoretical ideal type. In recent years numerous commentators have described, and in many instances decried, the decline of the solo practitioner and the rise of the firm attorney. Concomitant with this shift has been an apparent trend toward larger and larger law firms, with a proportional increase in the degree of specialization. In his study of occupations Hall notes that "for most fields [including law], therefore, individual practice is probably just an image of the past, and like many such images, revered, but somewhat irrelevant" (Hall, 1969, p. 99). Our survey of the practicing bar supports Hall's contention and further confirms the growth in law-firm size. With different kinds of clients likely to be served within different practice contexts, such changes in the distribution of lawyers have broad public policy implications. Any consideration of the socialization of the profession must take these trends into account.

Limits of the Research Design

Ideally an inquiry into the professional development of lawyers would include persons who were subject to the same influences but did not enter or did not remain in the practice of law. At a minimum, one would certainly want to include those who entered law school but did not become practicing lawyers. As designed, this study neglects such individuals. In considering a number of factors that might contribute to such career patterns, we wish to acknowledge the limits of our research and in so doing to encourage future research on the legal profession.

Among students who enter law school a certain proportion never graduate. Attrition rates no doubt vary by law school, but the following aggregate figures are indicative.

	No. of First-Year Students Enrolled 1958 & 1966	No. of First Law Degrees Conferred
Class of 1961	16,651	9,957
Class of 1969	26,552	17,240

SOURCE: *Review of Legal Education* (1958, 1961, 1966, 1969).

14. The nature of percentages is such that the overrepresentation of any part of the whole means that at least one other part must be proportionally underrepresented. Thus the figures on practicing attorneys in the other categories are also affected. The small discrepancy in the government category may be partly a reflection of this. If anything, however, the similarity between the *Lawyer Statistical Report*'s government figures and our own is somewhat surprising. A kind of balancing out may have occurred. The broader category of "government" used by *Martindale-Hubbell* (including more than our government category) in the data through 1970 may have been more than compensated for by the expansion of public employment in general and attorneys employed by government in particular since that period.

These data show attrition rates of 40 percent and 35 percent respectively.[15] Some individuals surely dropped out because of academic difficulties, but still unknown are the various influences that might have contributed to that failure. In addition, there are presumably many who
choose to leave law school before graduation for a myriad of other reasons, some of them possibly related to the effects of the law school experience itself or to a changing perception of the profession. Indeed,
even among those who graduate from law school, many never actually
practice law.[16]

The data from our study indicate that those who are academically less
successful in law school are less likely to practice law. Approximately 50
percent of the sample reported having been in the top 20 percent of their
classes in comparison with less than 10 percent reporting being in the
bottom 40 percent.[17] The skew in these data may cause some concern
about the reliability of responses.[18] It may simply be that self-aggrandizement is to be expected when individuals are asked to relate measures
of their own performance, even anonymously. However, a more careful
examination of the data and comparisons with other data sets provide
alternative explanations.

15. In a discussion of these data Olavi Maru (1972) attributes some of this apparent attrition to part-time programs (which take longer than three years to complete) and tempo-
rary leaves due to military service or financial difficulties. However, those factors ought
not to affect the data very much. In the aggregate, for every part-time student who
entered in 1958 but did not graduate in 1962, there is one who entered in 1957 whose degree will be reflected in the 1961 figures. The military situation, of relevance only in certain historical periods, has a similar effect. Thus, the bulk of the attrition reflects permanent dropouts. We could speculate on a variety of causes, some implicitly more critical of
legal education than others. We prefer, however, to call for research that will make such
speculation unnecessary.

16. Figures on law school graduates who do not practice law are sparse. One source is
the *Michigan Alumni Survey Cumulative Report*, which provides figures on the status of
University of Michigan Law School graduates 15 years after graduation. With an overall
response rate of 78 percent from nine consecutive graduating classes, 11 percent report
nonlaw jobs (excluding judges and legal educators). It could be argued that this figure underestimates the nonlawyers because of their diminished likelihood of responding to a law
school survey. In any case they constitute a population that is significant for understanding the influences affecting entry into the profession.

17. The exact figures are as follows:

Class Standing (Percentile)		%Reporting (N = 514)
(Top)	1–10	24.7
	11–20	25.5
	21–40	26.8
	41–60	15.8
	61–80	4.5
(Bottom)	81–100	2.7
		100.0

18. This distribution does not differ for graduates of full- and part-time programs, nor
does it vary by law school attended. Perhaps most interesting, given hypotheses about
selective memory, is the failure of newer attorneys to report significantly different class
standings.

The most obvious post–law school limitation on entry to the profession is the bar examination. Recent data that indicate a strong relationship between Multistate Bar Examination scores and law school grade-point averages would predict that the academic performance pattern of practicing attorneys would be skewed away from the lowest class standings.[19] The validity of the positive skew in class standing is further supported by the similarity between the 24.7 percent of the sample who reported their standing in the top 10 percent of their class and the 24.1 percent who participated in law review.[20] Finally, the data indicate that those with lower reported class standing had more difficulty finding a first job after graduation from law school.[21]

We can only speculate on the role that success in law school plays in the decisions taken by law school graduates themselves, namely the decision to take the bar exam and, if successful, the decision to enter the practice of law, assuming available employment. An assumed directionality of cause and effect that has yet to be substantiated has been implicit in this discussion. An alternative hypothesis might be that law school by the nature of its instruction, and the image of the law and the profession it projects, discourages some who were initially attracted to a career in the law.[22] Surely those filtered out of access to the profession bear study for a fuller understanding of the influence of formal legal education on the legal profession and its place in society. Nevertheless, for now we must be content to examine the making of the legal profession by concentrating on the practicing bar.

19. The Educational Testing Service reports a correlation of .46 between cumulative three-year grade average and scores on the Multistate Bar Examination (MBE), when controlled for the influence of the Law School Admission Test (LSAT) (Carlson & Werts, 1976, p. 49).

20. During the law school career of most practicing attorneys, membership on law review was indicative of high class standing; typically the top 10 percent of the class would have been eligible for participation. Participation in law review is also likely to be more reliably reported than class standing, both because it is a dichotomous variable and because memory of it is less likely to be affected over time.

21. Those with lower class standing were significantly more likely to mention "no other job offers" as an important reason for selecting their first employment after law school. (See survey questionnaire, pt. II, Q. 3, p. 7, appendix 1, for the question on which this is based.)

22. Another plausible rival hypothesis is that many of the law school graduates who never intended to practice law do not do as well in law school. Since the quality of law school grades (beyond the minimum necessary to avoid dismissal) is relevant only to finding certain kinds of employment in the practice of law, those not intending to practice may be less competitive and so perform less spectacularly. That group may constitute a substantial proportion of law school graduates. Even among practicing attorneys, close to one-third (32 percent) cite "good background for other occupational goals" as an important reason for their going to law school (questionnaire, pt. I, Q. 1.f., p. 2, appendix 1). It is reasonable to assume that many of those who went to law school because of the background it provided for other occupational goals never entered the practice of law and so are not reflected in the sample. Like a number of other interesting questions raised herein, this interpretation, while reasonable, is still a matter of conjecture and in need of further research for substantiation.

Chapter 3

ROUTE TO THE LEGAL PROFESSION

Introduction

Despite the dominance of law school in both preparation for and access to the legal profession, it constitutes but one stage in the professional development of lawyers. The adoption of a perspective on socialization which acknowledges the potential influence of all life experiences on subsequent values, attitudes, and behavior dictates a much broader scope for our inquiry. Although the impact of law school will be a major focus of study, we shall consider early experiences and influences before law school as well as continuing socialization within the context of practice in order to trace the making of professionals through its entire course. The wisdom of this approach is supported by the views of the practitioners themselves, who continue to remind us that much of what they perceive to have been important in their professional development has occurred outside of formal schooling.

In this chapter we begin with an inquiry into the attractions of a career in the law and the perceived influences on the decision to pursue it, giving particular attention to the legal profession as a route to higher social status. This will be followed by an analysis of the factors influencing selection of law schools—a decision, as we shall see in chapter 5, that is critical in determining subsequent legal careers and the distribution of lawyers within the profession.

Attractions to a Career in the Law

By simply asking practicing lawyers to select and rank factors important in their decisions to attend law school, we can develop a composite picture of the attractions of a career in the law. These data are presented in table 3.1.[1] It appears that the most important factors are those central to the practice itself, as expressed in the most frequently checked items: "interest in the subject matter" and "wanted to practice law." These are rather more strictly professional goals than most of the others in that they are peculiar to law and, unlike the others, could not have been

TABLE 3.1
Rank Order of Factors Important in the Decision to Attend Law School ($N = 495$)

Rank	Factor	% Citing Important[a]
1	Interest in the subject matter	48
2	Wanted to practice law	40
3	Good background for other occupational goals[b] . . .	32
4	Prestige of the profession	28
5	Influence of family	23
6	Uncertainty about future plans	16
7	Opportunity to be helpful to others and/or useful to society in general	18.2
8	Prospects of above-average income	19.6
9	Influence of friend or teacher	8.9
10	Stable secure future expected	9.1
11	Relative freedom from supervision by others	9.1
12	Opportunity to work with people rather than things	10.1
13	Like to argue and debate	5.5
14	Opportunity to have an influence on the settlement of legal questions	4.2
15	Wanted to postpone military service	3.4

[a]Percentage of respondents ranking item 1, 2, *or* 3 in importance in the decision to attend law school. The ranking of the percentages is slightly different from the rank order in the left-hand column because of differences in the calculation of the figures. The percentages give equal weighting to each respondent's top three items, whereas the composite rank order weights them according to their precise ranking. Ranks 1 through 3 were selected because the drop in response rates after that makes comparisons less valid.
[b]This item includes responses in either the general category "good background for other occupational goals" or any of the subcategories: politics, business, judiciary, government work, legal education. All the items can be found in pt. I, p.2, of the questionnaire in appendix 1.

easily, if at all, satisfied by alternative career choices. Interest in the subject matter of law and desire to practice law as reasons for attending law school apparently do not extend to playing a conscious role in law's impact on the society. Neither the "opportunity to be helpful to others and/or useful to society in general" nor the "opportunity to have an influence on the settlement of legal questions" were rated very highly by

1. The precise question we asked can be found on page 2, part I, of the questionnaire (appendix 1). The equation employed to determine the important aggregate attractions to law school is as follows:

N_1 (number ranking item first) $\times$ 3 + ($N_2 \times 2$) + ($N_3 \times 1$) = score

The aggregate ranking scores were then ranked in order from 1 to 15.

practitioners as attractions to careers in the law. The predominance of the more technical aspects of legal practice will emerge again when we consider both the sources of skills important to the practice of law and the behavior appropriate to a professionally responsible bar.

These findings are consistent with the results of two previous studies of legal education. In his study of part-time legal education in the mid-1960s, Kelso asked full- and part-time law school seniors from a number of schools the most important reason for their decisions to study law. Of the 10 options provided, only "wanted to practice" received a substantial number of positive responses.[2] Stevens found that for the 1970 graduates of six law schools the two most important reasons for going to law school were interest in the subject matter and professional training. These are virtually identical to the items ranked 1 and 2 by Chicago practitioners across all age cohorts.[3]

"Uncertainty" as an important reason for going to law school ranks only tenth among the items mentioned by Stevens's respondents as important for attending law school.[4] Employing a comparable "percentage citing as important" rating, Chicago practitioners in our sample similarly rank "uncertainty about future plans" as only eighth among their reasons for attending law school (table 3.1). Of much greater importance to Chicago practitioners was law school as a good background for other career goals. Although this too reflects some uncertainty, we think it is a much more positive statement about the expected benefits of legal education.[5] Stevens implicitly acknowledges this in a footnote reference to Thielens's findings based on the views of law school entrants. Thielens found:

> Some 62 per cent of the law school student body . . . thought that "a legal training will be very useful regardless of what career I go into" had been a "very important" element in their decisions to come to law school . . . . Some 23 per cent of the entering class report that their decision "to try law school" resulted at least in part from being "indecisive about what to do" (Thielens, 1957, p. 141; Stevens, note 131, pp. 623–24).

Like our practitioners, Thielens's law students acknowledged the poten-

2. See table 122, "Most Important Reason 1965 Seniors Had Decided to Study Law," in Kelso (1972, p. 402). The other original categories were: "disliked job I had," "aid in business," "aid in government job," "public service," "further education," "always wanted to," "satisfy family," "no specific reason," and "other." The questions appeared on page 1 of the Law Student Questionnaire (Kelso, appendix B, p. 486).

3. Stevens's data are based on the denotation of each item as of "great" importance, "some" importance, and "none" rather than rank order data. The findings cited are based on his dichotomization of the data into "important" and "not important" reasons for going to law school. His data are reported in tables 8–19 (1973, pp. 576–83).

4. Given his findings, it is curious that Stevens finds support in his data for Mr. Justice Frankfurter's assertion about law students that "On the whole they came by default" (quoted in Warkov and Zelan (1965, p. xv), picked up by Stevens (1973, p. 623)).

5. Unfortunately, Stevens does not have comparable data, so there is no way to discover how similar his respondents might be to practicing lawyers on this item.

tial contribution of formal legal training to a variety of careers, but many fewer entrants were "indecisive" in the true sense of the word.[6]

The relative standing of a number of the factors important in the decision to attend law school provides some indication of the values held by students attracted to law school. For example, the item "prospects of above-average income" is substantially more important in the decision to attend law school than such other frequently discussed factors as independence ("relative freedom from supervision by others"), competitiveness ("like to argue and debate"), or "desire to work with people rather than things." The low rating of the last item is consistent with the findings of a 1961 study of the career plans of college seniors by the National Opinion Research Center (NORC),[7] in which various professions were compared according to three possible characteristics that had attracted the student respondents: making a lot of money, opportunity to work with people rather than things, and opportunities to be original and creative. Those planning careers in the law showed a distinctly different value pattern, compared with those entering other professions, in their "high interest in making money and a low interest in originality" (Davis, 1965, p. 140). According to Davis, the value "people" shows no

6. The percentage differences between our data and Thielens's in terms of preparation for other careers are to a large extent due to the different universes sampled. Thielens's sample was of law students, including both those who went on to practice and those who did not. It is not surprising, then, that among the practitioners we sampled, a smaller proportion cited background for other occupational goals as an important reason for going to law school. It is fair to assume that some portion of those students who mentioned other career goals actually pursued them and so would not fall within the universe of practitioners sampled for this study. What is perhaps more interesting is the closer comparability between the data sets for those "uncertain" or "indecisive" about their future plans: there is only a 7 percent difference between our data and Thielens's (16 percent versus 23 percent). This compares with a 30 percent difference (32 percent versus 62 percent) for background for other career goals. See Thielens (1957, pp. 140–43).

An obvious question about these distributions is whether there are any career differences between practitioners who cite background for other occupational goals as a reason for going to law school and those who do not. Both first jobs after law school graduation and serious contemplation of leaving the practice of law were investigated to determine whether or not they were related to an "other career" reason for attending law school. No substantial differences were found. While it would certainly be worth knowing whether those who pursued careers other than legal practice after law school graduation had those intentions before entering law school or whether some other factors, perhaps within the law school environment itself, deterred these individuals from practice, our data base is not appropriate for that inquiry. Answers to such questions would require a longitudinal study of law school entrants whose aspirations upon entrance could then be compared with their subsequent careers.

7. In the spring of 1961, NORC surveyed graduating college seniors at 135 colleges and universities. A year later it followed up the entire sample, in another survey, to discover the respondents' academic and employment situations and to determine to what extent their plans and expectations had been fulfilled. For a description of the study and a more complete report of the findings, see Davis's *Great Aspirations* (1964) and *Undergraduate Career Decisions* (1965). For an analysis of the survey data confined to future lawyers, see Warkov and Zelan's *Lawyers in the Making* (1965).

relationship to choice of legal career, although "one would expect off-hand that wanting to work with people as clients or opponents would be one of the attractions of legal work" (p. 140).

Davis reports that freshmen planning careers in the law, like those who plan to enter business, are particularly likely to highly value making money.[8] Yet, as shown in table 3.1, only 19.6 percent of the respondents in our sample cited the "prospects of above-average income" as among the three most important reasons for their career choices. This apparent inconsistency may simply reflect career choice as a two-stage decision-making process, with preferences for above-average income affecting the narrowing of career choices but not the selection of law in particular. Consistent with this interpretation, and with Davis's findings, more than half of those who entered law school with other career goals had business in mind. For these attorneys at least, expectation of above-average income, even if they highly valued it, may not be what drew them to the law specifically; it may, rather, have led to the choice of a whole range of careers. "Prestige of the profession," in contrast, is more prominent among the reasons for seeking careers in the law, for few occupations attain the prestige accorded the legal profession in American society.

Several factors cited as important in the decision to attend law school imply an understanding of and attraction to the high status enjoyed by the legal profession. An analysis of the "prestige of the profession," the "influence of family," "prospects of above-average income," and expectations of a "stable secure future" will assist us in evaluating the role of a career in the law as a perceived and actual route to or means of maintenance of high social status. Attraction and aspiration, while necessary, may not be sufficient to ensure access to a career in the law. Thus, in conjunction with our analysis of social status attractions of the law, we will consider limits on access to law school and ultimately to the legal profession.

8. Students' expectations about the relative remuneration received by doctors and lawyers is curiously out of touch with reality. In Chicago with incomes generally above those for comparable practice in small communities, the average annual income of a private legal practitioner in 1975 was $34,118 ("Economics of Legal Services in Illinois," 1975, p. 79). This contrasts with a 1975 national figure for doctors of $56,361. For the east north central states (Illinois, Indiana, Michigan, Ohio, and Wisconsin) the figure is an even higher $59,888 (*Profile of Medical Practice 1978,* table 60, p. 246 (published by the American Medical Association Center for Health Services Research and Development)). No doubt part of the public image in the minds of the students is related to media coverage of lawyers' earnings of the kind appearing in *Newsweek* magazine (1978) in an article entitled "The Super-Billers." The hourly fees cited as charged by various law partners in the Penn Central bankruptcy case ranged from $110/hour to $250/hour with a total of $50 million having been billed to the bankrupt corporation. Hourly fees of course are not the equivalent of income, although they are related. Even accounting for the overhead costs included within those figures, they represent a very select segment of the bar, thus providing an extremely skewed image of the monetary rewards of law practice.

Social Mobility and the Legal Profession

As early as 1835 the high social status of lawyers in the United States was observed by Alexis de Tocqueville, who commented: "If I were asked where I place the American aristocracy, I should reply without hesitation that it . . . occupies the judicial bench and bar" (1963, v. 1, p. 278). Later analyses confirm the continuing high status of the legal profession. On the basis of a socioeconomic index for occupations developed out of National Opinion Research Center (NORC) survey data, Albert Reiss finds lawyers among the highest prestige occupational groups (1961, p. 263).[9] In fact the high status and prestige of the legal profession have long been assumed to be part of its attractiveness.

Yet at the same time that participation in the legal profession has been pictured as a path to higher status, it has been characterized as a profession likely to draw its members from high-status backgrounds. This issue is of more than mere academic curiosity. As Alfred Reed noted in his early study of legal education, "the interests not only of the individual but of the community demand that participation in the making and administration of the law shall be kept accessible to Lincoln's plain people" (1921, p. 418). Of particular relevance to legal education is the implication, and sometimes outright conclusion, that as law schools become the single means of access to the profession, individuals from lower status backgrounds will be barred from the profession. Unlike the apprentice system under which one could both learn and earn simultaneously, formal schooling requires three years of increasingly high tuition and, in most cases, the loss of three years' income.[10] In addition, academic requirements for law school admissions further restrict entrance to the profession. Although law school enrollments have grown in recent years, the supply of spaces in law schools has nowhere matched the increased demand. The result has been that access to legal training has been increasingly restricted to the academic elite.[11]

9. An occupation's socioeconomic *status* and its *prestige,* while very highly correlated, are not identical. *Status* can be objectively determined from census data on educational requirements and economic rewards, while *prestige* ratings are derived from public opinion survey data. But, as Jencks points out, prestige evaluations tend to be high for occupations including the highly educated and the well paid (1972, pp. 177–78). The legal profession enjoys both high prestige (as we have shown in chapter 1) and high socioeconomic status.

10. Law school tuition varies substantially. For the nine law schools (seven in Illinois plus Harvard and Michigan) that educate most of the practicing bar in Chicago, the average nonresident full-time tuition in 1975 was just over $2,700. Tuition was lower for residents at state schools, with the University of Illinois charging only $700. Northwestern's tuition was the highest at $3,870. (Source: *Review of Legal Education,* 1976.) In addition every state except California requires a college degree, which means additional costs in both time and money.

11. The increase in quality of undergraduate performance required for law school admissions has also been influenced to some extent by general grade inflation in recent years. Perhaps a better indicator of increasingly stringent academic requirements is the LSAT scores now demanded for law school admissions.

Undergraduates have always understood the importance of social background to legal careers. Among college seniors aspiring to careers in the law in 1961, father's occupation has been shown to affect the likelihood that they actually enroll in law school the next fall. Students' chances increase, moving in ascending order through the father's occupations of blue collar/farm, sales/clerical, proprietor/manager, and professional, with the greatest variance found among students with low academic performance (Warkov & Zelan, 1965, pp. 32–33, 39). Further, Warkov and Zelan's study of the NORC data finds that the academic performance of college seniors planning careers in the law is essentially equivalent to or substantially higher than that of those planning to enter all other fields save medicine (p. 40).[12] The aggregate relationship between social status and academic achievement means that strict academic requirements will necessarily skew the backgrounds of lawyers toward the higher end of the social status continuum.[13]

We turn now to an examination of legal education and the law as a route to upward mobility and the changes over time in the role of a legal career as a means of access to higher status. The practicing bar is overwhelmingly white (98 percent) and male (97 percent). Although law schools have recently accepted and in some cases recruited more women and members of racial minorities, that change in policy has as yet had little impact on the actual composition of the practicing bar. It may be that those policies are too recent to have significantly affected the access of these groups to the legal profession, or it may be that later hurdles, such as bar examinations and job recruitment practices, have restricted their entry into the practicing bar.[14] For now we must rest content with evaluating access to the bar by social status as reflected in the occupations of the fathers of practicing lawyers.

The distribution of social backgrounds of practicing attorneys is, not surprisingly, skewed toward the upper end of the scale. It is clear from the figures displayed in table 3.2 that most lawyers have not strayed

12. On nine predictor items, including both demographic variables and selected value preferences in addition to academic performance, prelaw students are more similar to premed students than to students in any other category, including education, social sciences, humanities, biological sciences, physical sciences, business, engineering, and other professions. They differ substantially only in academic performance (prelaw students are lower) and valuation of money (prelaw students are higher). Law students are also slightly lower in valuation of people. Compared with students planning a career in business, law students share the same values but have higher academic performance indicators and higher social-status backgrounds (Davis, 1964, pp. 36–39).

13. The Academic Performance Index (API) used in the NORC reports is "a composite measure based on the student's cumulative grade point average and the quality of his school in terms of the intellectual calibre of its freshmen" (Davis, 1964, p. 256). See Davis's comments on the validity of this measure and the intervening effect of socioeconomic variables (appendix 3, pp. 256–68) and Jencks (1972) for a discussion of the relationship between academic achievement and social status.

14. Unfortunately there are, as yet, no available data that speak to this issue. As a topic of study it most certainly merits attention.

from the generally high status of their fathers' occupations.[15] In other words, they have not been, nor has it been possible for them to be, particularly upwardly mobile. To some extent, of course, this reflects a "ceiling effect": when using broad categories advancement cannot be reflected, even if it occurs, when the starting point is the highest cate-

TABLE 3.2

Occupations of Fathers of Chicago Lawyers

	% of Sample	No. of Lawyers
Professional	25.0	134
Managerial and administrative	27.5	147
Technical	5.6	30
Sales	16.6	89
Clerical	3.0	16
Craftsman, skilled laborer	13.1	70
Farmer, farm worker	1.9	10
Laborer	6.7	36
Multiple occupations	0.6	3
Total	100%	535

gory. While our data confirm the often-cited contention that lawyers generally come from the upper strata of society, still the fathers of 41.3 percent of the lawyers were in lower status occupations (i.e., sales, clerical, farmer, laborer), about equally divided between lower white-collar and blue-collar jobs. Figures similar to these are often cited to illustrate a kind of elitism among the bar, yet some interesting results emerge from a closer examination and comparison with the social mobility of other professions and the population in general.[16]

Pavalko, in a sociological analysis of work and professions (1971), gathered data on fathers' occupations from a number of studies of professions. Since these studies are drawn from different data bases and gathered with varying goals in mind, his figures are not strictly comparable either with each other or with our own. Still, it is worth observing that the proportion of lawyers with professional fathers (25 percent) is not very different from the proportion of doctors whose fathers were professionals.[17] Interestingly, according to Pavalko's compilation, doctors and lawyers fall somewhere in the middle of the scale of professions ranked in terms of the percentage among their numbers whose fathers were also professionals.[18]

The interpretation of these findings may be a matter of perspective. The 25 percent who come from professional families can be compared with the proportion of professionals in the population at large to illustrate the apparent strictures on access to the legal profession as a

15. This is similar to Handler's findings in a small midwestern city, where almost 80 percent of the lawyers came from a business, professional, or managerial background (1967, p. 23).

16. An example of such references is found in Mayer's *The Lawyers,* in which he compares the paternal occupations and incomes of law students of the mid-1960s with those of the general population (1967, p. 160).

mechanism of social mobility. On the other hand, the more than 40 percent who come from lower status, and particularly the more than 20 percent from blue-collar families, can be lauded as illustrating that the law is a continuing route to upward mobility that many of Carlin's solo practitioners saw as the cheapest and easiest way to become a professional.[19] A further examination of our own and others' data indicates that a large proportion of this status stability is attributable to children following directly in the footsteps of their fathers.

The NORC study of college seniors found that a lawyer parent was the most important variable in determining aspirations to a career in law, with socioeconomic status having little independent predictive value.[20] Among practicing attorneys, 56 percent of those who come from a professional background have (had) a lawyer parent. These individuals ac-

---

17. The following table was taken from Pavalko's *Sociology of Occupations and Professions* (1971, table 6, p. 72):

Occupational Inheritance in Terms of Broad Occupational Categories

	Percent with Fathers in "Professional" Occupations
Medicine	28[a]22[b]
Clergy	
Catholic	12[c]
Protestant	36[d]
Military	50[ef]
Dentistry	24[g]
Social Work	19[h]
Teaching	14[ij]
Engineering	19[k]
Academicians	16[l]

Sources:

[a](Medical Students) Helen H. Gee, "The Student View of the Medical Admissions Process," in Helen H. Gee and John T. Cowles (eds.) *The Appraisal of Applicants to Medical Schools,* Evanston, Ill.: Association of American Medical Colleges, 1957, p. 143.

[b](University of Kansas Medical Students) Howard S. Becker, *et al., Boys in White: Student Culture in Medical School,* Chicago: University of Chicago Press, 1961, p. 61.

[c]Joseph H. Fichter, *Religion as an Occupation,* Notre Dame, Ind.: University of Notre Dame Press, 1961, p. 62.

[d](Protestant Clergymen under age 50 listed in *Who's Who,* 1958–59) James Otis Smith and Gideon Sjoberg, "Origins and Career Patterns of Leading Protestant Clergymen," *Social Forces,* 39 (May, 1961) pp. 290–96.

[e](1960 Class of West Point) Morris Janowitz, *The Professional Soldier,* New York: The Free Press, 1960, p. 96.
[f]Includes professional and managerial.

[g](Dental Students, 1958) Douglas M. More, "Social Origins of Future Dentists," *The Midwest Sociologist,* 21 (July, 1959), pp. 69–76.

[h](Social Work Students, 1969) Arnulf M. Pins, *Who Chooses Social Work, When and Why?* New York: Council on Social Work Education, 1963, p. 44.

[i](Sample of elementary and secondary teachers), *The American Public School Teacher, 1960–61,* Washington, D.C.: National Education Association, 1963, p. 15.

[j]Includes professional and semiprofessional.

[k]Douglas M. More, "The Derivation of Hypotheses Relating Occupational Mobility and Job Performance," *The Midwest Sociologist,* 19 (May, 1957), pp. 87–92.

[l](Teachers in Minnesota Colleges, 1956) Ruth E. Eckert and John E. Stecklein, *Job Motivations and Satisfactions of College Teachers,* U.S. Dept. of Health, Education, and Welfare, U.S. Office of Education, Cooperative Research Monograph No. 7 (OE-53009), Washington, D.C.: U.S. Government Printing Office, 1961, p. 11.

18. It is worth noting that the importance of father's occupation to one's own occupation is not restricted to professions. See Blau and Duncan (1967).

19. See chapter 1 of Carlin (1962b).

20. Of those with a lawyer parent, 35 percent chose law as a career in contrast to 5 percent with no lawyer parent (Zelan, 1967, p. 46).

count for 14 percent of the entire sample, a finding consistent with other studies. In fact, a large proportion of the professional backgrounds of members of a number of different professions is accounted for by a father in the same occupation.[21] In a comparison of law school and medical school entrants, Thielens found that nearly identical proportions have at least one parent in the same profession, a pattern that holds for relatives in general. Fifteen percent of the law students and 17 percent of the medical students had one parent in the profession; 51 percent of the law students, and 50 percent of the medical students had at least one relative in law or medicine, respectively (Thielens, 1957, p. 134).

This intergenerational occupational pattern helps explain some of the social stability of the bar but also helps us understand more about the factors influential in the decision to seek a career in the law. Pavalko concludes that exposure to and familiarity with an occupation functions as a subtle and indirect influence on occupational choice (1971, p. 73). The figures in table 3.3 indicate that much of the influence is perceived to come directly from the family. It is clear that family influence is a significantly more important factor in the decision to enter law school for those whose fathers were also lawyers.[22]

21. Pavalko's compilation indicates that the proportion of high-status background accounted for by parents in the same profession is higher for doctors, lawyers, and professional soldiers than for other groups. The table below appears in Pavalko (table 5, p. 71) and can be compared with the table on father's occupational status in note 17 *supra:*

Direct Occupational Inheritance

	Percent with Fathers in Same Occupation
Medicine	11[a]19[b]17[c]
Clergy	13[d]
Military	25[e]
Lawyers	15[f]
Dentistry	8[g]
Social Work	3[h]
(father or mother)	

Sources:

[a](Medical Students) Helen H. Gee, "The Student View of the Medical Admissions Process," in Helen H. Gee and John T. Cowles (eds.) *The Appraisal of Applicants to Medical Schools,* Evanston, Ill.: Association of American Medical Colleges, 1957, p. 143.

[b](University of Kansas Medical Students) Howard S. Becker, *et al., Boys in White: Student Culture in Medical School,* Chicago: University of Chicago Press, 1961, p. 61.

[c](Medical Students, Eastern University) Wagner Thielens, Jr., "Some Comparisons of Entrants to Medical and Law School," in Robert K. Merton *et al., The Student Physician,* Cambridge: Harvard University Press, 1957, p. 134.

[d](Protestant Clergymen under age 50 listed in *Who's Who,* 1958–59) James Otis Smith and Gideon Sjoberg, "Origins and Career Patterns of Leading Protestant Clergymen," *Social Forces,* 39 (May, 1961), pp. 290–296.

[e](1960 Class of West Point) Morris Janowitz, *The Professional Soldier,* The Free Press, 1960, p. 96.

[f](Law School Students) Wagner Thielens, Jr., "Some Comparisons of Entrants to Medical and Law School," in Robert K. Merton, *et al., The Student Physician,* Cambridge: Harvard University Press, 1957, p. 134.

[g](Dental Students, 1958) Douglas M. More, "Social Origins of Future Dentists," *The Midwest Sociologist,* 21 (July, 1959), pp. 69–76.

[h](Social Work Students, 1960) Arnulf M. Pins, *Who Chooses Social Work, When and Why?* New York: Council on Social Work Education, 1963, p. 44.

22. The importance variable was constructed out of the rank order of reasons for going to law school, found on page 2 of the questionnaire (see appendix 1). Ranks 1, 2, and 3 were considered important ranks, below that as not important. The top three were used because the number of respondents ranking that number of items was very close, with

Consistent with a view of the law as a path to upward mobility, family influence would be expected to be more important among lower status families. The data however do not support this view. If we look at the proportion of lawyers from different status backgrounds who rate family influence as an important factor in their decision to enter law school,

TABLE 3.3
Importance of Family Influence in Decision to Attend Law School by Father's Occupation as Lawyer or Nonlawyer

	Lawyer Father	Nonlawyer Father
% citing important	53.0	18.7
% not citing important	47.0	81.3
	100%	100%
	(N = 66)	(N = 417)

$$\chi^2 = 35.57; p < 0.001$$

the results are in the opposite direction. As table 3.4 indicates, the higher the parent's status, the more likely the family is viewed as having an influence on the child's choice of a career in the law.[23] While most of the responses indicating family influence in the "professional" category

TABLE 3.4
Importance of Family Influence in Decision to Attend Law School by Father's Occupational Status

	Father's Occupation			
	Professional	Managerial, Administrative, Technical	Sales, Clerical	Blue Collar
% citing important	34.2	23.6	23.7	11.0
% not citing important	65.8	76.4	76.3	89.0
	100%	100%	100%	100%
	(N = 117)	(N = 161)	(N = 93)	(N = 109)

$$\chi^2 = 17.31; p < 0.001$$

Somers' $D = 0.113$ (asymmetric with family influence dependent)[a]

[a]Somers' D is a measure of association, used with ordinal data, which, like gamma, can be compared to assess the relative strength of different relationships. However, gamma is a symmetrical measure of association, while Somers' D is calculated taking cognizance of the directionality of the relationship, i.e., the independent versus the dependent variable.

While the numerators of the two measures are identical, the denominators differ with Somers' D including pairs tied on the dependent variable. This has the effect of making Somers' D a generally more conservative (smaller) estimate of the strength of association than gamma. See note a, table 3.13, *infra* for a description of gamma. For a more complete description of Somers' D see Robert H. Somers, "A New Asymmetric Measure of Association," 27 *American Sociological Review* 799 (1962).

---

many fewer respondents ranking any factors fourth or less in importance. The figures for absent or missing responses for the ranks are as follows: rank 1, 0; rank 2, 7; rank 3, 24; rank 4, 76.

23. In an attempt to discover the extent to which this is a generational phenomenon influenced by changes in respect for parental opinion, we repeated the analysis by age cohort and found no relationship between number of years out of law school and family influence on career choice.

are attributable to children following directly in the careers of their lawyer fathers (indeed those from other professional backgrounds in our
sample do not rate family influence highly), it is clear that lower status
families are not perceived by their children to have influenced the decision to seek a career in the law, at least not directly. In addition to the
tendency for careers to maintain themselves across generations in
families, it may be that higher status families are influential in encouraging their children to maintain their status by choosing high status
careers—that is, families make clear what careers are appropriate for
their children. It is highly likely that the lower one's status, the more acceptable a full range of possible career choices will be. Thus, while a
blue-collar family might well be pleased, and even proud, if one of their
progeny chooses to pursue a high-status career in the law, they are likely
to be considerably more amenable to a blue-collar career choice than a
higher status family would be. The tendency for higher status families to
be more influential in the choice of careers in the law may simply reflect
the narrower range of options they deem acceptable for their children,
with pressure more specifically directed to selected careers.[24]

This conclusion of course implies, as we think the data indicate, that
the traditional notion that more options are open to an individual as
social status and education increase needs restatement. In addition to
the ceiling effect on upward mobility at the top, the range of acceptable
choices is also limited. Davis makes a similar point about occupational
limits imposed by higher education: "While being barred from low
paid, less pleasant, low prestige jobs is a tolerable limitation, it is a
limitation, and the decision to attend college is in itself a major voca-
tional decision" (Davis, 1965, p.5).

The importance of father's occupation to one's career in the law is
not simply a matter of continued high status; it is centrally a reflection
of the tendency of children to follow the careers of their parents. Yet the
argument over the background of lawyers does not end here. There is
the further question of whether the backgrounds of attorneys and thus
the nature of the profession have changed over time, most particularly
whether the legal profession has become more elitist.

An interesting contradiction appears in the literature with regard to
the replacement of apprenticeships by law schools as the central route to
a career in the law. The debate is over the impact of this change on the
social backgrounds from which the legal community is drawn. Unlike
the earlier apprenticeships that even paid the apprentice a small wage,

---

24. Consistent with the view that professional socialization begins early in life, the
overall importance of family influence in the decision to attend law school is quite considerable. More lawyers cited family influence as important (i.e., among the top three factors) than 16 of the other 20 possible factors. The only items considered important by
more respondents are "interest in the subject matter," the desire "to practice law,"
"good background for other occupational goals," and the "prestige of the profession"
(48 percent, 40 percent, 32 percent, and 28 percent, respectively, compared with 23 percent considering family influence important).

law schools require three years of tuition, with very little scholarship assistance available. In addition, full-time law schools do not encourage students to work at jobs to support themselves. As a result, concludes Jacob (1978), "the sons and daughters of those Americans who earn less than the median family income usually cannot afford law school" (p. 38). Alternatively there is evidence "that the rise of the law schools was linked to a social change in the character of the bar—from strongly aristocratic to middle class in family background" (Friedman, 1973, p. 526).[25] In one sense there is no disagreement between these perspectives: both cite the middle-class nature of the law school population and ultimately of the bar. The literature as a whole predominantly views this as reflecting an increasingly restricted profession. Focusing on the costs attendant to the requirement that law students be college graduates, it is widely concluded that "the law as a career has become much less a vehicle of upward mobility than it was in the past" (Jacob, 1978, p. 38).[26] The data, however, show *no significant change* in the law as a route to upward mobility.

Table 3.5 compares years out of law school and status of father's occupation. Among those out of law school fewer than 36 years, there is clearly no trend toward more professional backgrounds from older to newer attorneys. While substantially fewer of those out of law school more than 35 years come from professional backgrounds compared with

TABLE 3.5
Father's Occupation by Years Out of Law School

Father's Occupation	Years Out of Law School			
	5 or Less	6–15	16–35	36 or More
Professional	26.2%	23.1%	31.4%	18.1%
Managerial, administrative, technical	36.4	33.3	28.1	38.6
Sales, clerical	21.5	20.4	17.6	19.3
Blue collar	15.9	23.1	22.9	24.1
	100%	100%	100%	100%
	(N = 107)	(N = 186)	(N = 153)	(N = 83)

$$\chi^2 = 9.28; \; p \leqslant 0.41$$

25. Friedman (1973) concludes that established lawyers in Philadelphia who prevented the creation of a law department at the University of Pennsylvania in the 1830s wished "to preserve their private prerogative of training the bar" (p. 526). Despite their efforts, however, the social make-up of the bar changed. During the first half of the nineteenth century, an increasing percentage of lawyers came from the middle class, with a sharp increase in the trend by 1900 (p. 550). Friedman bases his conclusions on the work of Gary B. Nash (1965).

26. Stevens (1973) concurs by concluding that "the students sampled appeared to come from better educated, as well as richer, families than in the past" (p. 573). While he acknowledges that educational levels have been rising in the nation as a whole, and that inflation has resulted in an increase in dollar income, he still concludes that the data "may . . . suggest that the schools studied drew their students from increasingly elite family backgrounds" (p. 573).

more recent graduates, this difference does not appear to be significant. It may be that the rather sharp break at the 35-year mark is due more to the smaller number in that category than to any real difference in the population they represent. If we combine the professional and managerial categories (add rows one and two in table 3.5), the figures for all age groups differ by only a few percentage points (62.6 percent, 56.4 percent, 59.5 percent, and 56.7 percent, respectively). Among practicing attorneys at least, more than half have always come from higher status backgrounds, and that proportion has remained relatively constant.[27]

Lawyers themselves acknowledge upward mobility as an attraction to the profession. A number of factors influential in the decision to go to law school reflect the pursuit of high status: "prestige of the profession," expectations of "a stable secure future," and "prospects of above-average income." Lawyers from blue-collar backgrounds are significantly more likely than those from professional backgrounds to cite these upward mobility reasons, considered in the aggregate, as important in their decisions to attend law school ($\chi^2 = 5.77$, $p < 0.05$).[28] This is, of course, consistent with the view that lawyers from lower status backgrounds have been attracted to careers in law as a means to improve their social status.

An analysis of the individual indicators also provides insight into the attractions of professional careers (table 3.6). While only the importance of a stable, secure future varies significantly (at a 0.05 level) by father's occupation for the whole sample, the *order* of importance of self-reported socioeconomic status reasons for selection of a career in the law is the same irrespective of father's occupation. Among those from the same social background, the prestige of the profession is more important than the prospect of above-average income, which in turn is more important than the expectation of a stable, secure future in the decision to attend law school. This ordering reflects realistic expectations of the likely benefits of a career in the law, with general social prestige virtually guaranteed but the other goals subject to specific circumstances.

27. Blau and Duncan (1967) reach a similar conclusion in their study of the American occupational structure as a whole. Comparing father's occupation with first job for four age cohorts (25–34, 35–44, 45–54, 55–64), they conclude "that the influence of social origin on career beginnings has not changed at all in the last forty years" (p. 424).

Among the practicing bar the only other sizable discrepancy in the figures is the percentage of attorneys coming from a blue-collar background. There appears to be a gradual decline in the likelihood that law school graduates who practice law have come from blue-collar families. The difference, however, is not significant. It may simply reflect a general upward mobility in the American work force due to an expanding volume of positions at high-status levels and contracting positions at a lower status, which, together with variances in birth rates (lower at higher status levels), create an impression of an upwardly mobile population (Blau & Duncan, 1967, pp. 426–35).

28. When all four occupational status categories are included in the analysis, there is no statistically significant relationship between father's occupation and reasons of upward mobility.

TABLE 3.6
Upward Mobility Reasons Important in Decision to Attend Law School by
Father's Occupation

Reasons for Attending Law School	Father's Occupation			
	Professional	Managerial, Administrative, Technical	Sales, Clerical	Blue Collar
Prestige of profession...........	26.5%[a]	24.2%	29.0%	34.9%
Above-average income..........	17.1	16.1	18.3	25.7
Stable, secure future...........	2.6	11.2	12.9	9.2
	$(N = 117)$[b]	$(N = 161)$	$(N = 93)$	$(N = 109)$

[a]Figures represent percentages of respondents, with fathers in each occupational group, who cited the given reason as one of the three most important in the decision to enter law school. For example, 26.5% of lawyers with professional fathers rate "prestige of the profession" as an important reason in their decisions to attend law school, as compared with 17.1% of lawyers with the same background who cite "above-average income." Since each category includes respondents marking any of the items in the top three ranks, the groups are not mutually exclusive. See table 3.1 for the distribution across all factors important in the decision to attend law school.

[b]Number of respondents whose father's occupations were in each of the categories; number on which percentages in each column are based.

If this analysis is restricted to the most recent law school graduates, who may be assumed to have the clearest memory of their reasons for entering law school, only prestige is significantly related to father's occupation. As table 3.7 shows, the distribution is statistically significant but not linear. For those out of law school five years or less, prestige of the profession was an important factor in the decision to attend law school for only 18.5 percent and 17.1 percent, respectively, of the children of professionals and of the children of managers, administrators, and technical personnel. In contrast, a full 42 percent of the children of sales and clerical personnel and 47.1 percent of the children of blue-collar workers cite prestige of the profession as important in their decisions to enter the law. Thus, somewhat contrary to the conclusions reached in other studies (Jacob, 1978; Stevens, 1973), we find that young lawyers from lower status backgrounds are still consciously seeking and achieving higher status for themselves by pursuing careers in the legal profession.

TABLE 3.7
Importance of Prestige of Profession by Father's Occupation for Recent[a] Law
School Graduates' Decisions to Attend Law School

	Father's Occupation			
	Professional	Managerial, Administrative, Technical	Sales, Clerical	Blue Collar
% citing important[b]	18.5	17.1	42.9	47.1
% not citing important..........	81.5	82.9	57.1	52.9
	100%	100%	100%	100%
	$(N = 27)$	$(N = 35)$	$(N = 21)$	$(N = 17)$

[a]Recent law school graduates are those who had graduated within the previous five years at the time of the interview—i.e., between June 1970 and June 1975.

[b]The important category includes respondents who cited prestige of profession as one of the three most important reasons in the decision to enter law school.

In contrast to the implications in the literature, we do not find any change in the extent to which a career in the law serves as a route to upward mobility. Neither social backgrounds of practicing attorneys nor self-perceptions of the desire for upward mobility as an important influence on decisions to attend law school have changed much over the years. The questions of social mobility, however, may not be limited solely to entry into the profession. For while the law in comparison with other occupations carries with it relatively high social status, the legal profession is far from monolithic. In fact, there are important status differences within the legal profession. When we consider intrabar status in detail in chapter 5, we will discover that the selection of law school is a critical decision. Thus for a fuller understanding of a legal career as a route to high status we must also consider the factors that enter into the decision to attend a particular law school.

Selection of a Law School

Once the decision has been made to seek a career in the legal profession, there remains the question of which law school to attend. The rank order of factors important in the selection of a law school is displayed in table 3.8 (questionnaire, pt. I, Q. 4, p. 3, appendix 1). The "quality of the school" stands out as substantially more important than other factors. This finding is consistent with Stevens's study of the 1972 graduates of six law schools, 80.3 percent of whom cited "quality of law

TABLE 3.8
Rank Order of Factors Important in Selection of Law School

Rank[a]	Factor in Selection of Law School	% Ranking Important[b]
1	Quality of the school	55.1
2	Classes scheduled to allow opportunity to work full or part time while attending law school	23.5
3	Wanted to practice law in that community or state .	24.3
4	Prestige	23.1
5	Cost	15.7
6	Opportunity for financial aid	10.5
7	Relative or friend who attended	9.9
8	Liked the community	8.0
9	Graduates had good record passing local bar exam	7.8
10	Only school at which accepted	4.0
11	Special professors or area of specialization	2.1
12	Diploma privilege (diploma from law school sufficient for admission to state bar)	0.6
		(N = 477)

[a]The ranks are based on scores that were calculated as $S = N_1 (2) + N_2$, where N_1 equals the number of respondents ranking the item as most important and N_2 equals number ranking the item second most important. Thus a first choice gets twice as much weight as a second choice. Ranks 1 and 2 were used because missing values increase significantly after the second rank, making comparisons more difficult.

[b]The percentages represent the proportion of the respondents ranking each item *either* 1 or 2. The only change in rank order is between ranks 2 and 3 in the table; the difference is less than one percentage point.

school'' as influencing law school selection (1973, pp. 624-25).[29] Indeed, despite substantial differences between Stevens's study and ours,[30] quality of the school is only one of seven factors that the two samples ranked quite similarly, in some cases indentically.[31]

The comparable items in relative agreement and their respective rankings in the two studies appear in table 3.9. Location and prestige of the

TABLE 3.9

Comparative Importance of Factors Influencing Selection of Law School by Practicing Attorneys and Law Students

Practicing Attorneys Factor in Selection of Law School	Rank	Rank	*Law Students (Class of 1972)*[a] Reason
Quality of the school	1	1	Quality of law school
Wanted to practice law in that community of state	3	4	Expected to practice in this state
Prestige	4	3	Prestige
Cost	5	6	Cheaper tuition
Opportunity for financial aid	6	8	Offered more (some) financial aid by this school
Only school at which accepted	10	9	Couldn't be admitted to one or more schools which I would have preferred
Special professor or area of specialization	11	10	Attracted by certain professor or group of professors at school

[a]Data on class of 1972 compiled from Stevens (1973, p. 625, table 38).

law school maintain their importance, followed by cost factors, including both direct costs and opportunities for financial aid. These findings are perfectly consistent with the stability of the law as a route to upward mobility, as documented earlier. It is clear that the relative importance of many of the factors (and most of the very important ones) which influenced the selection of law school has not changed very much over

29. In Stevens's data, as in our findings, this factor was considered influential by substantially more respondents than the second most important factor (''attracted to community or area in which school is situated''), which was selected by only 48.6 percent of the law students (1973, p. 625).

30. The following differences should be noted: (1) the universe for each study was quite different (Stevens's data are drawn from law students who were to graduate in 1972, ours from practicing attorneys who graduated as recently as 1974 and as long ago as 1907), (2) many of the preselected items were different (the number of items differed only by one, 12 in our study, 13 in Stevens's), and (3) our figures are based on a ranking derived from only the two most important factors influencing the decision, while Stevens's are based on yes/no responses to the question of importance of each of the items.

31. Of the eight items included in both studies, the only one on which the two samples substantially disagreed was the importance of the community in which the school was located (as distinguished from the desire to practice in that community or state). We termed the item ''liked the community''; Stevens called it ''attracted to community or area in which school is situated.'' As reported in table 3.8, only 8 percent of our respondents considered location important; in contrast, 48.6 percent of the class of 1972 considered this factor influential in their selection of a law school. The comparative rankings are eighth (our study) and second (Stevens's study).

time, and that those who actually entered the practice of law, compared with new law students as a whole (some of whom we can assume will never practice law or choose it as a long-term career), have been similarly influenced in the selection of a law school. In sum, although law school curricula have changed over recent decades, it is general reputation and extracurricular factors (location and costs), rather than any special substantive training provided by particular law schools, which have attracted and continue to attract students. An examination of these factors and their correlates will help us to more clearly understand the distribution of law students among the various law schools and, due to the strong relationship between law school attended and subsequent legal career,[32] the distribution of lawyers within the legal profession.

Costs and Law School Selection

The importance of costs in the selection of law school is further evidence that access to the law has not been restricted exclusively to those from high socioeconomic status backgrounds. For those who find the direct costs of law school and/or the loss of income during the years of attendance burdensome, there are several options. First, law school tuition is extremely variable. Among the nine law schools that educate the bulk of the Chicago bar, the most expensive cost almost six times as much as the least expensive at the time of the study.[33] It is important to note that tuition costs are not directly proportional to the school's reputation or the career chances of its graduates. As for higher education in general, the greatest discrepancy in costs is between public and private institutions. This will be important to remember when we consider the credentials for the practice of law provided by different law schools. While costs surely limit access to the formal training required for entrance into the legal profession, direct tuition costs alone do not necessarily prohibit less well-to-do students from attending relatively high-status law schools.[34]

One obvious alternative for less expensive legal training is part-time legal education, usually but not exclusively restricted to evening hours. Among the practicing bar we find, as expected, that lawyers from lower status backgrounds are significantly more likely to have attended law school part time than those from higher status backgrounds (table 3.10).[35] To some extent these data support Auerbach's concurrence with Alfred Reed (1921) that night law schools have "kept the privilege of

32. See chapter 5 for an analysis of the impact of law school attended on subsequent legal career.

33. See note 10 *supra* for a discussion of tuition.

34. The issue of law school status will be considered in detail in chapter 5.

35. In the sample as a whole, there is a statistically significant trend away from part-time legal education, with the younger, more recent graduates less likely to have attended law school part time. Since this trend has not been accompanied by change in the status groups from which the lawyer population as a whole is drawn, it may reflect an increase in the availability of financial aid.

practicing law from becoming a class monopoly" (Auerbach, 1976, p. 110). Still that conclusion substantially overstates the role of part-time legal education in providing entry to the bar for those from lower status backgrounds. While the data in table 3.10 show that background and

TABLE 3.10
Full-Time or Part-Time Law School Attendance by Father's Occupation

	Father's Occupation			
	Professional	Managerial, Administrative, Technical	Sales, Clerical	Blue Collar
Full-time attendance	92.7%	88.0%	90.0%	73.6%
Part-time attendance	7.3	12.0	10.0	26.4
	100%	100%	100%	100%
	($N=124$)	($N=167$)	($N=100$)	($N=110$)

$$\chi^2 = 21.01; \, p < 0.001$$

Somers' $D = 0.09$ (with law school type dependent)

part-time attendance at a law school are significantly related,[36] it is equally clear that the overwhelming proportion of lawyers from all social backgrounds attend law school full time.

Whether attendance at law school is full or part time, the costs of legal education have been important in the selection of law schools. Like attendance part time, the importance of costs in the choice of law school varies by social background. As expected and as table 3.11 illustrates,

TABLE 3.11
Importance of Costs[a] in Selection of Law School by Father's Occupation

	Father's Occupation			
	Professional	Managerial, Administrative, Technical	Sales, Clerical	Blue Collar
% citing important[b]	30.1	50.0	46.1	72.4
% not citing important	69.9	50.0	53.9	27.6
	100%	100%	100%	100%
	($N=113$)	($N=158$)	($N=89$)	($N=105$)

$$\chi^2 = 39.46; \, p < 0.001$$

Somers' $D = .20$ (with cost factors dependent)

[a]Three indicators of costs were measured: opportunity for financial aid, cost of schooling, and classes scheduled to allow opportunity to work full or part time while attending law school. Respondents ranking any of these three indicators as the first, second, or third most important factor in selecting a particular law school are included among those for whom costs were important in law school selection.

[b]Factors ranked 1, 2, and 3 are counted as important in tables 3.11 and 3.13. Since these first three ranks have not been weighted, individuals checking but not ranking three or fewer reasons were included. (Table 3.8 requiring rank information to calculate scores does not include those cases. This difference in variable construction accounts for the discrepancy in the Ns between table 3.8 and tables 3.11 and 3.13).

36. See chapter 5 for a discussion of the distribution of lawyers from different backgrounds among law schools of varying prestige.

costs increase in importance as a factor in the selection of a particular law school as one moves from higher to lower status backgrounds.[37] A comparison of tables 3.11 and 3.10 shows that while costs were important in the choice of law school for substantial proportions of the practicing bar, only some lawyers attended part-time law schools. The appropriate comparison is between those who attended part-time law school (table 3.10) and those for whom costs were important in selection of law school (table 3.11). This reveals that for lawyers from every background many more considered costs in selecting a law school than entered a part-time program (ranging from a difference of 46.0 percent for those from blue-collar backgrounds to 22.8 percent for those from professional backgrounds).[38]

If, as the literature implies, increasing costs are further reducing access to the legal profession, we might expect to find differences among age cohorts as to the importance of costs in the choice of law school. In the composite costs variable we find no such relationship. Costs have been important in law school selection for about half of all law school graduates studied regardless of years since graduation. But the importance of individual cost indicators has changed: class scheduling to allow for the opportunity to work has become less important in law school selection, and the availability of financial aid has become more so. In the composite, of course, the changes in importance of these factors would have the effect of canceling each other out and would explain why no relationship was found between years out of law school and composite costs. Since we did not find any significant change in the status of law graduates' backgrounds over the years, it may be that the increased availability of financial aid for legal education has merely reduced law students' dependence on outside work.[39]

The documented relationship between cost limitations and choice of law school is no small matter. Although access to the status of the profession as a whole may be insured irrespective of law school attended,

37. The costs variable includes items b, h, and i from question 4, pt. I, p. 3, of the questionnaire (appendix 1): "opportunity for financial aid," "cost," and "classes scheduled to allow opportunity to work full or part time while attending law school." We counted a factor as "important" if it ranked 1, 2, or 3. Using three ranks gave all three items an equal chance of being included.

38. Among the indicators of costs, the scheduling of classes to allow for the "opportunity to work full or part time while attending law school" is the most closely related to father's occupation. This may help explain the data concerning part-time legal education. Any trends away from part-time legal education must be considered in light of the option to attend a full-time law school (carrying a full load and completing the curriculum in three years) with class hours arranged (usually mornings) to allow working an eight-hour job. DePaul University Law School, whose graduates constitute close to one-fifth of the Chicago bar, has such an arrangement. Thus night law school (by definition part time) is not the only option for those who cannot afford to attend law school without keeping an income-producing job.

39. In addition, opportunities for lucrative summer employment in law firms have increased, particularly after the second year of law school.

we will see in subsequent chapters that there is substantial variability in the practice of law and that career routes are strongly influenced by the source of a lawyer's professional degree. Thus to the extent that cost considerations restrict the schools available to individuals from particular backgrounds, they will indirectly affect careers within the profession as well.

Geographic Considerations in Law School Selection

As indicated in table 3.8, the desire to practice law in a particular community or state is rated as an important factor in the selection of law school by more practitioners than any other factor except quality of the school.[40] One need only peruse the distribution of law schools attended shown in table 3.12 to appreciate the localism of the practicing

TABLE 3.12
Law Schools Attended by Chicago Lawyers

	% of Sample	No. of Lawyers
DePaul[a]	18.2	98
Northwestern......................	11.5	62
Chicago	10.2	55
John Marshall	9.5	51
IIT-Chicago Kent	7.8	42
Illinois..........................	6.9	37
Loyola	6.3	34
Harvard	6.0	32
Michigan	5.0	27
Other schools[b]...................	18.6	99
Total	100%	537

[a]The schools are listed in the order in which they have contributed graduates to the practicing bar.

[b]All other law schools have each trained less than 3% of the Chicago bar with only four of those schools each contributing more than 1% (Wisconsin 2.4%, Notre Dame 1.9%, Yale 1.5%, and Columbia 1.3%).

bar. The overwhelming majority of practicing lawyers in Chicago attended law school within the city limits. There is in fact a strong relationship between the desire to practice law in the area and the decision to attend a law school in Chicago. As indicated in table 3.13, twice as many lawyers who attended law school in Chicago, as compared with those attending schools elsewhere, cite the desire to practice law in the community or state as important in their selection of law school. Chicago is the center of a major metropolitan area with a strong base of economic activity that generates demand for legal services and attracts a high concentration of lawyers. But why choose Chicago over another

40. As indicated in the notes to table 3.8, the community factor is ranked third because the ranking weights the importance ranking of individual items, while the percentage figure treats both importance ranks (rank 1 and rank 2) equally. In any case the importance attributed to "classes scheduled to allow opportunity to work full or part time while attending law school" and "wanted to practice law in that community or state" is virtually the same.

TABLE 3.13

Importance of Plans to Practice Law in Community or State as Factor in Selection of Law School, by Location of School[a]

	Location of Law School	
	In Chicago	Outside Chicago
% citing important[b]	41.4	19.5
% not citing important	58.6	80.5
	100%	100%
	(N = 297)	(N = 87)

$$\chi^2 = 13.35; \ p \leqslant 0.001;$$
$$gamma^c = 0.49$$

[a]Includes only respondents with *some* prior contact with Chicago. In addition to those represented in the table, 22 other respondents rated this item important and 28 more mentioned it.

[b]See note b, table 3.11, *supra* for an explanation of the construction of the importance variable.

[c]Gamma is a symmetrical measure of association used with ordinal data. It can range in value from -1 to $+1$. A positive value indicates a tendency for the same rank ordering of cases on both variables. A negative value indicates a tendency for the opposite rank ordering of cases on the two variables. Gamma $= (Ns - Nd)/(Ns + Nd)$, where $Ns =$ concordant pairs, $Nd =$ discordant pairs. For further description of gamma and its interpretation see Herman J. Loether and Donald G. McTavish, *Descriptive Statistics for Sociologists* (Boston: Allyn & Bacon, Inc., 1974), pp. 221–29.

major American city? The answer can be found by examining where today's lawyers spent their time prior to law school.

One of the most striking demographic features of the practicing bar is its extremely limited geographic mobility. As illustrated in figure 3.1, the overwhelming proportion of Chicago lawyers had some contact with the city before entering the practice of law. Much of this is simply a reflection of the earlier documented extent to which law schools within Chicago have educated the Chicago bar.[41] In addition, since Chicago is significantly larger with proportionally more economic activity than any other midwestern city, Chicago may be a "local" place to practice law for those from elsewhere in the Midwest. This is particularly true for those pursuing certain specialties that depend upon a high degree of economic activity for sufficient demand to constitute a specialty. If those attending midwestern law schools, including those in Chicago, are viewed as a group, 398, or 83 percent of the 477 lawyers, have not strayed very far from the location of their law schools.[42]

Furthermore, it is clear that even most of those who attended law

41. The figures in figure 3.1 are limited to those respondents for whom all the reported data in the graph are available. For example, table 3.12 shows 342, or 63.7 percent of the Chicago bar sample, as having attended law school in Chicago. The 309 in the graph are those for whom information on undergraduate school and location of childhood residence were also available. However, since this should not, and in fact did not, affect Chicago law school graduates more than others, the proportions remain essentially the same (309 = 64.8 percent of the 477 lawyers in figure 3.1).

42. Again this figure is based on those members of the sample for whom all geographic indicators were available. If we include the rest of the sample the figures are 442 out of 537, or 82.3 percent.

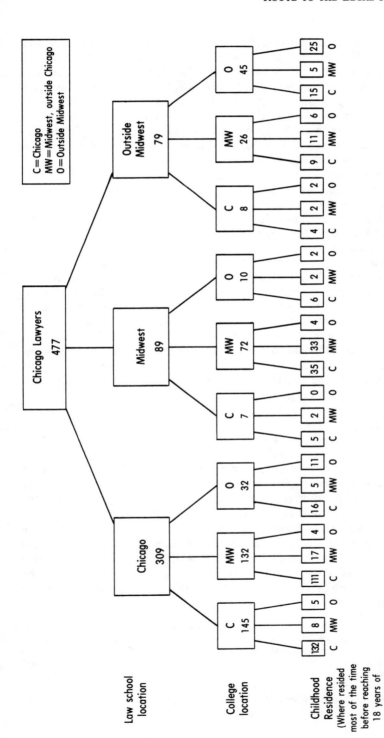

Fig. 3.1. Geographic mobility patterns

school outside the Midwest had some prior contact with the area. For example, undergraduate education also tends to be localized, although not nearly as much so as legal education. To some extent this difference is due simply to the geographical distribution of law schools as compared with colleges and universities.[43] In fact most of the localism of the Chicago bar extends back much earlier, with 69.8 percent having resided in Chicago during their childhood. Indeed only 5.2 percent of the practicing bar in Chicago did not grow up, go to college, or attend law school in Chicago or the Midwest.

In order to examine whether the geographic mobility of our sample was affected by age, we looked for an association between age and each of the individual components of the geographic mobility variable: birthplace, childhood residence, location of undergraduate education, and law school location. Only the relationship between area of undergraduate school and age is statistically significant ($p < 0.005$), with older attorneys more likely to have attended college in Chicago than the younger attorneys (22.6 percent of the attorneys under 35 years of age, 32.0 percent from 35 to 49, and 41.4 percent of those 50 or over attended college in Chicago). Although younger attorneys appear to be more geographically mobile with respect to their higher education, when it comes to choosing a law school and/or settling into the practice of law, there is virtually no difference among generations. Young attorneys, like their predecessors, tend to practice law where their parents raised them; entering practice is simply more often a *return* home for them than for older attorneys.

To go back to the very strong relationship between law school attendance in Chicago and practicing law in Chicago, as reflected in table 3.13 and figure 3.1, one should note that Chicago lawyers are not much more provincial in this regard than are lawyers in other cities and the graduates of law schools in the same locale.[44] In his study of the 1960 class of six law schools, Stevens (1973) found that the alumni tended to practice law in the general region of their law schools. While the graduates of the more "regional" schools (such as the University of Iowa and the University of Southern California) are more likely to have worked in the same geographical area (67 percent and 74 percent in the Midwest and the West, respectively), the figures for Yale and Pennsylvania graduates are not very dissimilar: 45 percent of the Yale graduates practiced in the Northeast, and 56 percent of the Pennsylvania graduates practice in the mid-Atlantic region. If the region is expanded, the figures increase sub-

43. For example, at the time of the survey there was only one law school (the University of Illinois) in the state of Illinois outside Chicago which had any graduates. Several new law schools have not yet graduated their first class, and only two of them, Southern Illinois University and Northern Illinois University College of Law (formerly Lewis University), are ABA approved, making graduates eligible to take the Illinois bar examination.

44. Handler's finding of localism within the bar of a middle-sized midwestern city ("Prairie City"), a third of whom were born there (and three-quarters of whom were born in the same state), was not as surprising (1967, p. 22).

stantially. "Of the Pennsylvania graduates, 88 percent were located in the northeast, mid-Atlantic or southeastern states, as were 70 percent of the Yale graduates. To some extent, therefore, all of the schools are 'regional' in terms of training for geographical areas" (Stevens, pp. 562-63).

This view of regionalism is substantially supported if examined from the opposite perspective—that is, looking at practicing attorneys in given cities and noting where they attended law school. Jerome Carlin (1962b) organized that type of data for seven cities (Chicago, New York, Boston, Philadelphia, Cleveland, San Francisco, and Los Angeles) to show that individual practitioners, regardless of city, are much more likely to have attended a non-Ivy League school, and particularly a night law school, than practitioners in firms of more than 25 lawyers. What is of interest for our purpose is the rather remarkable localism of all the practitioners which Carlin inadvertently documented. A full 82 percent of all lawyers in firms with more than 25 members in Boston attended Harvard Law School, in contrast to a range of 21 percent to 32 percent for lawyers with firms of the same size in the other six cities. If graduates of Yale and Columbia (for which New York is the closest large city) are added to the group from Harvard, the tendency to localism is supported further: 74 percent of New York lawyers and 87 percent of Boston lawyers in firms of more than 25 attended law school at Harvard, Yale, or Columbia. The range for the same practice context in the other cities is from 25 percent to 46 percent. In Carlin's figures for individual practitioners, the pattern repeats itself, though on a lesser scale. More specifically, 27 percent of the solo practitioners in New York and 35 percent in Boston graduated from Ivy League law schools. These contrast with a range of from 2 percent to 8 percent of the individual practitioners in the other six cities who graduated from an Ivy League law school.[45] Thus, irrespective of practice context, lawyers tend

45. The following tables from Carlin (1962b, table 11, note 13, and table 12, note 14, pp. 32-33) show the law school background of both firm lawyers and individual practitioners in the seven cities.

The law schools attended by lawyers in firms with more than 25 lawyers are as follows:

	Chicago	New York	Boston	Phila-delphia	Cleve-land	San Francisco	Los Angeles
Ivy League:							
Harvard	21%	32%	82%	20%	32%	29%	28%
Yale	3	16	4	3	11	5	8
Columbia	1	26	1	1	3	2	1
Total	25	74	87	24	46	36	37
Other full-time university	60	12	8	64	51	54	54
Night	15	14	5	12	3	10	9
	100	100	100	100	100	100	100
No. of lawyers	(581)	(70)	(232)	(361)	(244)	(167)	(166)
No. of firms	16	--	7	10	5	5	4

The law schools attended by individual practitioners are as follows:

to be drawn from law schools within the same general geographic area in which they practice.

This finding of localism is of particular interest because of the role of geography in prestige ratings of law schools. Law schools are typically categorized according to the student clientele they serve, "national" law schools appealing to students from around the country and "local" law schools generally drawing their students from a narrower geographic area.[46] National law schools are said to be preparing their graduates to practice anywhere in the nation, while local schools expect their graduates to practice in the same state in which the school is located (and so orient their curricula). Consequently, it is generally assumed, with some validity, that the law school attended affects a lawyer's geographic mobility (e.g., York and Hale, 1973, p.15). Yet while it may be true that graduates from certain schools have greater *opportunities* for mobility, the evidence suggests that their *actual* mobility may not be as great as assumed.[47]

Prestige and Law School Selection

Law school prestige is cited by about one-quarter of the practicing bar

	Chicago	New York	Boston	Phila-delphia	Cleve-land	San Francisco	Los Angeles
Ivy League	2%	27%	35%	5%	4%	3%	8%
Other full-time university	29	3	23	45	54	59	42
Night	69	70	42	50	42	38	50
Total	100%	100%	100%	100%	100%	100%	100%
No. of lawyers	(109)	(103)	(79)	(75)	(70)	(65)	(119)

Carlin's source for these data was the *Martindale-Hubbell Law Directory* (1958), volumes 1 and 2. For all cities except New York, his figures were based on total listings in the biographical section. Since similar listings were not available for the larger New York City firms, these figures were based on information obtained in his survey of New York City lawyers (based on a random sample drawn from the alphabetical listings in the 1960 *Martindale-Hubbell* directory).

While the data rely on the *Martindale-Hubbell Law Directory* and so suffer from the limitations discussed in chapter 2, they are sufficiently skewed that the distributions would not change significantly.

46. The dichotomization of law schools into "national" and "non-national" categories is taken up in detail later in the text at note 49 and in the discussion of table 3.14. See appendix 2 for a review of the complexities of ranking law schools.

47. These findings do not eliminate the possibility that attendance at a national law school has an effect on geographic mobility. First of all we are dealing only with those who practice in Chicago and not all of the graduates of some law schools as compared with others. In addition, Chicago has two "national" law schools within its city limits: the University of Chicago and Northwestern University. Given the previously cited figures drawn from Carlin (1962b) and Stevens (1973) about the lack of geographic mobility of law graduates, there is a substantial likelihood that graduates of these two law schools will practice in Chicago. The hypothesized likelihood for those with no prior contact with Chicago to have attended national law schools thus cannot be accurately evaluated with these data. A similar sample in another major American city that does not have any locally based national law schools might yield different results.

as having been an important factor (rank 1 or 2) in their decisions on which law schools to attend. As such, prestige is ranked fourth in importance in the aggregate and is as influential as the scheduling of classes to allow for work and the desire to practice in the same geographical area in attracting students. Like these other factors, the influence of the law school's prestige in attracting its students has not been equally distributed within the bar. Lawyers from blue-collar families are significantly less likely than other lawyers to have been attracted by the prestige of the particular law schools they attended ($\chi^2 = 12.39$, $p < 0.01$). If, as discussed previously, these lawyers are more likely to have been attracted to a career in the legal profession because of its general social standing, then gradations among law schools, all of which provide access to the profession, may be relatively less important to them.

This school-prestige factor is entirely distinct from the earlier discussed prestige of the profession which attracts students to careers in the law, and we have found, moreover, that there is no relationship between them. That is to say, individuals drawn to the legal profession because of its prestige are no more or less likely than other attorneys to have considered prestige as an important factor in the selection of a law school.

As table 3.14 shows, law schools vary significantly in the extent to which their students are attracted by the schools' reputations.[48] Where

TABLE 3.14
Rank Order of Law Schools Educating Most of Chicago Bar by Importance of Prestige of Law School as Factor in Selection of School
($N = 425$)

Law School[a]	% Citing Important	N
Harvard	86.7	32
Michigan	65.4	26
Chicago	37.8	52
Northwestern	32.7	61
Illinois	12.5	35
Loyola	7.4	33
IIT-Chicago Kent	3.1	38
DePaul	2.6	97
John Marshall	2.3	51

$$\chi^2 = 142.01;$$
$$p \leqslant 0.001;$$
$$gamma = 0.81$$

[a]Law schools whose graduates represent 5% or more of the sample.

48. Because of the localism factor, University of Chicago and Northwestern graduates may appear in our Chicago sample to be more alike than they would if all alumni of both schools had been sampled. As discussed above, most law school graduates come from and practice in the same geographical area as the law school, with many who come from elsewhere returning there to practice law. The University of Chicago draws a substantially greater proportion of its students from outside the area, with 71.1 percent outside Illinois

appropriate we shall employ this self-ascribed prestige ranking of law schools in the remainder of the analysis and will see that it is a powerful predictor. The advantages of this ranking lay in its source (the consumers of legal education), its unidimensionality, and the individual variability it provides—a variability typically not provided in law school ratings.[49]

While the ranking of law schools shown in table 3.14 will provide the basis for parts of the subsequent analysis, particularly that restricted to the nine law schools from which most Chicago lawyers graduate, it excludes many law schools that have contributed to the shaping of the local bar. Unfortunately the number of graduates in the sample from any of these schools individually is too small to expand the same ranking technique.

In an effort to develop a categorization appropriate for all the data, we did several analyses of variance among graduates of the same nine law schools on the importance of prestige as a factor in choice of law school.[50] We analyzed the school data in two steps, first divided into four categories along the traditional "elite," "prestige," "regional," and "local" lines as best as we could apply them, and then dichotomized along the national/non-national dimension. The national/non-national distinction gave the best (140 percent larger F score: 135.98 versus 57.57) and most consistent results.[51] Thus we achieved a classifica-

---

and 60.1 percent outside the Midwest, than does Northwestern, with 49.9 percent outside Illinois and 36.5 percent outside the Midwest ("Residence of Members of the Student Body During 1977–78," *University of Chicago Law School Catalog 1978–79*, p. 79; telephone interview March 6, 1979 with Patricia Miller, Registrar, Northwestern University School of Law, providing figures for full-time J.D. candidates in 1978–79). Therefore, our sample of the local bar would tend to underestimate the percentage of Chicago alumni drawn by the school's prestige. The same phenomenon would probably lead to an overestimate for Harvard and Michigan. The central point, however, in terms of the general ordering of the importance of prestige is not altered.

49. See appendix 2 for discussion of the limitations of various attempts to rank law schools.

50. An analysis of variance compares the mean of the responses of members of different groups to determine whether the difference between groups is greater than the difference within groups, so as to evaluate the validity of the groupings. The Student-Newman-Keuls procedure was employed.

51. The analysis of variance was calculated by three methods: Student-Newman-Keuls Procedure, Modified LSD Procedure, and Scheffe Procedure. By most consistent results, we mean where all three procedures were likely to give the same result, where each method requires a different degree of variation to produce significant results. In addition to Harvard, Michigan, Chicago, and Northwestern, in alphabetical order the following law schools appearing in our data were later classified as national: Columbia, Georgetown, New York University, Pennsylvania, Stanford, Virginia, Wisconsin, and Yale. Although developed through a different analysis, these results would be consistent with those of Heinz et al. (1976) if they were to reduce their four categories to the national/non-national dichotomy. For the reasons discussed we think our dichotomous version is more realistic. This is particularly true in a study of the Chicago bar because the large number of Northwestern graduates overwhelm other schools similarly categorized as "prestige." As a result the prestige category would essentially represent the graduates of a single school.

tion of law schools based upon ascription by the schools' practicing graduates.

The importance of law school ratings, and the rancor with which they tend to be greeted, is in part due to the assumption that the reputation of the law school is both related to the quality of education provided and an important determinant of graduates' career chances (see appendix 2 for an extended discussion of the ranking problem). Whether those chances, as determined by law school rankings, are better or worse, or simply different, has been one aspect of the debate. We shall be evaluating several possible roles that law schools play in the professional lives of their graduates. First, we will inquire into the differences in law schools' goals as perceived by their graduates. In subsequent chapters we will consider the contributions of law schools, as compared with other sources, to the distribution of lawyers within the bar, to the development of skills requisite to the practice of law, and to professional responsibility.

Differences Among Law Schools in Educational Goals

There is a good deal of common wisdom about the differences in emphases among law schools. The higher prestige law schools are said to concentrate on the theoretical aspects of the law, with only slight attention to more practical, career-oriented concerns. In contrast, the less prestigious law schools are said to be concerned mainly with qualifying their graduates to take and pass the bar examination. There is considerable divergence in the extent to which the goals we examined are regarded as the major goals of American law schools (questionnaire, pt. I, Q. 5, p. 3, appendix 1). Table 3.15 shows the percentage of practicing

TABLE 3.15
Major Goals of Law School Attended as Perceived by
Chicago Lawyers

Goal	% Indicating
Teach students to think analytically	74.0
Provide good basis for the practice of law	64.1
Provide theoretical basis of the law	51.7
Instill high level of respect for the judicial process.....	46.0
Prepare graduates to pass the bar examination........	36.9
Prepare students for practice in a particular specialty ..	4.0
	($N = 543$)

lawyers who view each goal as having been a major goal of the law school attended, in the order in which they are cited. Not surprisingly, "teach students to think analytically," or in common parlance "thinking like a lawyer," is perceived as the most predominant law school goal. In contrast to this general basic skill, the preparation of students for practice in particular specialties is only very rarely attributed to law schools. Both these appraisals are consistent with the view that law schools prepare generalists in the law who, with additional experience, should be able to practice any specialty. While these data support that view, they also imply that lawyers and law schools recognize that the socializing role of law schools is rather narrowly limited, with much of the role behavior expected of a legal practitioner left undeveloped by law schools. This is a theme to which we will return subsequently.

With the exception of preparation of students for practice in a particular specialty, there is sufficient variance in the respondents' perceptions of law schools' goals to merit investigating these differences among the graduates of different types of law schools. In responses on all five goals on which analysis is possible, those who attended national law schools differ significantly from those who attended non-national law schools. These data appear in table 3.16, arranged in the same order as in table

TABLE 3.16
Perceived Major Goals of Law School Attended by National and
Non-national Law Schools

Goal	% Indicating Major Goal		χ^2	Probability of Bivariate Distribution Occurring by Chance	Gamma[a]
	National $(N=212)$	Non-national $(N=319)$			
Teach students to think analytically ..	91.5	63.0	52.8	< 0.001	.73
Provide good basis for the practice of law............	50.0	73.4	29.16	< 0.001	− .47
Provide theoretical basis of the law....	76.9	34.5	89.99	< 0.01	.73
Instill high level of respect for the judicial process....	52.8	42.0	5.57	< 0.05	.21
Prepare graduates to pass the bar examination	4.7	58.6	155.58	< 0.01	− .93

[a]Positive gammas indicate that lawyers who attended national law schools are more likely than those who attended non-national law schools to have agreed that the goal under consideration was a major goal of their law school. Negative gammas indicate that lawyers who attended non-national law schools are more likely than those who attended national law schools to have agreed that the goal under consideration was a major goal of their law school.

3.15 to facilitate comparisons (with preparation for a specialty excluded because of insufficient variance). The picture presented here in table 3.16, with the national/non-national breakdown, is substantially different from the impression given of law schools as a whole in table 3.15. While it is no less true that close to three-quarters of the practicing bar think that teaching students to think analytically was a major goal of their law schools, graduates of national law schools account for significantly more of the positive responses on this question than do graduates of other law schools. The national law schools are, according to their own graduates, significantly more likely to emphasize analytical thinking and the theoretical basis of the law than are other law schools. At the same time, the national law schools are substantially less likely to be viewed by their graduates as being centrally concerned with either providing a good basis for the practice of law or preparing students for the bar examination.

These findings are consistent with previous interpretations of the differences among law schools. What is most interesting here is that practicing lawyers speaking only about their own experiences, and not attempting to compare themselves with other lawyers, fall into distinct patterns according to the law school attended. The one goal not yet mentioned is instilling a high level of respect for the judicial process. While the difference is statistically significant, there is only a 10 percent difference in responses. The idea that national law schools are more "professional" in orientation might lead one to suspect that their graduates would have been even more likely to have mentioned inculcation of respect for the judicial process as one of their schools' major goals. As it is, fewer than 50 percent of the practicing bar think that instilling a high level of respect for the judicial process was a major goal of their law schools.

A good deal of attention has been given to the differences in both methods and goals of part-time and full-time law schools. This has been true of both defenders and detractors of part-time legal education. One reflection of the intensity of the debate was the proposal by the executive committee of the Association of American Law Schools (AALS) as late as 1957 to deny AALS membership to law schools with evening programs (Cox, 1975). Since national law schools do not have part-time programs, and since the goals they seem to emphasize are different from those of other law schools (including some with part-time programs), any simple full-time/part-time comparison would be likely to reflect national status. If we look only at the graduates of law schools with *both* full-and part-time programs, we find that graduates who attended law school full time do not perceive the major goals of their law schools any differently than those who attended part time. While the most prestigious law schools may not have part-time programs, there is nothing inherent in part-time education that requires or even promotes goals different from those of the regular three-year law school program. While it might be argued that those going to school part time are less likely to be interested in goals that do not directly relate to the practice of law, with the part-time law school obligated to fulfill its customers' needs, no such differences were found among graduates of schools offering both full-time and part-time programs.

In addition to differences among law schools, even within law schools there have been substantial changes in emphasis over the years. Yet of the five goals discussed, only two have been found to vary in perceived importance by the years since graduation from law school: instilling respect for the judicial process and providing the theoretical basis of the law. Both differences are in the expected directions: according to law schools' graduates, as respect for the judicial process has declined as a perceived major goal of law schools, the theoretical basis of the law has increased (see table 3.17). Decreasing emphasis on respect for the judicial process may say something more about changes in generational attitudes toward institutions both inside and outside law schools than about legal education in particular.[52] The increasing number of references to the theoretical basis of the law, however, may reflect actual increased curricular emphasis on the theoretical underpinnings of the law.[53]

TABLE 3.17
Perceived Major Goals of Law School Attended by Years
Since Graduation

Years Out of Law School	% Indicating as Major Goal ($N = 536$)	
	Instill Respect for Judicial Process	Provide Theoretical Basis of Law
5 or less.................	32.1	60.6
6–15....................	44.7	50.5
16–35..................	52.9	52.3
36 or more	53.6	40.5
	$\chi^2 = 13.51$; $p \leqslant 0.005$	$\chi^2 = 7.76$; $p \leqslant 0.05$
	Somers' $D = -0.114$ (asymmetric with goal dependent)	Somers' $D = 0.076$ (asymmetric with goal dependent)

For both substantive and analytic reasons, it is important to move beyond the national/non-national distinction to determine the impact of individual law schools on the findings. Substantively, we are interested in individual differences among law schools. Analytically, we do not want to miss differences that are suppressed because of domination of categories by individual schools. A one-way analysis of variance among the nine schools revealed highly significant differences ($p < 0.001$) for each of the five goals. Having determined that the perceived goals of the nine law schools are more different than they are alike, we need to explore further the extent to which this reflects a national/non-national split among the law schools.[54]

52. Consideration of generational change in attitude as a linear variable may mask some important variation, particularly with respect to graduates' attitudes about their law schools. Although, as we have noted, the tension between the practicing bar and legal academia has had a long tradition, the criticisms of legal education reached a crescendo in the turbulent sixties. The critics of the sixties concentrated particularly on law schools' failure to address the inequities of the legal system and their collusion in perpetuating them. It appears that since that era, law students, like other students in higher education, have returned to many of the presixties concerns and values. Analysis reveals no significant differences between the sixties cohort and the rest of the practicing bar with respect to law schools' goals. (The sixties cohort includes those out of law school four to nine years as of the time of the data collection in 1975. That category would include all those who were in law school or college in the last half of that decade, when rebellion of all forms reached its height.)

53. An alternative hypothesis might be that these two findings are interrelated with criticism of the courts increasing as more emphasis is put on theoretical consistency in the schools.

On the whole there is substantial linearity among law schools in terms of the goals emphasized. Yet there are some striking individual differences, illustrated in table 3.18, which deserve some attention. Loyola University Law School, not a "national" law school by any definition and a "local" one by most, does not act as might be predicted. The average Loyola graduate is significantly more likely to report instilling respect for the judicial process as a goal of the law school attended than are graduates of any other school. In addition, on two other goals, preparation for the bar examination and providing the theoretical basis of the law, Loyola graduates stand alone: they are significantly different from both the other "local" law schools and from all others. We think that Loyola holds a unique place among Chicago's "local" law schools and that this is reflected in the responses of its graduates. As indicated in table 3.14, Loyola graduates are more likely to have selected Loyola for reasons of prestige than graduates of other non-national law schools in Chicago. Whether those who select Loyola differ from those who select other local law schools, or Loyola offers a different program, or a combination of both, Loyola is a special case.

The University of Chicago Law School, while staying firmly within the national category, represents the extreme case for four of the five goals. The average graduate is either most or least likely to attribute a particular goal to that law school. The average Chicago graduate is least likely to agree that providing the basis for the practice of law or passage of the bar examination is a major goal of the law school. In fact, not a single graduate of the University of Chicago Law School in the sample views preparation for the bar examination as a major goal of the law school. On the positive side, the average Chicago graduate is the most likely to see providing the theoretical basis of the law and teaching analytic thinking as important goals of the law school. Apparently the University of Chicago's reputation for an academic orientation both precedes and follows actual attendance there.

---

54. A two-way analysis of variance using both the nine largest law schools in the order of their self-ascribed prestige and the years since graduation from law school reveals substantial variance in the proportion of the differences explained by the selected variables. Differences in preparation of graduates to pass the bar examination and providing the theoretical basis of the law as goals of the law schools are explained substantially more than other goals examined. (Actually the variance for these two goals is almost entirely accounted for by the law school prestige variable.)

Percentage of the Variance Explained by Two-Way Multiple
Classification Analysis for Goals of Law Schools

Goal	% Explained
Instill respect for judicial process	9.5
Prepare graduates to pass the bar exam	46.0
Provide theoretical basis of the law	29.3
Provide good basis for the practice of law	14.6
Teach students to think analytically	16.1

NOTE: The two factors are the nine largest law schools ranked by self-ascribed prestige and the years out of law school (5 or less, 6–15, 16–35, and 36 or more years).

TABLE 3.18 One-Way Analysis of Variance of Law School Goals by Law School Attended

Goals	Significantly Different Groups[a]			F Ratio for Anova	Probability of F Ratio
Instill respect for judicial process	Loyola[b] (1.3636)[c] Harvard (1.3750)	John Marshall (1.7255)		3.314	0.001
Prepare graduates to pass the bar examination	John Marshall (1.2368) DePaul (1.2708) IIT Chicago-Kent (1.2745)	Loyola (1.5758)	Illinois (1.8286) Harvard (1.9375) Northwestern (1.9516) Michigan (1.9600) Chicago (2.000)	43.292	0.0001
Provide theoretical basis of the law	Chicago (1.1887) Northwestern (1.2258) Michigan (1.2692) Harvard (1.2813) Illinois (1.2857)	Loyola (1.5758)	DePaul (1.8229)	19.754	0.0001
Provide basis for practice of law	John Marshall (1.0980)	Chicago (1.6038)		6.603	0.0001
Teach students to think analytically	Chicago (1.0189)	DePaul (1.4896)		9.066	0.0001
					N = 426

[a] The groupings indicate significant differences between the mean responses of the graduates of the schools in one grouping and those in another grouping. Schools not mentioned for a particular goal are those significantly different from a school in one group or another but not from all groupings shown. The exclusion of schools does not necessarily indicate that they are related to each other. The Student-Newman-Keuls (SNK) test was employed to determine the significant a posteriori contrasts. The SNK test is appropriate for comparing groups of unequal size: the larger the potential subset, the larger the difference in means must be to be declared significant.

[b] Schools are listed from low to high in the order of their mean responses to the question.

[c] Mean response for graduates of each school. A mean of 1.0 (low) would indicate that all graduates of a particular school noted the item as a major goal of their law school, a mean of 2.0 would indicate that none did.

Another way to see the same pheonomenon is to simply look at the percentage of each school's graduates who agree that the individual goals were major ones at their law schools. While we lose the ability to determine significantly different groupings displayed in table 3.18 above, this may be a simpler visual representation of the differences among schools. The same pattern reflected in the analysis of variance appears in table 3.19 in the percentages of graduates responding positively. Consistent with the findings of the earlier analysis, the exact ordering of schools varies according to the goal being discussed. There is not a single goal for which the precise ordering of percentage agreement by graduates exactly matches the self-ascribed prestige ranking. In addition, any attempt to divide the schools into more general categories based on the responses to the goals query fails. Perusal of table 3.19 indicates that a simple dichotomization of the schools would be different for different goals and, further, that such a split makes little sense for some of them.

Where does this leave us? Do prestige rankings mean nothing in terms of the perceived goals of the law schools? The data show very marked trends; the prestige rankings are related to the evaluation of goals, and generally in the expected direction. But categorizations always mask some differences, and this case is no exception. Many law schools are apparently unique in their emphases. In addition, as often occurs, the borderline cases provide the greatest difficulty.

The four law school goals for which there is substantial variance provide some interesting implications in light of the likely career differences of graduates of these schools. Two of the goals, providing a good basis for the practice of law and preparing graduates to pass the bar examination, speak to meeting the minimal requirements for access to the profession. The other two goals, teaching students to think analytically and providing the theoretical basis of the law, have more to do with the quality of legal expertise. The differences appear both in the comparison between the national and non-national law schools and in the analysis of variance by individual law school. Indeed the most extreme case in both analyses is preparing graduates to pass the bar examination (as reflected in a gamma of .93 for the cross tabulation, and an F ratio of 43.29 for the analysis of variance (Anova)). This clearly minimal achievement is most skewed toward schools whose students were least likely to have been attracted by the schools' reputations. Both the schools and their students may be in mutual agreement that the basic function of the school is to provide access to the legal profession for its graduates. Schools of greater prestige on the other hand may presume (although not always accurately) that access to the profession is readily available to their graduates. Consequently they are more likely to orient their approach toward a certain level of expertise that will result from an

TABLE 3.19 Perceived Major Goals of Law School Attended for Law Schools Educating Most of the Chicago Bar

Law School[a]	Instill Respect For Judicial Process	Prepare Graduates to Pass the Bar Examination	Provide Theoretical Basis of Law	Provide Basis for Practice of Law	Teach Students to Think Analytically
Harvard	62.5	6.3	71.9	59.4	96.9
Michigan	61.5	4.0	73.1	69.2	92.3
Chicago	47.2	0.0	81.1	39.6	98.1
Northwestern	46.8	4.8	77.4	45.2	80.6
Illinois	57.1	17.1	71.4	68.6	77.1
Loyola	63.6	42.4	42.4	69.7	66.7
IIT-Chicago Kent	36.8	76.3	28.9	84.2	57.9
DePaul	34.4	72.9	17.7	68.8	51.0
John Marshall	27.5	72.5	25.5	90.2	74.5
N	426	425	426	426	426
χ^2	25.47	193.08	117.08	47.90	63.11
p	0.001	0.0001	0.0001	0.0001	0.0001
Somers' D[b]	.13[c]	-.39	.31	-.15	.18

[a]Law schools are listed in decreasing order of ascribed prestige as established in table 3.14.

[b]All Somers' D coefficients presented were calculated with the law school goal under consideration as the dependent variable.

[c]A positive coefficient indicates a tendency for lawyers who attended law schools with higher self-ascribed prestige scores to have said that the goal under consideration was a major goal at their law schools more than those who attended law schools with lower self-ascribed prestige scores. Negative coefficients indicate the opposite tendency.

understanding of the theoretical basis of the law and highly developed analytic skills. It is most interesting that the expertise envisioned is essentially technical, with a professional concern with respect for the judicial process of substantially less importance. While a lay person might assume that professional training in law would be likely to value highly and therefore promote such respect, the products of law schools are simply not receiving a very strong message in this regard. The different careers that law schools apparently anticipate for their graduates and to which they ultimately move will be the subject of a subsequent chapter, in which the credentials for intrabar status are evaluated.

Conclusion

In this chapter we have examined the attractions of the legal profession. Our analysis has affirmed the existence of intergenerational occupational stability among lawyers and at the same time has documented the consistent role that the legal profession has played in providing access to higher status. Upward mobility has continued to be a strong attraction to the legal profession although naturally not equally so for lawyers from different social backgrounds.

With graduation from law school a nearly universal requirement for access to the profession, it was important to evaluate the factors entering into the selection of a school. We found that costs remain a very important factor in the choice of law school. So too, we have discovered, do the location of the law school and its prestige. We have refined our understanding of the geographic stability of the bar and the limits to viewing degrees from certain universities as determinative of subsequent geographic mobility. And we have developed a prestige ranking (and classification) of law schools that can be used for the remainder of the analysis. We further evaluated these rankings in connection with the perceived goals of the various law schools to determine whether the law school experience can be delineated along the prestige dimension.

There remains the question of whether the socializing effects of various law schools differ significantly. We shall be seeking to evaluate the effects of formal schooling in the law as compared with other influences on the distribution of lawyers within the bar, on the skills important in the lawyer's practice, and finally on the professional responsibility of the bar. Before examining the credentialing effects of law school on intrabar status, we must first portray the bar and its distribution among different practice contexts and different specialities. It is to this task that we now turn.

Chapter 4
PORTRAIT OF AN URBAN BAR

Introduction

The available picture of the practicing bar is not very clear. With a few important exceptions sociologists concerned with occupations in general, and the professions in particular, have not given lawyers the attention that their important social role dictates.[1] In addition, except for distinctions between solo and firm attorneys, discussions of the practicing bar typically fail to acknowledge the diversity of careers in the actual practice of law.[2] Our task in this chapter is to describe an urban bar, including the areas of law and the practice contexts within which professional careers unfold. We will then analyze the stability of legal careers and examine its implications for the profession.

The Context of Practice

The literature contains frequent references to the "traditional" lawyer, a small-town, independent solo practitioner who represents clients on a case-by-case basis and whose reputation is his most productive calling card. Although it is clear that such an image hardly represents the contemporary bar, the appropriate image is somewhat less clear. In accordance with population trends in general, the bar has become urbanized. Indeed, because legal activity is directly related to economic activi-

---

1. The best-known exception is Jerome Carlin, whose *Lawyers on Their Own* (1962b) and *Lawyers' Ethics* (1966) remain the best and most frequently cited works in the field. Like Carlin's work, Jack Ladinsky's study of Detroit lawyers, published as "Careers of Lawyers, Law Practice, and Legal Institutions" (1963a), is more than a decade old.

2. For an introduction to different legal careers, see Ehrlich and Hazard's readings, *Going to Law School?* (1975), in which the titles in the section "Some Profiles and Life Styles of Lawyers" indicate the range of practice covered: "The Small Town Lawyer," "The Individual Practitioner," "The Legal Aid Lawyer," "The Wall Street Lawyer," "The Legislative Assistant," and "The Public Interest Lawyer."

ty, the bar has become particularly concentrated in urban centers (York & Hale, 1973, pp. 10–11). Concomitantly, urban lawyers have become increasingly likely to practice in law firms.[3] While technically lawyers are still overwhelmingly (more than 75 percent) "independent" practitioners not directly employed by either government or private enterprise, the distinction between the independent and the employed attorney has become blurred. Associates (as opposed to partners) in law firms are salaried employees, although they do not legally represent their employers as would be the case with a staff attorney in government or business. While partners in law firms appear to fit more closely the image of the independent practitioner, in practice they often lack the professional independence implied by that term.[4] Therefore, where distinctions in the context of practice are appropriate, we will refer to "private" rather than "independent" practitioners. In general, however, we will attempt to be even more specific in references to private-practice context, making distinctions among solo practitioners and lawyers in firms of various sizes. Indeed, we will see that these more precise distinctions have substantial predictive power with respect to the professional development of lawyers.[5]

Since notions of what a small or a large firm is vary dramatically by location, it seemed appropriate to let the practicing bar determine for us the limits of each category.[6] Thus in addition to being asked to cate-

3. While there is a general trend for more recent law school graduates to practice in larger law firms, it is not statistically significant at an acceptable level ($p < 0.09$).

4. Law firms built on the representation of a small number of continuing corporate clients may well become as dependent upon those clients for their professional survival as the employed attorney. This development, however, has been curiously neglected in inquiries into the nature of the profession and its place in society. Although we cannot directly address the implications of relative degrees of professional independence in the practice of law, we wish at least to call the reader's attention to the importance of this issue.

5. Discussions of the distribution of attorneys in the practice of law have centered on the issue of firm affiliation. The steadily increasing proportion of firm over solo attorneys, coupled with indications that firms are more likely to handle the legal problems of corporate entities than of private citizens, has raised some voices of concern. Yet the solo/firm distinction is extremely problematic, potentially contributing greater confusion than clarity to an understanding of the distribution of lawyers in various practice contexts. Although law firms range in size from two to hundreds of members, they are generally discussed as a monolith. What is particularly bothersome is the tendency to describe the very large law firms (such as those depicted in Smigel's *The Wall Street Lawyer,* 1964), which typically cater to a corporate clientele, then to cite figures on the increase in firm over solo practice, all to bolster the conclusion that the legal needs of the private citizen are increasingly being left unmet. The inherent implication of course is that all law firms are more like the very large firms than they are like solo practitioners. It may be that this is not at all the case. Cavers (1968) in fact concludes that the legal practice of small-firm attorneys resembles that of solo practitioners more than it does that of large-firm lawyers (p. 141).

6. For example, Handler (1967) found that the largest law firm in "Prairie City" (code name for a midwestern town of 80,000) had only eight members. However, it is interesting to note that if all firms are treated as one category, the distribution of lawyers in various practice contexts in Prairie City is virtually the same as in Chicago (pp. 6, 13).

gorize their practice, those in firms were requested to indicate the number of attorneys in the firm (questionnaire, pt. II, Q. 8, p. 8, appendix 1). On the basis of the aggregate responses to the various kinds of firm practice and the accompanying number of members, we developed the categories displayed in table 4.1.[7] For now we will focus on those figures

TABLE 4.1
Distribution of Lawyers Among Kinds of Practice

	% of Sample	No. of Lawyers
Solo.	16.2	88
Small firm (2–8)	26.7	145
Medium firm (9–49)	16.6	90
Large firm (50 or more)	14.9	81
Government attorneys[a]	10.1	55
Business legal staff	11.6	63
Other.	3.9	21[b]
Total	100%	543[c]

[a]Consistent with the definition of practicing attorney, these include only those who represent the legal status of others. In the Chicago survey these respondents included city corporation counsel, state's attorneys, United States attorneys, or public defenders, or they represented one of the following government agencies: the Internal Revenue Service, the Securities and Exchange Commission, the Air Force, the Treasury Department, or the National Labor Relations Board.
[b]More than half of these are legal aid attorneys. Most of the remainder have a combination of careers such as "part-time prosecutor and own practice."
[c]The five missing cases, all of which involve respondents associated with firms, are not included because they failed to provide information on the size of their firms.

as simple descriptions of the distribution of the practicing bar and the trends they represent. Later in this chapter we will discuss the organization of substantive specialties and the degree of specialization within these various practice contexts. In subsequent chapters recruitment to different practice contexts and its implications for the professional development of lawyers will be considered and evaluated.

The distribution in table 4.1 reflects the current practice of the Chicago bar. If we are to evaluate assumptions about recent and continuing changes in the distribution of attorneys in different practice contexts, it is necessary to distinguish attorneys by stages in their careers. Figure 4.1

7. We developed our categories through a simple scatterplot of the size category of firm practice by the number in the firm. Although there was the occasional odd response (e.g., the respondent who checked "large" firm and then noted less than 10 persons in the firm), boundaries between categories became visually quite clear. Although 50 is a higher minimum number for the large-firm category than is usually found in this kind of analysis, a comparison with the study of the Chicago bar by Heinz and Laumann confirmed our categories. Although they set a substantially smaller number—30 in contrast to our 50—as the minimum for a "large" firm, our distributions vary hardly at all. In our sample 14.9 percent are in large law firms (using 50 as the minimum criterion) as compared with 16 percent in their sample (Heinz et al., 1976, p. 726). Our scatterplot confirms (with only 4 out of 548 lawyers in firms of 30 to 50) that at least in Chicago there are not many firms in the 30-to-50 member range. We hypothesize that once a firm reaches a certain size it continues to grow to meet new demands. Given the division of labor within a large firm, the 30-to-50 range is apparently not a very stable size. These parameters would not of course be appropriate in a nonurban setting.

illustrates the relationship between the years out of law school and the nature of the practice context. It is apparent that while the proportion of attorneys in firms is relatively constant, the proportion of solo attorneys drops dramatically, the more recent the law school graduation.[8] It is also true that the attorneys who have been in practice longer are likely

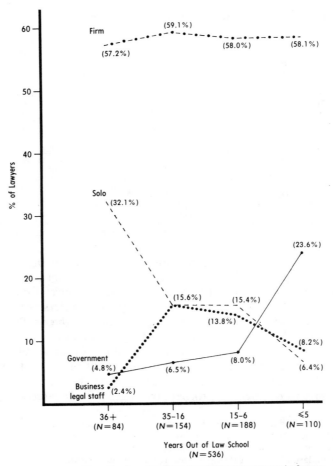

(Percentages in graph based on number of lawyers in each of the "years out" categories. For example, 32.1 percent of those out of law school 36 years or more are solo practitioners.)

Fig. 4.1 Context of practice by years out of law school

8. Here again the data may be somewhat skewed as a result of sampling from law directories, whether *Martindale-Hubbell* or *Sullivan's*. Young attorneys in firms are somewhat more likely to be listed than young solo practitioners, since their firms are already listed and take the initiative to add the new member's name. However, since postcards to add one's name to the law directories are distributed (at least in Illinois) at the bar admission ceremony, it is not likely that this factor significantly affects the data.

to be more settled into a career and so are not comparable with new attorneys still "looking for experience." This finding about the influence of stage of career is conceptually important because of the common wisdom that firms and government jobs serve as training grounds providing skills not obtainable in law school. Thus the greater porportions of government attorneys and smaller proportions of solo attorneys among newer lawyers in figure 4.1 may simply reflect newer graduates' choice of government jobs for supervised experience and similarly their avoidance of solo practice. An evaluation of that hypothesis requires a comparison of first law jobs after law school graduation for older and newer attorneys.

The distributions of first law jobs shown in figure 4.2 indicate more

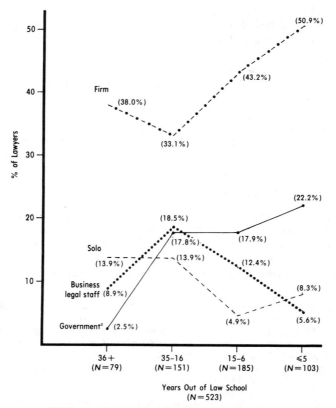

NOTE: The percentages add to less than 100 percent for each group of graduates because the graph does not include lawyers whose first law-related employment was other than the four listed.

[a]Government category includes both advocacy roles and other law-related government jobs. If we were to consider only government advocates, the figures would all drop, but the constancy of the government as first employer remains. In place of the 17.8 percent, 17.9 percent and 22.2 percent, the new figures would be 9.9 percent, 11.4 percent and 15.7 percent respectively, with the 36+ category at zero.

Fig. 4.2 Context of first law job by years out of law school

clearly any changing trends in the pattern of law careers. Government attorneys provide the clearest example of the point. While figure 4.1 gives the impression of a sudden increase in government attorneys, a comparison with figure 4.2 illustrates quite clearly that for first jobs after law school government has been a relatively constant employer for some time. On the other hand, a closer look at the solo and firm attorneys on these two graphs reveals major trends in the patterning of legal careers. Solo practice has apparently never been extremely popular as a first job out of law school (a maximum of 13.9 percent of any of the cohorts—those out of school more than 35 years—began their careers as solo practitioners).[9] Still the proportion of new lawyers choosing solo practice has decreased over the years. Figure 4.2 also documents that more and more law graduates are joining firms directly from law school.[10] In the past 5 years more than half of the law school graduates who have remained in the practice of law began their legal careers as members of law firms. The trends are both readily apparent and statistically significant.[11]

This trend toward firm practice has important implications for the nature and the structure of the legal profession in light of the continuing stability in legal careers, a matter we will consider later in this chapter. That stability, moreover, is greatest for individuals who begin their careers in law firms. Thus any tendency toward firm practice in the first job after law school is more likely to have a long-term effect on the nature of the legal profession than changes that have occurred in other practice contexts.

Specialization Within the Bar

Specialization is not new to the practice of law. As early as 1933 Karl Llewellyn voiced concern over the growing specialization among the bar in a law review article entitled "The Bar Specializes—with What Results?" Since that time specialization has continued to increase. Its rise has been variously attributed to population density and urbanism, in-

9. Like all the data reported here, these are based on attorneys still in practice. It is possible that many more new attorneys began their careers as solo practitioners but did not remain in the practice of law. One can speculate that simple market factors have operated to change the distribution of lawyers in various kinds of practice. If so, it might mean that more new attorneys began their careers as solo practitioners than reflected in the data but that fewer of them succeeded and so pursued other careers. As noted previously, the greatest failures are probably not currently practicing law, and any attempt to include them would require a different research design.

10. To ensure that the data represented in figure 4.2 reflect actual trends and not simply age-cohort categorization, figures for individual years since law school graduation were similarly evaluated, and they confirmed the findings. Although fluctuations naturally occur, the trend toward firm employment in the first job after law school graduation is unmistakable. It should also be noted that the career patterns of the large law school classes of recent years will have a proportional impact on the nature of the legal profession. See chapter 2, figure 2.1, for national trends.

11. Based upon a chi-square evaluation, the bivariate distribution illustrated is significant at a 0.01 level of probability.

creasing complexity in the law, need for greater efficiency in the face of rising demand for legal services, trends toward monopolization of goods and services, and numerous combinations and permutations thereof.[12] By 1952 an ABA committee had concluded that de facto specialization already existed, leaving as the only question for consideration the wisdom of certification and/or training for specialty practice and how they might best be achieved.[13] Recent figures support that conclusion: a survey of the California State Bar in the late sixties found that two-thirds consider themselves specialists (Thorne, 1973, pp. 111–12); a survey of the Chicago bar in the mid-seventies found that 70 percent identify themselves as specialists (Laumann & Heinz, 1977, p. 155).[14]

Despite observers' characterization and the self-identification of the bar as increasingly specialized, the legal profession is not nearly as specialized as many other occupations, with the medical profession the most obvious example.[15] Among practicing lawyers specialization most typically means that a large share or most of one's time is devoted to a particular area of the law. Only rarely, with the exception of prosecutors and public defenders, does it mean a practice that is exclusive to a single field of law. Recognition of this characteristic of legal specialization is implicit in research efforts to identify specialists. One American Bar Foundation study considers practitioners specialists if they devote 25 percent or more of their time to a particular area of law (Laumann & Heinz, 1977, table 2, p. 169). By that definition, of course, one can be a "specialist" in four areas of the law simultaneously.

Similarly cognizant of the nature of legal specialization, we asked legal practitioners to list the areas of law in which they did a *significant* amount of work (questionnaire, pt. II, Q. 6, p. 8).[16] While only 15.5

12. For discussions of the various causes and correlates of specialization see Christensen (1967), Greenwood and Frederickson (1964), Hochberg (1976), and Johnstone and Hopson (1967, pp. 142–59).

13. At the 1977 midyear meeting of the ABA the chairman of the Standing Committee on Specialization considered "widespread adoption of formal specialization 'inevitable' " ("ABA Midyear Meeting Wrapup," 63 *American Bar Association Journal*, pp. 307, 309 (1977)). For a description of regulatory schemes in operation and under consideration in various states, see Zehnle (1975). A more recent review with particular attention to the approved plans in California, New Mexico, and Florida can be found in an article by David Fromson, "Let's Be Realistic About Specialization" (1977). Much of the continuing debate over specialization within the legal profession centers on whether and how to certify specialists. Central to the negative view is the question of what impact certification has on the availability of legal services to people of moderate means. For a particularly vituperative attack on this trend see Nicholas von Hoffman's article "Legal Specialty Newest Ripoff?" in the *Chicago Tribune* (January 2, 1975, sec. 2, p. 4).

14. While the extent of specialization varies by the degree of urbanism (Deitsch & Weinstein, 1976), some degree of specialization is also found in smaller communities (Handler, 1967, ch. 2, pp. 35–69). The discussion of specialization therefore has relevance beyond metropolitan centers.

15. For comparisons of specialization in the legal and medical professions see Greenwood and Frederickson (1964) and Christensen (1970, ch. 3).

16. The specialties were ranked to show the area of law in which each lawyer spends more time than any other. This first-ranked specialty will provide the basis for subsequent analysis.

percent ($N=542$) indicate that they devote their time exclusively to a single area of the law, most of the sample limit their practices to a few substantive legal areas. Most do not cite more than three fields (45.6 percent rank four or more, with only 24.5 percent ranking more than four areas of law in which they do a *significant* amount of work).[17] It should be noted that these rankings somewhat understate the degree of specialization among the practicing bar. For we shall see later that for those attorneys who rank more than one specialty, the areas of the law cited are typically related to each other either in substance or by virtue of the similarity of the clientele served.[18]

Areas of Specialization of an Urban Bar

The work of practicing lawyers is not equally distributed among various areas of the law; market factors skew specialization toward selected fields. Table 4.2 displays the distribution of fields of law in which Chicago lawyers do a significant amount of their work and the percentages of lawyers who rank each specialty as the most important to their practices.[19] While there is a wide range in areas of specialization represented, corporate, real estate, and personal injury work (in that order) predominate, and more than two-thirds of the practicing bar (67.0 percent) concentrate their work in seven areas of the law.

As mentioned previously most lawyers do a significant amount of work in more than a single area of the law. We know further that some specialties are more likely to constitute an entire practice than are others. Among the Chicago bar, criminal law and patent law are the specialties most likely to be practiced to the exclusion of all others. The next most specialized practitioners are those who rank labor law or antitrust work as their predominant work. Conversely, creditor-debtor law, municipal law, family law, and corporate law are most likely to be practiced in conjunction with a number of other specialties.[20]

17. Another indicator of the importance of legal specialty to the practice of law is reflected in the factors considered important in deciding which cases and/or clients to accept (questionnaire, pt. II, Qs. 9 & 10, p. 9). For those who actually select cases, more than half (53.4 percent) cite the subject matter and its consistency with current work as the most important factor.

18. We shall also see later in this chapter (around fig. 4.3) that these specialty categories, while widely recognized, probably paint a picture of the bar with too broad a brush, and that clientele in combination with the substantive area of the law are important to understanding the actual work of lawyers.

19. The rankings of these specialties vary only negligibly if rankings are based on first-ranked specialty as in table 4.2, or on weighted ranks 1 through 4, or on mere mentions of significant work done in each legal specialty. We think, therefore, that these figures fairly represent the legal work currently engaging the practicing bar in Chicago.

20. The relationships among specialties have been determined by an analysis of the mode and median number of specialties cited as constituting a significant amount of the work done by lawyers who concentrate in each of the mentioned specialties (i.e., rank first among areas of law in which they work). For criminal and patent law the mode is 1.000, and the medians are 1.368 and 1.8333, respectively. The modal response is 5 (i.e., five specialties mentioned) for creditor-debtor, municipal, family, and corporate law, with medians ranging from 4.750 to 3.913.

TABLE 4.2
Distribution of Lawyers Among Legal
Specialties

Specialty[a]	%[b]	No. of Lawyers
Corporate...............	19.0	103
Real estate	12.4	67
Personal injury	10.5	57
Trusts and estates	8.1	44
Tax	6.3	34
Criminal	6.1	33
Family..................	4.6	25
Labor	4.4	24
Litigation	4.4	24
Patent	3.7	20
Administrative...........	3.5	19
Insurance	2.9	16
Commercial	2.4	13
Antitrust................	2.2	12
Municipal...............	1.5	8
Proverty	0.7	4
Bankruptcy	0.6	3
Creditor-Debtor	0.6	3
Other[c].................	6.1	33
Total	100%	542

[a]Specialties are listed in order of their prominence in the practice of law.

[b]Percentages are based on the 542 respondents who cited at least one specialty in which they do a significant amount of work, and represent the proportion of practitioners who rank each of the listed specialties as number one.

[c]The remaining 6.1% who rank specialty mention other areas, e.g., hospital, constitutional, etc.

The degree of specialization varies not only by area of law but by practice context as well. For example, two-thirds of the Chicago lawyers specializing in criminal law are employed by the government and thereby limited in their opportunities for other work. Government employment, however, is not the only practice context that is correlated with a high degree of specialization in practice. As shown in table 4.3, consistent with the argument that the rise of firm practice (and particularly the growth of large firms) is related to the trend toward specialization, we find that the larger the firm, the more likely the lawyer is to concentrate in fewer areas of the law. Although much of the literature claims that firm attorneys are more likely to be more specialized than solo

TABLE 4.3
Number of Areas of Specialization of Private Practitioners by Size of Practice Context

Practice Context	No. of Areas of Specialization (%)					Total %	N
	One	Two	Three	Four	Five		
Solo........................	4.5	11.4	19.3	27.3	37.5	100.0	88
Small firm (2–8)	9.8	11.9	21.0	25.2	32.2	100.1	143
Medium firm (9–49)	12.4	15.7	31.5	27.0	13.5	100.1	89
Large firm (50 or more)	17.3	34.6	19.8	17.3	11.1	100.1	81

$\chi^2 = 50.78$; $p < 0.001$;
gamma $= -0.33$

practitioners,[21] the degree of specialization among solo and small-firm practitioners varies only slightly. Rather it is the large firms in which lawyers are most likely to become highly specialized.[22] More than half (51.9 percent) of the lawyers affiliated with large firms do a significant amount of work in only one or two areas of the law; comparable figures for medium-firm, small-firm, and solo practitioners are 30 percent, 20 percent, and 15 percent, respectively.

Relationships Among Specialties

In the sample as a whole, 84.5 percent of the practitioners cited more than one specialty as occupying a significant amount of their time. Figure 4.3 reports the way that the seven largest specialties relate to each other in actual practice. The percentages in figure 4.3 are calculated on the basis of the number of lawyers citing more than one specialty as significant in their practice who rank each of these seven specialties as rank 1. Thus, for example, of all the attorneys ranking more than one specialty in their practice, 98 rank corporate law as the area of law that occupies the greatest proportion of their time. The percentage then represents the proportion of those attorneys who rank the specialty noted at the point of the connecting arrow as the second most important specialty in their practice. To use the same example, of those specializing in corporate law who mention a second specialty, 26.5 percent spend the next largest share of their time in real estate work. The relationships represented are limited to those for which more than 20 percent of the lawyers specializing in each area of practice cite another particular area as second most important. All other possible linkages that are not illustrated fall below those figures.

The pattern displayed in figure 4.3 illuminates the dynamics of specialization. With the same denoted substantive legal specialty, there are in fact substantially different kinds of practice. The figure also provides information as to the direction and nature of those differences. For example, real estate is the second-named specialty for more than one-third of those whose primary specialty is in the area of trusts and estates, and close to that for those concentrating in corporate law. In both of these cases the relationship holds in the reverse as well. That is, approximately one-third of the real estate lawyers spend the second largest share of their time on trusts and estates and another third on corporate law. But in contrast to the symmetry of those relationships, only small proportions of corporate attorneys spend much time on trusts and estates, and

21. For example York and Hale (1973) state categorically that "the reason for the relative decline of the solo practitioner and the boom of the partner-and-associate law firm is the need for lawyers to band together so that each can specialize and hence provide the service demanded by clients" (p. 8).

22. Using percent of time devoted to a single area of the law as his indicator, Carlin (1962a) similarly found that the larger the law firm, the greater the degree of specialization, with solo practitioners and small-firm attorneys most alike on this dimension (table 16).

vice versa. At least two different kinds of practice in real estate law are reflected in these data. One practice largely serves individual clients, in estate planning and transfers of property, both of which may require knowledge of real estate law. The other serves corporations or partnerships whose business is real estate and involves quite different work, although still doctrinally in the real estate field. We would not be at all surprised to find that the dollar value as well as the complexity of the legal matters with which these two different sets of real estate lawyers

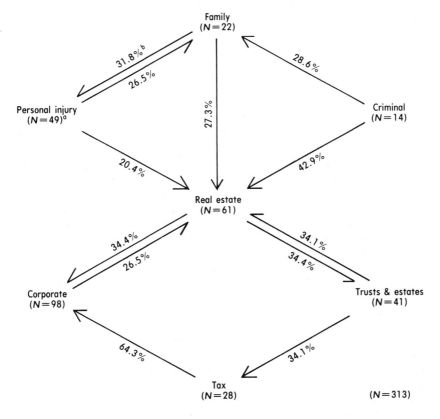

Note: Includes respondents whose first-ranked specialty is among the seven practiced by the largest proportions of attorneys in Chicago.

[a]Number of attorneys who rank each specialty as occupying the greatest part of their time of those who rank more than one specialty.

[b]Percentage of attorneys whose first-ranked specialty appears at the base of the arrow for whom the specialty at the top of the arrow is ranked second. Arrows included only where percentage is greater than 20 percent.

Fig. 4.3. Relationship between first- and second-ranked specialties in the practice of law

deal are correspondingly diverse. When time is billed on a per-hour basis, complexity and cost are directly proportional to one another. Thus, although an individual's real estate issue may have the potential for complexity, if the dollar value in the transaction or income of the holding does not justify the cost, the issue will necessarily be handled at a simpler level of legal analysis and will likely involve a more limited range of tasks.

A similar analysis of those specializing in trusts and estates reveals that one-third rank tax law as second most important in their practices and another third cite real estate law. This analysis implies that there may be some differences between these two sets of attorneys, although in this case clientele would probably not be the appropriate dimension along which they could be delineated. Or take the tax lawyers, almost two-thirds of whom mention corporate work as their second-ranked specialty but only small numbers of whom mention trusts and estates. Thus, although lawyers in a number of different areas may do some or even a substantial amount of tax law in their practices, tax lawyers—those who spend the largest share of their time doing tax work—work for corporate clients, with only small numbers mentioning any other area of practice in which they do a significant amount of work.

Two other observations should be made about the patterns revealed in figure 4.3. One is that criminal law is generally practiced either as a predominant specialty or not at all. Very few attorneys cite criminal law as constituting a significant share of their practice if some other specialty predominates. In fact less than half (42.4 percent) of the criminal bar even mention a second area of the law. To some extent, then, those in the criminal law are the most specialized urban lawyers.[23] These figures again reflect the fact that most criminal lawyers are employed by the state to concentrate exclusively on criminal cases as either prosecutors or public defenders.

A second observation is the obvious centrality of real estate law. With the exception of those specializing in tax, real estate law is the universal second specialty. To some extent this simply reflects the demands of the marketplace, with lawyers more likely to cite real estate law than any other legal specialty save the rather ambiguous catchall of corporate law. In addition, however, real estate law as currently defined is not confined to either a corporate or individual clientele. Therefore, its practice is not dependent, as are some specialties, on access to a particular client pool.

In sum, we have seen quite clearly that certain specialties—although not necessarily doctrinally interrelated—are very likely to be practiced in tandem. These patterns demonstrate that traditional substantive categories only broadly characterize the diversity of legal practice and that

---

23. Although only 6.1 percent of the bar rank criminal law as their first-ranked area of specialization, the criminal bar constitutes 22.6 percent of those who mention only a single specialty as significant to their practices.

additional factors, such as clientele served and tasks performed, need to be considered in understanding the nature and structure of the legal profession.

Specialization: Selection or Drift?

Despite the importance of specialty to the skills needed in practice, to the doctrines of law relevant to practice, to the clientele served, and to intrabar status,[24] we know very little about the factors that influence lawyers to concentrate their practices in specific areas of the law. Responses to our inquiry about influences on specialization indicate that drift and opportunity may best describe the process. Clearly legal education is not playing much of a role. Only 17.2 percent of the bar credit their law school experiences with influencing their selection of a field or fields of specialization, with the percentage dropping to 12.2 percent for private practitioners out of law school more than three years.[25] This attribution does not vary by the particular specialty most prominent in practice. Indeed there is little expectation on the part of law school applicants that law schools will provide particular instruction in areas of specialization. Only 3.6 percent of the sample cite "special professors or area of specialization" as one of the three most important reasons for choosing a particular law school (questionnaire, pt. I, Q. 4, p. 3, appendix 1). Law schools' failure to directly influence the selection of an area of specialization is perfectly consistent with the perceptions their students have of the schools' goals. As noted in chapter 3, only 3.9 percent of the bar think that preparing students for practice in a particular specialty was a major goal of their law school.

Another possible influence on specialty practiced could be jobs held before and/or during law school. An example would be a respondent who served in the merchant marine and later specialized in admiralty law. Yet of the respondents ($N = 357$) who explained how such jobs contributed to their practice, only 17.9 percent mentioned learning or developing an interest in a specific type of law.[26]

In the selection of a first law-related job after law school, only 15.3 percent cited the opportunity to learn a specialty as an important factor, and even that low figure may imply greater importance given to specialty than is warranted.[27] For as shown in table 4.4, the role of specialty in

24. See chapter 5 for a discussion of intrabar prestige rankings.

25. More than half of those crediting law schools with influence in their selection of a specialty mention course work as the influential factor (see questionnaire, pt. I, Q. 9, p. 4, appendix 1).

26. Other important contributions were learning practicalities of law practice (e.g., learning one's "way around the courthouse") and learning to deal with people (see questionnaire, pt. II, Q. 1, p. 6).

27. See part II, question 3, page 7 of the questionnaire. Although this question asked respondents to indicate the most important factor in the selection of their first law-related employment after graduation from law school, 15 percent of the respondents mentioned more than one factor. The 15.3 percent include all those who checked the item "chance to learn a specialty"; only 8.6 percent of the respondents cited only this item.

TABLE 4.4

Chance to Learn a Specialty as an Important
Factor in Selection of First Law Job by
Specialty Practiced in That Job

Specialty[a]	% Citing Important	N
Corporate...............	7.1	70
Criminal................	17.8	45
Family.................	0.0	24
Personal injury	17.1	70
Tax	46.2	39
Trusts and estates	14.3	35
Real estate	11.8	68
Other..................	14.9	175

$$\chi^2 = 37.08; \ p \leqslant 0.001$$

[a]Includes only the seven specialties practiced by the
largest proportion of the bar.

the selection of first law career employment is extremely skewed.
Almost half of all attorneys who concentrated on tax law in their first
law-related employment after law school cited the chance to learn a
specialty as an important factor in the selection of that employment; the
figures for other specialties are quite low. This is an indication that the
timing and the pattern of the professional development of lawyers are
far from uniform. Tax lawyers are inclined toward their eventual careers
relatively earlier than most lawyers, as reflected in their undergraduate
concentrations. Of the lawyers with undergraduate majors in business,
42.9 percent are now tax lawyers; another 38.6 percent concentrate on
corporate law. There are no similar relationships for any other undergraduate major or legal specialty for which their are sufficient numbers
to allow valid measurement.[28]

Despite the centrality of legal specialization in defining one's legal
career, with rare exceptions it is an identity developed only after beginning the actual practice of law. Specialization has been and continues to
be unimportant in the selection of first career experiences after law
school. Specialty does not compare particularly favorably with other
factors important in first job selection (questionnaire, pt. II, Q. 3, p. 7).
Essentially equivalent proportions of the sample mentioned geographical considerations or simply the lack of other job offers as reasons for
selecting their first jobs.[29] More importantly, the "opportunity to learn
practice from other attorneys" was an important reason for selection of

28. Patent law has not been included in the analysis because of the limited number (17).
But there are the expected relationships: 35 percent of the lawyers specializing in patent
law were attracted to their first law job in part by the chance to learn a specialty, and 88
percent majored in engineering as undergraduates. The same argument of pre–law school
career decisions and preparation for career and of early determination of eventual career
holds here.

29. The importance of "no other job offers" in the selection of first law job is interestingly not significantly related either to the prestige of the law school attended or to
academic standing therein.

first law job for 24.4 percent of the respondents and the single most important reason for 13.8 percent. As that attraction increases, as it has over recent decades, the practice of a particular substantive specialty may become even less important in the selection of a first law job.

Although the attraction to a first job may be a general one—that is, the desire to learn the whole gamut of practical lawyering skills given only cursory attention in law schools—because of the extent of specialization in law firms the new attorney attracted to a firm context will be taught those skills that are peculiarly important to the areas of the law predominating in the particular firm or the section of the firm where he or she is first placed. As the lessons learned are often rather narrow, and not equally applicable across all specialties, options for practice in other areas of the law become circumscribed. While this occurs in any field with a high degree of specialization, the point here is that the factors influencing a lawyer's route to a *particular* specialty are typically unrelated to the specialty itself. Rather, the field of specialization is most likely to be determined by virtue of the nature of the first job setting.[30] While specific specialties are not determined by the context within which a lawyer works (except for prosecutors and public defenders), in general terms there is a strong relationship between the kinds of specialties practiced and the contexts of practice to which lawyers have been attracted.[31] More precisely, practice contexts provide broad parameters within which certain kinds of specialties tend to be practiced.

Specialization and the Organizational Context of Practice

The relationship between context and substance of practice is partly due to economies of scale necessary for certain kinds of law. In addition, specialties, or variations thereof, are usually tied to a particular client pool. If specialists in different areas of the law but dependent upon the business of the same client pool are joined together, then most if not all of the legal needs of that clientele can be handled by the same firm.[32] The firm is then assured of maintaining the ongoing relationships necessary to support a firm of substantial size. With new lawyers attracted to particular contextual settings and with no good indicators of why most lawyers enter particular specialties,[33] we are inclined to think that specific substantive specialization for a large proportion of the bar is largely a result of circumstances. These include the needs of

30. A study of law students similarly finds that they characterize their anticipated careers in terms of practice context rather than substantive specialty (Pipkin, research in progress on Law Student Activity Patterns, a project of the American Bar Foundation).

31. See chapter 5 for a discussion of the factors that influence access to careers in selected contexts of legal practice.

32. This is similar to Ladinsky's argument that the rise in large law firms is related to the development of large corporations that demand highly specialized legal services (1963b, p. 128).

33. As discussed, specialists in tax law, corporate law, and patent law are exceptions.

the firm at the time the new lawyer begins employment and may in fact be related to a single "big case" on the current agenda. In smaller firms and in solo practice, too, the demands of the initial clientele will influence the development of expertise in particular areas of law. As we shall see, once a predominant specialty is established, it is likely to remain central to the rest of one's legal career.[34]

Beyond the obvious connections between criminal law and government employment, and corporate law and corporate employment, there are a number of other relationships between substantive specialty and context of law practice. Tax law and antitrust work are most likely to be done within the context of large law firms, although tax work is also frequently done by lawyers employed by the government as well as within all other contexts examined. In contrast, patent law is relatively rarely practiced in large firms. Rather it is most often found in small and medium-sized firms and on the agenda of business legal staffs. Corporate law, while most likely to be practiced in medium-sized and large law firms and among business legal staffs, is also very often the predominant specialty of solo and small-firm as well as government attorneys. Labor law is rarely found in solo practice but is found in all other contexts. Real estate law is a universal specialty except for government practice. Personal injury, while concentrated in private practice, is also often practiced by lawyers employed by government or business. Both family law and trusts and estates work, reflecting the individual clientele for which those areas of the law are relevant, are practiced exclusively in private practice. Administrative law in contrast is generally the work of government or business legal staffs.

The strong relationship between the substance of an attorney's legal work and the context within which it is practiced is important. We shall see in chapter 6 that the very skills and knowledge important to the actual practice of law are closely related to the substantive specialty practiced. In addition, area of specialization often determines the nature of one's clientele, including how much they pay for legal services and the lawyer's status within the bar. Yet the dimension along which lawyers are distributed within the job market is the organizational context of practice, with area of specialization generally developing on the job. We have already intimated the importance of practice context in recruitment of young lawyers and will discuss that issue in depth in chapter 5. An examination of the stability of law practice will demonstrate just how important recruitment practices are to the shaping of the profession, with respect to both the organizational context of practice and related areas of specialization. The stability of the law practice of most lawyers, in conjunction with the relationship between context and substance, means

---

34. This is not to say that there is no self-selection at a more general level. Desires for substantial remuneration, for example, may lead to seeking a practice with largely business clientele. While that selection may preclude some specialties (e.g., criminal or family law), it still leaves one's choice of eventual field of law quite open.

that early recruitment and career experiences have the effect of determining not only the form of legal services but also the actual substantive expertise available. For the lawyers themselves, early career options and choices will influence if not determine their status within their chosen profession.

Career Stability in the Legal Profession

In *Occupations and the Social Structure,* Richard Hall (1969) refers to five stages of career development: (1) preparatory (school and family), (2) initial (full- and part-time jobs during the educational process), (3) trial (first full-time job, frequent job changes until more or less permanent position—around three years duration), (4) stable (job permanence and ties to occupational position and related social structure), and (5) retirement (p. 315).[35] There are, of course, some features in this development which are unique to a legal career. Unlike many occupations, it entails a lengthy and costly training period. Because of the requisite academic preparation, lawyers choose their occupation relatively early. In addition, since most lawyers are private practitioners, retirement is often not dictated by company policies or labor negotiations—indeed, for many lawyers that career stage never comes.[36] More importantly, however, the frequent job changes that supposedly typify the trial stage of career development either never occur or do so in a substantially truncated fashion in legal careers.

Comparing first jobs with subsequent careers in the law, we shall observe a great deal of stability. Few practitioners expect any change in either the nature of their employment or the substantive legal work in which they are currently engaged. Although such expectations are directly related to age, with the more recent law school graduates most likely to anticipate career changes ($p < 0.001$), even they do not generally expect to change either their employment or their work in the next five years or later. In the aggregate, approximately 85 percent of the practicing lawyers in our sample expected to be in the same *employment* five years from the time of the study, and approximately 80 percent anticipated the same for subsequent years. Comparable figures for the *fields of law* in which attorneys are engaged are similarly 84.1 percent and 79.8 percent, respectively. An examination of the actual career patterns of practicing lawyers will substantiate the validity of these expectations.

To avoid overweighting stability in careers, the sample for this part of the analysis has been restricted to those who had been out of law school more than three years at the time of the data collection. Among this large subsample (87.8 percent of the whole sample), 52.8 percent were in the same organizational context of practice, and 74.0 percent were spending the largest share of their time in the same specialty as in their

35. This typology was originally devised by Miller and Form (1951, p. 517).
36. Approximately 10 percent of the practicing bar are over the age of 65.

very first law jobs after law school. Thus restricting the analysis is consistent with Hall's conclusion that after the first three years of trial and change, substantial stability occurs in occupational careers. Using a very limited Chicago sample, Lortie (1959) confirmed the infrequency of position changes by the fourth year after law school. Actually the stability of law careers is characteristically determined even earlier. In the entire sample, including those just out of law school, 56.0 percent are in the same kind of practice, and 75.2 percent are spending the largest share of their time in the same specialty as they did in their very first job after law school. These figures vary only slightly from the more restricted sample employed in the analysis. Although there is some decrease in career mobility after three years in practice, it is most certainly insufficient to characterize this period of time a career "stage" in the practice of law.

Stability in the Organizational Context of Practice

The movement of lawyers among different contexts is an important indicator of the mobility of the urban bar. Table 4.5 illustrates that there is in fact a statistically significant relationship between the organizational contexts within which lawyers practice in their first law-related jobs after law school and later in their careers.[37] That is, the organizational context of a new lawyer's first law-related job after law school is likely to restrict the subsequent legal career within either the identical context or a limited number of other contexts.

Like so much of the data analyzed here, it is not only the general results descriptive of the bar as a whole but the individual differences that are of great interest. Only very few (6.1 percent) of the government lawyers, at all levels, began their legal careers in private law firms. Rather, 51.6 percent of them entered government service of one kind or another immediately upon graduation from law school.[38] In contrast, 76.2 percent of those currently practicing in large law firms began their legal careers either in firm practice or as judicial clerks (with 61.9 percent attributable to firm practice).[39] For practitioners in small firms, the comparable figure is 49.6 percent (with 36.2 percent attributable to firm practice). Indeed solo practitioners are as likely to have started their

37. As in the evaluation of stability of specialty, the data are limited to those attorneys who graduated from law school more than three years before the survey.

38. With only government lawyers who represent the legal rights of others included in the sample, we do not know what proportion of those who first entered some form of government service remain in a nonadvocate government position. For an explanation of the limits of the sample of lawyers included in the study see chapter 2.

39. Unfortunately, we do not have data on size of firm for the first job. The differences observed would no doubt increase were that factor entered into the analysis. Without it, the reported results have provided a conservative picture of the actual stability of the nature of law practice for the 39.5 percent of the bar (in practice more than three years) whose first jobs after law school were with law firms.

TABLE 4.5 Nature of First Law Job by Nature of Current Practice for Lawyers Out of Law School More than Three Years

First Law Job	Current Job							Row N
	Solo	Small Firm	Medium Firm	Large Firm	Govt. Lawyer	Business Legal Staff	Other	
Solo practice	31.8[a] 17.9[b]	22.7 7.9	22.7 12.8	2.3 1.6	13.6 18.2	4.5 3.6	2.3 5.6	44
Firm practice[c]	16.8 38.5	25.7 36.2	21.8 50.0	21.8 61.9	1.1 6.1	10.6 33.9	2.2 22.2	179
Government[d] advocate	9.5 5.1	31.0 10.2	4.8 2.6	11.9 7.9	28.6 36.4	9.5 7.1	4.8 11.1	42
Other government[d]	24.1 9.0	20.7 4.7	13.8 5.1	10.3 4.8	17.2 15.2	10.3 5.4	3.4 5.6	29
Business legal staff	8.5 6.4	23.7 11.0	11.9 9.0	6.8 6.3	3.4 6.1	35.6 37.5	10.2 33.3	59
Law clerk	20.8 14.1	32.1 13.4	9.4 6.4	17.0 14.3	9.4 15.2	9.4 8.9	1.9 5.6	53
Other	14.9 9.0	44.7 16.5	23.4 14.1	4.3 3.2	2.1 3.0	4.3 3.6	6.4 16.7	47
Column N	78	127	78	63	33	56	18	453

$p < 0.001$

[a]The first number in each cell represents current practice context as a proportion of first practice context. These figures sum across to 100%. For example, 31.8% of those who began their legal careers in solo practice are currently in solo practice.
[b]The second number in each cell represents first practice context as a proportion of current practice context. These figures sum down to 100%. For example, 17.9% of those whose current practice context is solo practice began their legal careers in solo practice.
[c]Firm practice is a single category in the first job because data on size of firm are not available.
[d]Question 8 (pt. II, p. 8, appendix 1) of the questionnaire provided for specification of type of government lawyer in first law job.

careers with a law firm as are those currently practicing in a small-firm context.

In sharp contrast to Carlin's findings, our data show that attorneys who began their legal careers as individual practitioners are no more likely to remain in that context than are lawyers who began their careers in other settings. Although in New York Carlin found that a full two-thirds of those who began their careers as individual practitioners remained so (1962a, table 36), table 4.5 shows quite clearly that to be the case for only 31.8 percent in the Chicago bar. But there is also substantial movement into solo practice. Of those now in practice by themselves, more than twice as many (38.5 percent as opposed to 17.9 percent) began their legal career in law firms than as individual practitioners. This is perfectly consistent with the earlier reported finding that a large number of attorneys select their first job precisely because they wish to gain experience and learn from other attorneys in their own offices.[40] Yet here again the large law firms are unique. Only 1.6 percent of large-firm practitioners began their legal careers as solo practitioners; that percentage represents a single practitioner among the 63 in the sample who practice in firms of 50 members or more. Another interesting limitation on the future careers of those who begin as solo practitioners is their relative exclusion from corporate legal staffs. This restriction is related to the stability of specialty practiced and the pattern of specialties that are practiced in concert. We shall see that specialties oriented toward the legal rights and duties of individuals, such as personal injury and divorce, tend to be practiced together; so too does there appear to be a stability of clientele reflected in patterns of the context of practice. Both the lack of movement from solo practice to either a large firm or business legal staff and the strong likelihood that business legal staff lawyers who began their careers elsewhere did so in a firm practice, reflect a stability in the clientele served, the areas of law relevant to its needs, and the tasks required.

Stability in Specialty Practiced

Although not generally attracted to particular specialties, once established lawyers remain extremely stable in the substantive areas of the law in which practice is concentrated. There is, however, a good deal of variation by individual specialty. Table 4.6 presents the actual distribution of lawyers among different specialties for both the first and current job in terms of the relationship between the two. The skew toward the diagonal is of course predictable from the 74.0 percent who currently concentrate their practice in the same substantive area of the law as their

---

40. It is not known how many of those who began careers in firms left that context of practice because they did not become partners. Yet not all who fail to gain partnership turn to solo practice. They may go to another firm, start their own firm, practice as an employed attorney, or leave the practice of law altogether. As noted previously, the sample is limited to current practitioners, thus excluding those practitioners who leave the practice of law. See chapter 2 for a discussion of the sample population

TABLE 4.6 Current Specialty (Rank 1) by First Specialty for Lawyers Out of Law School More than Three Years

Current Specialty	First Specialty																		Total
	Corp.	Crim.	Admin.	Fam. Law	Pers. Injur.	Tax Law	Pov. Law	T. & E.	Bank-ruptcy	Labor Law	Insur.	Pat. Law	Anti-Trust	Real Est.	Trial Litig.	Comm'l	Munic.	Cred./Debtor	
Corporate	29	2	4	2	11	4	1	6	–	–	2	3	1	8	5	3	–	2	83
Criminal	–	13	2	1	1	–	–	2	–	–	1	–	–	2	1	–	–	–	21
Administrative	2	3	2	–	1	–	–	–	1	–	–	1	–	2	–	1	–	–	13
Family law	3	2	–	9	–	1	1	–	–	–	–	–	1	3	1	–	–	–	21
Personal injury	2	3	1	–	33	–	–	2	–	–	2	–	–	5	–	1	–	–	51
Tax law	1	1	–	–	1	20	2	1	–	1	–	–	–	1	1	–	–	–	27
Poverty law	1	–	–	–	–	–	2	–	–	–	–	–	–	–	–	–	–	–	4
Trusts and estates	3	2	1	1	1	2	–	18	–	–	–	–	–	9	1	–	–	1	38
Bankruptcy	–	–	1	–	–	–	–	–	1	–	–	–	–	1	–	–	–	–	3
Labor law	–	1	–	2	–	–	–	–	–	11	–	–	1	1	1	–	–	–	19
Insurance	1	–	–	1	6	–	–	–	–	–	5	–	–	–	–	–	–	–	14
Patent law	1	–	1	–	1	–	–	–	–	–	–	17	1	–	–	–	–	–	19
Antitrust	1	–	–	–	–	–	–	–	–	–	–	–	6	–	–	–	–	–	8
Real estate	5	4	–	3	5	–	–	9	–	–	–	–	–	28	–	1	–	2	54
Trial/litigation	2	2	1	1	2	–	–	1	–	–	–	–	–	–	6	1	–	–	16
Commercial	2	–	1	–	1	–	–	1	1	–	–	1	–	2	–	3	–	1	11
Municipal	–	1	1	1	1	–	–	–	–	–	–	–	–	–	–	–	4	–	7
Creditor/debtor	–	1	1	–	–	–	–	–	–	–	–	–	–	–	–	–	–	1	3
Total	53	35	14	20	64	30	7	31	4	14	10	22	9	62	15	10	4	8	412
Direction & % change, First to current[a]	↑56.6	↓40.0	↓7.1	↑5.0	↓20.3	↓10.0	↓42.9	↑22.6	↓25	↑35.7	↓40.0	↓13.6	↓11.1	↓12.9	↑66.6	↑10.0	↑75.0	↓62.5	

[a] ↑ indicates the specialty gained members from first specialty to current specialty. That is, there was movement into the specialty. ↓ indicates the specialty lost members from first specialty to current specialty. That is, there was movement out of the specialty. The percentage change was calculated as follows: $[(N_{First} - N_{Current})/N_{First}]\,100$.

$$\frac{N_{First} - N_{Current}}{N_{First}}\,100$$

first law-related job after law school. What is more interesting from this table is both the degree of variability in stability among different specialties and the distribution of stability among the substantive specialties.

Among the seven largest specialties, the greatest movement occurs in corporate law, the least specific of the specialties. This is indicated by the percentage change at the bottom of table 4.6 combined with the movement of individual lawyers into and out of corporate practice, as seen by comparing the corporate row and the corporate column. Since this category includes so many different kinds of substantive practices, it is not surprising that it appears to be the least stable. In addition, it is an area toward which careers in the law move. Of the specialties currently practiced by substantial proportions of the Chicago bar, corporate law practice has a greater percentage increase in practitioners from first jobs than any other specialty. To some extent this reflects the demand for legal services by corporations and their ability to pay for them; in sharp contrast there is a 40 percent attrition rate from first to current jobs in criminal law. That is, 40 percent of Chicago attorneys who began their legal careers concentrating in criminal law eventually shift to another area of the law. Since there is no particular pattern in the specialties toward which they move, it may be that the skills sought in that area with its high litigation rate have been learned and/or that the rewards of criminal practice simply are not sufficiently attractive to retain its practitioners. A proportion of this movement is from first jobs with the government, as prosecutors or public defenders, to private practice, where the economic demand for legal services in criminal law is sharply reduced. In contrast to those relatively more mobile areas, there are specialties such as tax law and patent law which are particularly stable. This is due to the highly specialized and therefore nontransferable skills inherent in their practice as well as to the requisite nonlawyer skills frequently acquired before law school. In addition, as seen previously, these specialties tend to be selected earlier and are set more firmly before one embarks on the first law job.

The figures in table 4.6 represent only the specialty ranked first by each practitioner in each job. Thus the calculations underestimate stability since they do not take into account the extent to which first-ranked specialties have simply become *relatively* less significant. An alternative analysis correlates the first four (ranks 1–4) predominant specialties in the first job for each respondent with specialties ranked 1 through 4 currently for each specialty.[41] The highly significant results ($p < 0.001$ for every correlation) are reported in table 4.7. These data confirm the findings reported in table 4.6. Looking at the correlation coefficients between relative rankings of the same specialty in first and current job, it

41. Four ranks were included because close to half of the bar (45.6 percent) do a significant amount of work in four different substantive areas, with less than a quarter (24.5 percent) ranking more than four of them.

TABLE 4.7
Correlation of First and Current Specialties,
Ranks 1–4 ($N = 461$)

Specialty	Correlation Coefficient[a]	Rank[b]
Corporate...............	.477	10
Criminal	.475	11
Administrative...........	.386	14
Family law	.491	9
Personal injury	.557	6
Tax law.................	.675	2
Trusts and estates	.575	5
Labor	.605	3
Insurance	.578	4
Patent law	.903	1
Antitrust...............	.509	8
Real estate	.540	7
Litigation	.454	13
Commercial	.462	12

[a]All correlations are significant at the .001 level.
[b]Ranks were scored as follows: rank 1 = 4; rank 2 = 3;
rank 3 = 2; rank 4 = 1.

is clear that patent law is by far the most stable legal specialty. That is, not only are those who spend a significant amount of their time on patent work in their first job likely to continue to do so, as in fact they are in most specialties, but they are also very likely to maintain the same *degree* of emphasis on it throughout their careers. The 0.903 correlation coefficient for patent law is much larger than the next most highly correlated specialty, tax, at 0.675. Other specialties have an average correlation coefficient of .509, with limited differences in stability among the various fields of law.

Stability and Change in the Legal Profession

The extent to which the bar is, as the Code of Professional Responsibility states, interested in the distribution of legal services and providing for the legal needs of the public, stability in the practice of law dictates that attention be given to both recruitment practices in law schools and the availability of opportunities in practice at the time of graduation from law school. An illustration of the importance of the latter can be found in Erlanger's examination of the effect of participation in social reform organizations on subsequent careers of early participants in the OEO Legal Services Program. He concludes that within the limits of the quasi-experimental design employed in the research, "the data for white male Legal Services lawyers clearly indicate that participation in the program leads to a redistribution of service among lawyers in private practice" (1977, p. 243). That is, the legal practice to which these young lawyers were exposed in the Legal Services Program significantly increased the likelihood that they would continue to concentrate in the same areas of law and serve similar clientele subsequently.

On the basis of our own research Erlanger's findings are not too surprising. For though movement into careers is subject to many influences, once an acceptable practice has been found, the likelihood is that such practice will continue. In part this is related to the establishment of a reputation among a relevant clientele. Further, the analysis of skill development to follow in chapter 6 indicates that specialty is significantly related to the post–law school development of skills that are so important to practice. Since, as we will demonstrate, the skills most important to practice are closely tied to the specialty practiced, first job experience develops the skills most appropriate to that kind of work. To switch specialties then may involve starting again to develop the package of skills requisite to practice in another field. The policy implication of this pattern, it seems to us, is that a broader distribution of legal services would be likely to occur if opportunities for practice in selected areas of the law serving the legal needs of individual citizens were provided at the time of law school graduation. It will be interesting to see, as an example, the impact that the Legal Services Corporation will have on subsequent careers of participating lawyers and thus on the distribution of legal services to the public.

There has been considerable speculation about the impact of the law students of the 1960s on the nature and form of the legal profession. It was anticipated that their proclaimed interest in social welfare would affect the distribution of lawyers in practice. To test that hypothesis Rita James Simon and her colleagues examined the career aspirations and occupational choices of 1950s and 1960s graduates of the University of Chicago and University of Illinois law schools as compared with earlier cohorts (Simon, Koziol, & Joslyn, 1973).[42] Their major finding was that career choices have not changed over time, with private law practice drawing 50–60 percent of each cohort. Indeed the major increases for all University of Chicago graduates and for the top University of Illinois graduates from the 1950s to the 1960s is in employment with large firms.

To some extent, of course, this simply reflects the absolute and proportional increases in the number of large firms and therefore available opportunities. Given the stability in legal practice so clearly illustrated by the Chicago bar data, the trends described in the first jobs after law school graduation are exceedingly important, for they tell us what the general picture of the practicing bar will be in the future. Indeed the trend toward larger firm practice mentioned earlier is simply an extension of the pattern illustrated in figure 4.2. Yet the same stability in legal practice which makes the main finding of Simon and her colleagues important also makes what they consider lesser findings quite important. Although legal aid jobs drew very small numbers, the proportional increase in graduates drawn to such careers is worth mentioning. While

42. The study was based on a mailed questionnaire sent to samples of graduates of the University of Chicago in odd years of the 1950s and 1960s (1951–69) and of the University of Illinois in even years (1950–68). In both cases the top and the bottom of the class standings were overweighted. For a more complete description of the sample see Simon et al. (1973, p. 96).

not a single one of the 1950s graduates chose legal aid, 2–8 percent of their 1960s counterparts chose legal aid. When considered in conjunction with the stability in legal practice and with a legal system where *stare decisis* means that broad policy making often occurs in the context of a single case, small changes in the pattern of legal practice can potentially make a substantial difference. Although all those who begin their legal careers in legal aid may not stay in the identical practice, the evidence indicates that initial law experience is likely to be the major influence on the nature of future legal careers.

Conclusion

Practicing lawyers go through an extended period of academic preparation. After four years of college, they continue their formal schooling for another three years to study law. Although the pattern of legal education is relatively uniform and may imply monolithic preparation, it provides only one stage in the process of socialization of lawyers. We have seen in chapter 3 that urban lawyers, while not representative of the population as a whole, do come from a wide variety of backgrounds. Since earlier experiences provide the backdrop for new encounters, even if all legal schooling were identical, which it is not, law school would be expected to be perceived and experienced differently, thus varying in its socializing impact.

Additionally we have seen in this chapter that experience in the practice of law is extremely varied. We shall see later that lawyers attribute much of their professional expertise as well as their sense of professional obligation to their lawyer colleagues. This is particularly true for lawyers practicing in a firm context. With the distribution of lawyers in practice having a continuing impact on their professional careers, it is important to know just how the bar is distributed in practice. We have seen that lawyers are likely to be concentrated in particular substantive areas of the law where their experience with the law and their clientele are substantially delimited. With legal careers increasingly law-firm based, and with context and substantive specialty empirically related, changes in the context of practice will have the effect of influencing the distribution of lawyers working in various fields of law. Additionally, with both context and specialty very likely to remain stable throughout professional careers, opportunities for diverse experiences and their contributions to professional development are severely limited. Although socialization no doubt continues, opportunities for counter-experiences providing challenges to current attitudes toward the law, the profession, and one's role therein are restricted.

There are within these conclusions some interesting implications, although not necessarily direction, for legal education. Part of the movement toward increased specialization and the growing pressure for more certification of specialties has been a heightened awareness of the "general" education received in law schools. There has been rising concern and interest in the possibility of specialization within law school so that new lawyers would not, as the data indicate, have to rely quite so heavily on other lawyers in their offices, or, failing that, on experience with clients, as a learning source. The difficulty with specialized training in law school of course is that it presumes the selection of substantive specialty earlier in career development than has been the case for the vast majority of the practicing bar. Whether earlier specialization will affect the distribution of specialists is hard to tell. No doubt the same market forces that now influence that distribution, and of which law students are aware, will continue to play the dominant role. Yet if our findings and those of others reported are correct, early job experiences must be added to the equation, for they seem to make an independent difference in lawyers' careers. The breadth of the distribution of lawyers among specialties partly expanded by on-the-job experience may well be restricted by earlier career decision making that would follow from specialized training in law school. Although in the aggregate the quantitative distribution of the bar may not, and probably would not, vary significantly from the extant arrangement, small numbers of lawyers can make a difference. Indeed newer structural arrangements, including prepaid legal services and the growing phenomenon of legal clinics, indicate that there is a demand for legal services for which the supply has previously been restricted. Lawyers in these forms of practice, like the predominant proportion of all practitioners, do not concentrate in a single area of the law alone. They may well spend more time on one area than another, but most practices include more than one narrowly defined substantive specialty. It seems requisite, therefore, that the law school graduate be conversant in at least several areas of the law. While the opportunity for early specialization may be efficient from the standpoint of some lawyers, it may have the effect of closing off alternative employment options too early, particularly with career patterns so dependent on the first job after law school.

To the extent that society wishes to encourage the availability of legal services in general, and selected areas and contexts in particular, then recruitment practices at the time of law school graduation need to be carefully examined. We have discussed individually pre–law school, law school, and post–law school stages in the professional development of lawyers. As yet we have left unexamined the relationships, if any, among these various stages. In the next chapter we will attempt to fit together these basic pieces of the puzzle of professional socialization.

Chapter 5
CREDENTIALS FOR PROFESSIONAL STATUS

Introduction

The legal profession has consistently enjoyed a high level of prestige in American society.[1] As documented in chapter 3, this has in fact been one of the primary attractions to careers in the law. To some extent the public prestige of the legal profession is related to the amount of education required for access. In his study of educational opportunity Jencks (1972) concludes that education has a credentialing effect on occupational prestige.

> Occupations that require a lot of schooling generally have higher prestige than occupations that require very little schooling. . . . This . . . implies that Americans are impressed by educational credentials and that credentials confer status. . . .
>   . . . To some significant degree, occupations acquire prestige because educated people choose them. Occupations like preaching and teaching, which pay badly but attract educated people, have as much prestige as occupations that pay much better but attract uneducated people (pp. 180–81).[2]

Such considerations of and references to occupational prestige treat occupational groups as monolithic. Thus the prestige ratings of the legal profession apply to the bar as if it were an undifferentiated whole without diversity or variability. While that may be a reasonable and necessary formulation for a survey of public perceptions intended to compare different occupations, it contrasts sharply with the portrait of the practicing bar presented in chapter 4.

1. See chapter 1 for a discussion of the prestige of the legal profession. For discussions of prestige allocation in society see Barber (1957), Bendix and Lipset (1966), and Dahrendorf (1968).
2. Part of the reason that occupations with more highly educated members are accorded prestige is perceptions about the types of people who pursue more education.

There are in fact internal hierarchies of prestige within the legal profession. Since most states now require lawyers to have the same *amount* of education, the number of years of schooling alone cannot provide the credential for achieving higher status positions within the bar. Still since not all legal education is perceived to be equal, it may confer status variously. As a surrogate for years of schooling we will employ law school prestige as a possible credential to intrabar status.[3] We shall examine what attendance at different types of law schools means to a graduate's career and how the effects of law school fare when compared with other variables, most particularly social background and academic achievement in law school.

In his now half-century-old examination of part-time legal education, Reed concluded that different law schools would train their students for different kinds of practice. While he was referring specifically to the day-time/night-time distinction among law schools, his central point was that "the general principle of a differentiated profession is something that we already have, and could not abolish if we would" (1921, p. 419). Under the assumption of the existence of a unitary bar, Reed's conclusions were not received with much enthusiasm.

While Reed distinguished among different kinds of practice according to the economic status of their clientele, later efforts—most notably those of Carlin (1962a, 1962b, 1966) and of Ladinsky (1963a, 1963b)—also distinguished between private practitioners in solo and firm contexts. That practice distinction was then evaluated in relation to lawyers' background characteristics as well as to the fields of law in which they specialized. In each study the same variables reappear: background, law school, context of practice, and area of specialization. In addition to these, we shall also consider intrabar specialty prestige and academic performance in our effort to evaluate formal legal education as a credential for practice.

For this analysis father's occupation will provide the indicator for social background; law school status will be measured by the ascribed prestige rankings of law schools discussed in chapter 3. The practice-context variable will generally be limited to the categories of private practice and will be distinguished according to the number of associates in a firm, as presented in chapter 4. The specialty ranked first among specialties practiced will constitute the area-of-specialization variable except where specifically denoted otherwise.

The measure of specialty prestige is derived from prestige scores developed by Laumann and Heinz (1977), based on the responses of Chicago lawyers to a query about the "general prestige of specialty within the legal profession at large" (table 1, note (1), p. 167). While similar to the general occupational prestige surveys, this is an intraoccupational

---

3. As in earlier chapters law school status will be based on ratings by practitioners of the prestige of their law schools as attractions to attendance. See chapter 3 for the development of the prestige rankings.

scale calculated only upon the opinions of lawyers.[4] This scale is particularly important if we are to determine the extent to which organizational context of practice and prestige of specialty are interchangeable as indicators of prestige (as the literature has often implied). More importantly, the distinction between organizational context and substantive specialty will allow a more precise evaluation of the credentialing effects of law school on legal practice. Finally, we will consider academic performance in law school (as reported by the respondents) as a factor in the distribution of lawyers in the practice of law.

After considering each variable separately, we shall determine the aggregate impact of social background, law school attended, and academic performance on the distribution of lawyers among various practice contexts and specialties and then assess the ultimate explanatory power of each factor.

Social Background

In *The American Occupational Structure* Blau and Duncan (1967) conclude that social origins directly affect careers, both in their early stages and subsequently (p. 49). Consistent with their findings, the literature is quite clear about the relationship between social background and the nature of one's law practice. Even with the paucity of studies on the legal profession, the virtually unanimous agreement about this relationship is impressive. Auerbach (1976), in his historical critique of the legal profession and its role in social change, states that "the emergence and proliferation of corporation law firms at the turn of the century provided those lawyers who possessed appropriate social, religious, and ethnic credentials with an opportunity to secure personal power and to shape the future of their profession" (p. 21). In his empirical study of Detroit lawyers, Ladinsky (1963b) found that solo practitioners are

4. Mean prestige scores from a 5-point scale were computed for each specialty. These were then standardized, resulting in a rank order of prestige of specialties within the profession. Since the Heinz/Laumann sample was drawn from virtually the same population as this study, there is no problem of external reliability. For some parts of the analysis to follow, the specialties have been divided into prestige categories. The ranked scores divided quite easily into three groups: high-prestige specialties include securities, tax, antitrust, patent, banking, corporate, and administrative law; middle-level-prestige specialties include real estate, trust and estates, labor, insurance, bankruptcy, commercial, civil litigation, and municipal law; and low-prestige specialties include criminal, family, personal injury, poverty, and creditor-debtor law.

It should be noted that the utility of any prestige ranking based on legal specialties is limited by the inclusion of quite different kinds of practice within single categories. As discussed in chapter 4, lawyers involved in a wide variety of tasks and dealing with very different clientele may be categorized together simply because their work involves the same doctrinal area of law. For specialties in which such differences can be delineated, prestige scores may simply reflect an averaging of two quite distinct scores, each related to one kind of practice within the same substantive area of the law. The middle-level-prestige ranking accorded specialists in real estate law may be an example. While this caveat does not negate the analysis, it means that the substantial differences found among specialty categories as currently constituted underestimate actual variability. See chapter 4 for a discussion of specialties.

more often from minority ethnic and working-class backgrounds than are firm practitioners: only 70 percent of the solo practitioners had fathers in nonmanual occupations, in contrast to 94 percent of the firm practitioners. Although there are no tests of statistical significance, he concludes that there is in fact an important relationship between father's occupation and law practice (p. 131). Together with the relationship he finds between solo practice and low-prestige specialties (e.g., divorce and criminal law), the implication is clear: the higher the status of one's background, the higher the status of one's future legal career.

In an infrequently cited work, *Current Research in the Sociology of the Legal Profession* (1962a), Carlin, too, presents data on the work context and family background characteristics of a representative sample of lawyers in Manhattan and the Bronx. Using father's education, country of family origin, and generation American, Carlin shows linear trends (there are no tests of statistical significance) from individual practitioners, to small-firm, to medium-firm, to large-firm practice.[5] In further analyzing his data (table 26), we find the relationship between practice-context size and father's occupation to be statistically significant ($\chi^2 = 26.88$, $p < 0.005$).

In contrast to the above-mentioned findings, the Chicago data yield quite different results. We find *no significant relationship* between the occupation of an attorney's father and his own legal practice, with respect to either the organizational context of the practice or the prestige of the specialty. Although large-firm attorneys are slightly more likely than other attorneys to come from professional backgrounds and slightly less likely to come from blue-collar backgrounds, the differences do not even approach statistical significance ($p \leqslant 0.78$). In terms of the prestige of specialty within the bar, there is no difference at all. While our results run counter to the best-known reports in the literature, they are not unique. In their study *Lawyers in the Making* (1965), Warkov and Zelan found family background to be much less important than had been previously assumed. They found no linear relationship between parent's occupational status and expected law work setting if the strata of law school was held constant (table 7.5, p. 107). Although these conclusions related to *expected* rather than *actual* work settings, the comparison is appropriate. A recent study of the legal profession undertaken by Handler, Hollingsworth, and Erlanger (1978) similarly found no relationship between background characteristics and career choice.

It could be argued of course that if law school is the kind of credential hypothesized, then social background may simply exert influence at an earlier stage in the process. Such an interpretation would be consistent with Blau and Duncan's findings (1967). Although speaking about a different point in time, Warkov (1965) shows that indeed socioreligious

5. Although he is usually cited for his discussion of individual practitioners, with his findings then contrasted to studies of firm lawyers, Carlin himself avoids that error here and recognizes the importance of firm size as an independent criterion.

origins affect the distribution of students among American law schools (p. 150). According to Warkov, however, origins come in a weak third behind attendance at the "right" undergraduate school and Law School Admission Test (LSAT) performance as predictors to entry into the top law schools.[6] This trend is generally supported by the bar data.

As shown in table 5.1 there is a statistically significant relationship be-

TABLE 5.1
Type of Law School Attended by Father's Occupation

Father's Occupation	% National	% Non-national	Total %	N
Professional..................	47.3	52.7	100	131
Managerial, administrative, technical...................	41.5	58.5	100	171
Sales, clerical.................	40.0	60.0	100	105
Blue collar	28.3	71.7	100	113

$\chi^2 = 9.53$; $p < 0.05$

Somers' $D = 0.093$ (asymmetric with law school type dependent)

tween the prestige of the law school and the occupations of its graduates' fathers.[7] Yet the distribution is perhaps not as dramatic as might have been anticipated. Subsequently we shall see that law school attended is the best predictor of the nature of one's legal practice, in terms of both setting and substance. Therefore, it is curious that despite the relationship observed in table 5.1 we found no relationship between father's occupation and the nature of law practice.

A more careful look at the relationship between father's occupation and law school attended suggests an explanation for these data. Looking again at only those respondents who attended the nine law schools from which most of the Chicago bar graduate, we see in table 5.2 that the relationship between father's background and the prestige of the school attended is not linear. Not only is there not a statistically significant relationship between the self-ascribed prestige of one's law school and father's occupation, the relationship is not even consistently in the expected direction. What is probably the most surprising is the proportion of IIT-Chicago Kent and John Marshall graduates with fathers in professions. IIT-Chicago Kent and John Marshall are apparently drawing their students from a population similar to the more prestigious law schools. The difference, we suspect, is in the academic credentials the students bring with them. If law school attended and academic standing affect career opportunities in the law, then IIT-Chicago Kent and John

6. A more recent study of law students confirms the same ordering of variables influencing the distribution of students among law schools. Not yet published, this study is part of the American Bar Foundation's Law Student Activity Patterns project, directed by Ronald M. Pipkin.

7. This is consistent with the finding reported in chapter 3 that a law school's prestige is significantly more likely to be important in the selection of law school for those from higher status backgrounds.

TABLE 5.2 Law School Attended by Father's Occupation

Father's Occupation	Harvard[a]	Michigan	Chicago	North-western	Illinois	Loyola	IIT-Chicago Kent	DePaul	John Marshall
Professional	33.3%	38.5%	22.0%	32.8%	19.4%	15.2%	27.0%	17.5%	29.2%
Managerial, administrative, technical	33.3	30.8	42.0	26.2	41.9	24.2	29.7	33.0	29.2
Sales, clerical	30.0	15.4	18.0	24.6	19.4	18.2	24.3	25.8	10.4
Blue collar	3.3	15.4	18.0	16.4	19.4	42.4	18.9	23.7	31.3
	99.9%[b]	100.1%	100.0%	100.0%	100.1%	100.0%	99.9%	100.0%	100.1%
	(N=29)	(N=26)	(N=53)	(N=62)	(N=35)	(N=33)	(N=38)	(N=97)	(N=50)

$p \leq 0.0863$

[a]The law schools are listed in decreasing order of ascribed prestige. See chapter 3, table 3.14, for an explanation of the basis of this ordering.
[b]Percents do not add up to 100 due to rounding.

Marshall graduates should be substantially less likely than graduates of high-prestige law schools to settle into high-prestige law jobs. This would help explain why there is no relationship between father's occupation and kind of law practice, even when significant relationships occur between law school attended and both father's occupation and law career.[8]

A possible alternative hypothesis is that this can be explained by differences among the careers of the lawyers' fathers who were themselves professionals. In particular, we explored the possibility that those who attended lower status law schools and subsequently practiced in smaller private practice contexts and less prestigious specialties were more likely to be the children of lawyers (perhaps in similar or the same practices) than of other profesionals (e.g., doctors), but we found no differences. The proportion of lawyers to other professionals among the fathers of practitioners does not vary significantly among the graduates of the nine law schools or by the nature of the legal practice, either substantively or in context. These findings support the interpretation that there are a group of progeny of professionals whose academic credentials would not be likely to provide entrance for them to a professional career. However, having low academic standing combined with a high-status background, they indeed do aspire to such a career and find a law school for their formal training. This is consistent with Warkov and Zelan's finding that although academic performance is more important, a high-status (as represented by father's occupation) background supports entrance to law school even with a low academic performance (1965, table 2.10, p. 39).

These data imply that family background has been somewhat overplayed in the literature, at least to the extent that it directly differentiates among careers in the law. It is most important at the point of general career choice, where family background clearly affects both aspirations and abilities to attend law school, including academic performance in high school and college. Yet standing alone, family background provides virtually no explanation of the distribution of lawyers within the bar.

Law School and Context of Practice

Since the manifest purpose of law school is preparation for careers in law, the linkage between law school as a credential and career context is basic to any inquiry into the legal profession. The differentiation in practice among graduates of different law schools first noted by Reed (1921) has been refined more recently by Cavers (1968):[9]

8. The data are insufficient to determine whether background predicts the practice context or the nature or prestige of specialty for graduates of the same law school.

9. Beginning with Reed's study in 1921 and continuing through studies in the 1960s (e.g., Cavers, 1968), descriptions of the legal profession dichotomized legal practice between solo and firm attorneys. Both Lortie and Ladinsky followed this practice and con-

> The fission in legal education . . . reflects fission in the American bar. The line of division (which must ignore many exceptions) falls between lawyers organized in the big firms which represent big interests and lawyers practicing "solo" or in small partnerships who serve chiefly small business and small people (p. 141).

Cavers goes on to draw the line of demarcation at from 8 to 10 lawyers, the number sufficient to permit some division of labor and specialization. The corresponding fission in legal education he describes as follows:

> Most knowledgeable law school professors would identify fifteen to twenty schools as having widely distributed student bodies with high academic credentials, offering curricula pointed to national problems and preparation for federal, corporate practice, being located in universities of high standing (p. 142).

As will become apparent, the Chicago data basically support Cavers's view but dictate a further refined typology on both the legal education and the law practice sides of the comparison.

Several respondents were in retrospect quite cognizant of the credentialing role of law school. Although we did not directly elicit any information on this point, in response to a query about whether the respondent would attend the same law school given the same circumstances, some interesting explanations were proffered—for example:

> The unfortunate and unjustified importance of attending a "big name" law school in terms of obtaining a position would have forced me to attend Harvard, University of Pennsylvania, or the like. Attending a small school like Villanova worked out for me, but in retrospect, I was taking a big chance.

Even more to the point is the following response to the same question:

> A qualified yes—because of the insane prejudice for a few eastern law schools, outside of the State of Texas my law school diploma was constantly questioned, assuming my résumé was looked at. I feel my legal education was first class, but I have had some difficulty in seeking employment because I did not graduate from Harvard, Yale, Columbia, etc. I have always found employment, and my employers have always been extremely satisfied with my legal education and my ability.

---

cluded that firm attorneys are more likely to have graduated from prestigious law schools. Ladinsky finds that only 14 percent of solo attorneys in Detroit in 1960 had attended "top national" law schools, in contrast to 73 percent of those in firm practice (1963b, p. 132). Lortie divides law schools somewhat differently: "university," "Catholic" (but also within universities), and "independent" law schools. He attributes some of the differences he finds in first jobs after law school to the active role played by different kinds of law schools in placing their graduates (1959, p. 362). The number of cases with which he works yields some interesting suggestions but is admittedly too small to permit any systematic analysis. In contrast to this work, Smigel's study of law firms reports substantial differences in the proportions of law firm partners who attended Harvard, Yale, or Columbia according to law firm size: 55 percent for small law firms (less than 50 lawyers but usually less than 20 lawyers) and 71 percent for large ones (50 or more) (1964, p. 191).

This respondent's views are interesting for a number of reasons. First, his law school, the University of Texas, is generally ranked well within Cavers's 15 to 20 top law schools. In addition, by all standards this practitioner has been quite successful. He graduated in the top 10 percent of his class (1966) and ranks his success and legal skills at the 95th percentile compared with other Chicago attorneys in his specialty with approximately the same time at the bar. He is sufficiently satisfied with his situation to report that he expects to stay in the same job doing the same work. His first job after law school was with a New York law firm, where he worked in corporate and securities law, in that order. He is currently employed by a business firm and has now added antitrust work to his early specialties. In the data to be reported below, he will be included among those who practice a high-prestige specialty. Yet despite evident success, this attorney believes that the law school he attended did not facilitate his career to the extent that it could have.[10]

Perusal of the distribution of law school graduates by law jobs is sufficient to see the credentialing effect of different law schools. There is a statistically significant linear trend for private practitioners from national law schools to work in larger organizational settings. As shown in table 5.3, the percentage of national law school graduates increases di-

TABLE 5.3
Distribution of National Law School Graduates
Among Practice Contexts

Practice	% National	N
Solo practice	22.1	86
Small firm (2–8)	34.0	141
Medium firm (9–49)	46.7	90
Large firm (50 or more)	72.8	81
Government lawyer	29.6	54
Business legal staff	35.6	59
Other	26.3	19
		530

$\chi^2 = 56.58$;
$p < 0.001$

rectly from solo, to small-firm, to medium-sized-firm, to large-firm practice. Employed attorneys, those working for either government or business in a legal capacity, are likely to have attended national law schools in generally the same proportion as solo practitioners and small-firm attorneys. The government category is not very surprising and is consistent with Cavers's reference to law for "small people"; that is,

10. Our data are insufficient to consider the relative ease or difficulty with which graduates of different law schools have managed to acquire similar jobs. The implication of this example is not only that graduates of high-status law schools have a greater chance of having a high-status legal career, as the data show quite clearly, but also that the differences may be underestimated since it has been implicitly assumed that those who found high-status jobs had done so with equal facility. This does not seem to apply to this University of Texas graduate, nor does it apply, in his view, to others like him.

government lawyers, like solo and small firm attorneys, serve individuals rather than business interests. This of course implies something about the substantive specialty practiced as well. Lawyers working on business legal staffs and advocating the position of business are, by both Cavers's and Laumann and Heinz's definitions, doing high-status work. Yet such attorneys are no more likely to have graduated from national law schools than are those who do the law of the "small people." Large law firms are apparently more concerned with hiring lawyers with the "right credentials" than are corporations. Alternatively, it may be the lawyers with the best credentials rather than the employers who are making the choice. They may be attracted by the salary and independence of large law firms over that of business legal staffs, despite the relative equality of the prestige of the substantive legal specialty practiced.[11]

The most striking figure in table 5.3 is the percentage of members of large firms (72.8 percent) who have received their formal training at a national law school. It is in fact the very large firms that look different from all the rest. With the large firm defined as that having 50 members or more,[12] this finding contrasts with earlier work (Ladinsky, 1963a, 1963b; Lortie, 1959; Thorne, 1973) that locates differences in legal education at the lower end of the practice scale (i.e., distinguishes solo practitioners from the rest of the bar). Although it never generated much discussion, Carlin's data in *Lawyers on Their Own* (1962b) show a similar pattern. For Ivy League law schools (Harvard, Yale, and Columbia), his most comparable category, the trends are the same: Ivy League law school graduates practicing in Chicago are not evenly distributed; they constitute 1 percent of the individual practitioners, 3.3 percent of the small-firm attorneys, 18 percent of the medium-sized-firm (10–25) attorneys, and 31 percent of the large-firm (26 or more) attorneys.[13] Evidently the larger the firm, the more likely its members are to be graduates of prestigious law schools—underscoring the importance of the law school credential to placement in private practice.

In our discussion of the geographic mobility of the practicing bar in chapter 3, we noted that with very few exceptions local practitioners had had previous contact with Chicago before their practice. We mentioned

11. This finding raises further questions about the validity of attributing prestige levels to broad categories of substantive specialty. In particular it leads us to reconsider whether specialty alone is a sufficient measure of intrabar prestige or whether practice context ought to be included within any such ranking. See note 3 *supra* for a discussion of the limits of specialty prestige rankings.

12. It should be noted once again that the actual size of a "large" firm will vary in different locations. See chapter 4 for a discussion of the derivation of the firm-size categories for Chicago.

13. Since he is including in his calculations only Ivy League law school graduates, Carlin's figures are, of course, substantially lower than ours in every category (1962b, table 13, p. 33; table duplicated in chap. 3, n. 44). Carlin's figures are based on a number of sources: individual practitioners are from his own study sample, and the firm data are drawn from a combination of both *Sullivan's Law Directory* and *Martindale-Hubbell* (see source note to Carlin's table 13).

then that those with no prior contact with Chicago are somewhat different from the rest of the local bar. They are more likely to practice in firms and to have had better law school credentials, including class standing. Since the outsiders are also more likely to have attended a national law school, we wanted to see whether the law school–practice relationship held if we considered only law schools within Chicago, where we would not have to add national recruitment practices and national reputation as factors in the equation. The distribution is the same. If anything, the differences are somewhat more extreme, with an even smaller proportion of national law school graduates in solo practice and a larger proportion in large firms.

That conclusion is confirmed by an analysis of the careers of graduates of individual law schools. As shown in table 5.4, among the nine law schools that train most Chicago lawyers there is a positive relationship between law school prestige and large-firm practice: graduates of the three elite schools (Harvard, Michigan, and Chicago) are much more likely (41.4 percent, 30.8 percent and 30.2 percent, respectively) than the graduates of the other six (Northwestern, Illinois, Loyola, IIT-Chicago Kent, DePaul, and John Marshall) to be in a large-firm practice. Among solo practitioners, the schools split somewhat differently, with the four "local" law schools (Loyola, IIT-Chicago Kent, DePaul, and John Marshall) significantly more likely to send their graduates into solo practice than are the others. In the same regard, the similarity in formal, legal training between solo practitioners and small-firm attorneys is most likely to be found among graduates of these same schools.[14]

The implications of these findings extend beyond the mere distribution of law graduates within various practice contexts. For in Illinois, as elsewhere, the size of private-practice context is directly related to the median income earned. Firm attorneys earn more than solo practitioners, and the larger the firm, the greater the median income.[15] In addition, there is a statistically significant relationship between the size of private-practice context and lawyers' evaluations of their own skills and

14. While there is a strong relationship between the law school attended and subsequent career, the difference often attributed to part-time legal education is in fact dependent on the school attended. We examined the careers of graduates who had attended part time as compared with those who had attended full time, controlling for law school. This analysis was thus limited to graduates of Loyola, IIT-Chicago Kent, DePaul, and John Marshall. Despite implications in the literature to the contrary, it makes little difference to one's career whether the law school experience was full time or part time. It is of course true that part-time programs are not evenly distributed across all law schools and that the need to attend law school part time generally consigns one to institutions lower on the law school prestige hierarchy. Yet it should be noted that other law schools are beginning to admit part-time students. At Northwestern, for example, a limited number of applicants have been admitted on a reduced schedule. In particular this has accommodated women with family responsibilities.

15. These are the findings of a survey of the Illinois bar by the Illinois State Bar Association. Net income of lawyers is also related to years since graduation, with peak earnings 25–29 years after admission to the bar. See "Economics of Legal Services in Illinois—a 1975 Special Bar Survey" (1975, pp. 86–91).

TABLE 5.4 Law School Attended by Private Practice Context

Practice Context	Harvard	Michigan	Chicago	Northwestern	Illinois	Loyola	IIT-Chicago Kent	DePaul	John Marshall
Solo	10.3%	3.8%	5.7%	12.9%	11.4%	24.2%	18.4%	24.7%	28.0%
Small firm (2–8)	6.9	26.9	15.1	35.5	28.6	27.3	50.0	33.0	28.0
Medium firm (9–49)	31.0	23.1	24.5	12.9	20.0	12.1	5.3	14.4	18.0
Large firm (50 or more)	41.4	30.8	30.2	17.7	11.4	9.1	5.3	0.0	4.0
Total	89.6%[a]	84.6%	75.5%	79.0%	71.4%	72.7%	79.0%	72.1%	78.0%
	(N=29)	(N=26)	(N=53)	(N=62)	(N=35)	(N=33)	(N=38)	(N=97)	(N=50)

[a]Figures do not add to 100% because lawyers who are not private practitioners are excluded from the table.

their own success (both probabilities ≤0.001). The larger the practice context, the more likely attorneys are to rate both their skills and their success in the law above the median.[16] Even with the substantial self-aggrandizement reflected in the overwhelming majority of the bar rating their own skills and success as greater than those of half of all comparable attorneys, the differences shown in table 5.5 are quite substantial.

TABLE 5.5
Lawyers' Self-Ratings of Success and Skills by Private Practice Context

Size of Organizational Context	% Rating Own Success Above Median[a]	% Rating Own Skills Above Median[b]
Solo........................	59.0	77.6
Small firm (2–8)	75.9	80.9
Medium firm (9–49)	81.9	86.7
Large firm (50 or more)	90.8	94.8
	$\chi^2 = 24.11$; $p < 0.001$; gamma = 0.43	$\chi^2 = 10.81$; $p < 0.001$; gamma = 0.34

[a]Percentage rating their own success as better than 50% of other Chicago attorneys in the same specialty with approximately the same time at the bar. For the total sample including those not in private practice, 75.6% is the comparable figure.

[b]Percentage rating their own skills as better than 50% of other Chicago attorneys in the same specialty with approximately the same time at the bar. For the total sample including those not in private practice, 85.3% is the comparable figure.

Sixty percent of the solo practitioners, as compared with 90 percent of large firm lawyers, rated their own success as greater than that of half of other Chicago attorneys in the same specialty and career stage. The skill ratings follow the same general pattern but with less variance. These findings are not merely secondary reflections of an underlying relationship between legal education and skills and success evaluations—despite expectations to the contrary, lawyers' evaluations of their own success and skills are either not related or show a very weak relationship to law school attended or to class standing in law school. The only significant relationship ($\chi^2 = 17.62$, $p < .05$) is between law school and skill ratings, for the graduates of the nine law schools only. Although there is a general trend toward higher self-ratings of skills for graduates of more prestigious law schools, it is not linear. In addition, those with higher class standing are somewhat more likely to rate their skills highly, but the relationship is not statistically significant ($\chi^2 = 3.41$, $p < .06$).

Government employment is the other career context of particular interest, partly because of its assumed relationship to positions of political influence. Since government attorneys constitute only slightly more than 10 percent of the sample, our analysis must be somewhat limited. There is much common wisdom in Chicago about the route to politics, and

16. Respondents were asked to compare their own skills and success in the bar with those of "other Chicago attorneys in my specialty with approximately the same time at the bar" (questionnaire, pt. II, Qs. 14 & 15, p. 10, appendix 1).

more particularly that a government law job is best secured by way of DePaul law school. To address this question the valid comparison is between the proportions of each law school's graduates who practice in different contexts. In proportion to its numbers, while DePaul is an important contributor to government practice in Chicago, it is in the same range as Northwestern, IIT-Chicago Kent, John Marshall, Loyola, and the University of Chicago, each of which contributes from 9.4 percent to 10.5 percent of their graduates.[17] These six schools all are located within the city limits, suggesting that Chicago area schools generally—and not any one in particular—are supplying lawyers for government positions in Chicago. "Government lawyer," however, may be too broad a category, representing substantially different tasks and concomitant levels of prestige. Unfortunately we do not have sufficient data to examine this question. For those interested in the direct role of lawyers as advocates in government this would be a most provocative research question.[18] Although we cannot answer it, we can say that government lawyers, like firm lawyers, are a mixed breed, and if we are interested in the role of law school as a credentialing agent to various positions in a status hierarchy, then that hierarchy needs to be clearly and independently defined.[19]

Law School and Specialty

The relationship between law school attended and the intrabar prestige of the predominant area of specialization parallels the data on practice context. As table 5.6 clearly shows, graduates of national law schools are significantly more likely to practice a high-prestige specialty than are graduates of other law schools. The linearity of the relationship is more perfect among graduates of national law schools. They are least likely to practice low-prestige specialties, next most likely to practice middle-level-prestige specialties, and most likely (48.5 percent) to practice high-prestige legal specialties. Still, because of the larger numbers of graduates from non-national law schools reported in chapter 3, approximately equal proportions of those practicing high-prestige specialties graduated from national and non-national law schools (50.5 percent and 49.5 percent, respectively).[20]

17. While it is true that government lawyers are more likely to have graduated from DePaul than any other single law school, this merely reflects the predominance of DePaul graduates in the Chicago bar. As discussed in chapter 3, DePaul graduates constitute 18.2 percent of the practicing bar in Chicago and so would be expected to play a dominant role in every practice context. With the exception of large-firm practice, DePaul graduates make up the largest share of every kind of legal practice context.

18. Any such research would, we think, have to take into account the political connections that are made *before* attending law school. These would necessarily include connections through one's family, attendance at Catholic schools in Chicago (which have educated most of the predominant political elite in Chicago), and political participation before law school.

19. The analysis of the relationship between law school and government practice was repeated by cohort to determine if the results were affected by the number of years since law school graduation. There were no significant differences.

TABLE 5.6
Type of Law School Attended by Prestige
of Specialty

Prestige of Specialty	Law School	
	National	Non-national
Low...............	12.2%	30.3%
Medium	39.3	39.4
High	48.5	30.3
	100%	100%
	(N = 196)	(N = 307)

$\chi^2 = 27.33$; $p < 0.001$

Somers' $D = 0.253$
(asymmetric with specialty
prestige dependent)

The differences in the prestige of specialties practiced by the graduates of different law schools is even clearer from an analysis limited to the nine law schools that train most of the Chicago bar. As shown in table 5.7, the rank order of law schools according to the percentage of graduates who practice specialties accorded high prestige within the bar is an almost perfect replica of the self-ascribed prestige ranking for law

TABLE 5.7
Law School Attended by High- and Low-Prestige
Specialties

Law School	Prestige of Specialty		N
	High[a]	Low[b]	
Harvard	61.5%	7.7%	26
Michigan	52.0	12.0	25
Chicago[c]...............	44.0	10.0	50
Northwestern...........	42.1	21.1	57
Illinois.................	34.4	21.9	32
Loyola	26.7	26.7	30
IIT-Chicago Kent	13.9	38.9	36
DePaul	31.9	31.9	94
John Marshall	32.0	40.0	50

$\chi^2 = 37.10$; $p < 0.005$

[a]Percentage of graduates from each school whose first ranked specialty is rated high as compared with other specialties, by the bar as a whole. The percentages do not add across to 100% because lawyers whose first-ranked specialty is rated of medium prestige by the bar as a whole have been excluded.
[b]Percentage of graduates from each law school whose first-ranked specialty is rated low as compared with other specialties by the bar as a whole.
[c]See chapter 3, note 48, for a discussion of a bias in this sample toward similarity between the Chicago and Northwestern graduates.

20. These differences can be delineated more finely if we look only at the seven specialties that have the greatest number of practicing attorneys in the Chicago bar. National law school graduates are more likely to be practicing corporate, tax, or trusts and estates law, and less likely than graduates of nonnational law schools to practice criminal, family, personal injury, or real estate law. The differences are statistically significant ($p < .001$).

school prestige presented in chapter 3; for the low-prestige specialty ranking it is a mirror image. Again the pattern is the clearest for graduates of the elite law schools.

It could be argued that the relationship between law school attended and specialty practiced merely reflects the links between each of these and practice context. Yet the tie between specialty and context is not as close as might have been assumed. The case of the business legal staff who practice high-prestige law but are not very likely to have graduated from top-prestige law schools has already been mentioned. Yet this is the single case where context and substance are most closely tied. They practice the specialty they do by virtue of their employment. The same of course can be said of at least a substantial proportion of government lawyers in Chicago, 40 percent of whom deal exclusively in criminal law. Not surprisingly a greater proportion of government lawyers (62.7 percent) are in low-prestige specialties than are lawyers in any other kind of practice. Admittedly government lawyers constitute only about 20 percent of the practicing bar and may not be the appropriate basis for examining the relationship in question; however, these examples do force us to reconsider the reliance on substantive specialty as the sole indicator of intrabar prestige. Prestige may prove better estimated by an evaluation of the interaction between specialty and context.

Before accepting that interpretation, and to properly evaluate the relationship between specialty and context of practice, it is most reasonable to consider only private practitioners who constitute the bulk (75 percent) of the legal profession as well as its core image. The relationship between specialty prestige and private-practice context is presented in table 5.8. As expected, the larger the private legal organization, the

TABLE 5.8
Prestige of Specialty by Private Practice Context

Prestige of Specialty	Solo	Small Firm	Medium Firm	Large Firm
Low.................	30.1%	34.1%	13.1%	5.1%
Medium	49.4	39.9	39.3	42.3
High	20.5	26.1	47.6	52.6
	100%	100%	100%	100%
	(N = 83)	(N = 138)	(N = 84)	(N = 78)

$\chi^2 = 44.06; p < 0.001$

Somers' $D = 0.262$ (symmetric)

more likely an attorney is to be practicing a high-prestige legal specialty. For high- and low-prestige specialties, Cavers's dichotomy (1968) is supported: the substantive specialties of firms of eight persons or less are at approximately the same prestige level as solo practitioners. A similar statement can be made with regard to large and medium-sized firms. The correlation of prestige score and exact size of context of private practice further support this dichotomy. While the Pearson's $r = 0.291$[21]

was positive and significant, it was not as large as would have been expected if there had been a strong linear relationship.[22]

If we look at individual highly prestigious substantive specialties, the limits of the broad categories that are the basis for the cross tabulation in table 5.8 become clear. As discussed in chapter 4, areas of specialization are not randomly distributed among different practice contexts. While certain high-prestige specialties are particularly likely to be practiced within large firms, others are located in other parts of the private practice spectrum. Antitrust law and tax law, for example, are peculiarly large-firm specialties, with 70 percent and 56.6 percent of their private practitioners, respectively, working within large firms, but patent law (another high-prestige specialty) is almost never practiced as a predominant specialty in a large firm or, for that matter, in solo practice. In contrast, those who cite patent law as their first-ranked specialty are split about two to one between medium-sized and small law firms. Corporate law, which is admittedly something of a mixed bag, is practiced in all contexts, with small and medium-sized firms the most likely places.

Thus we find that individual substantive specialties ranked as prestigious by the Chicago bar fall into quite different contextual arrangements. This does not in any way diminish the relationship between size of firm within which one practices law and the prestige of one's specialty, but it does indicate that some substantive specialties even of relatively equal prestige within the bar are not equally likely to be practiced in large firms. Looking at the data from the opposite perspective, it is not so much, as Ladinsky says in "Careers of Lawyers," that solo practitioners do the dirty work of the bar but rather, as Smigel points out in *The Wall Street Lawyer,* that members of large firms do virtually none of it. No large-firm lawyers in our sample of Chicago lawyers list any of the following as their predominant specialty: criminal law, family law, poverty law, creditor-debtor law. To the extent that graduation from certain law schools predicts large-firm practice, it also eliminates the

---

21. Pearson's *r* (Pearson's product-moment correlation coefficient) is a symmetrical measure of association appropriate to interval and ratio data. It measures the degree of straight-line relationship between two variables and can range from -1 to $+1$. A positive value indicates a tendency for respondents to score similarly, relative to the respective means, on both variables. A negative value indicates a tendency to score inversely. In the example in question, the positive correlation between specialty prestige and size of context of private practice indicates that those who practice relatively high-status specialties tend to practice in relatively large firms.

22. A Pearson's $r = .29$ means that the distribution of one variable (e.g., practice context) explains 8.7 percent of the variance in the other variable (e.g., specialty prestige). Actually not all of the variance explained is due to the size of the context of practice per se; rather, it is a surrogate for law school attended and academic performance therein. This conclusion is based on a regression analysis in which the variance in the prestige of the specialty explained increases by only 4.9 percent when office size is added to the equation *after* the law school and academic performance variables. See regression analyses in the text at tables 5.11 and 5.12.

possibility of concentrating one's time in work rated low in prestige by the bar.

Academic Performance

Any evaluation of educational credentials must of course give some attention to the academic qualifications presented by the individual graduate. Value in the marketplace of the degree granted by a particular law school is one part of that formulation, and we have seen the extent of its effects. Another part is how each graduate performed within the law school attended—that is, his or her academic ranking compared with other graduates. Smigel, in his study of large New York law firms, found that 53 percent of the Yale graduates in large firms graduated in the top 25 percent of their classes. This is evidence, he concludes, that the recruitment efforts of large law firms are geared to high academic averages (1964, pp. 38–39).

The self-reported class standing of Chicago lawyers indicates that 50.3 percent of the graduates of the nine law schools that contribute substantial proportions of the practicing bar report that they graduated in the top 20 percent of their classes, with only small differences among the individual schools. While these figures seem considerably skewed, excessive self-aggrandizement was not expected given the anonymity of the responses. Indeed these figures may not be inaccurate. As noted in the discussion of the research design in chapter 2, the 24.7 percent of the sample who report their class standing to be in the top 10 percent are closely matched by the 24.1 percent who report participation in law review. The latter information in particular is both less likely to be false and less likely to be affected by diminished memory. Therefore, the apparent skew in the distribution is probably due to the design employed in this research.[23] Most important in this context, however, is not the absolute class standing but the *relative* academic success of attorneys who are in different kinds of practice.

As clearly evident from table 5.9, relative class standing makes an important difference in legal careers. Given the distribution in class standing, the results are naturally skewed to the high end of the class standings for all categories. Nonetheless, large-firm attorneys stand out as having had much higher class standing than lawyers in any other kind of practice. This pattern is perhaps clearer still if we dichotomize class standing and look only at the private practitioners represented in table 5.10. The data generally confirm former Harvard Law School Assistant Dean John P. Wilson's profile of the Harvard alumni, which concludes that high grade average is positively correlated with working in a large firm and

23. See chapter 2 for a discussion of the research design and its effects on the class standing of respondents. Consider also that a telephone survey of a random sample of lawyers in Toronto, Canada, similarly yielded 31 percent claiming to have been in the top 10 percent of their classes, 52 percent claiming to have been in the top one-third (Arthurs, Willms, & Taman, 1971, p. 503).

TABLE 5.9
Class Standing by Nature of Legal Practice

Class Standing	Solo	Small Firm	Medium Firm	Large Firm	Govern- ment	Business Legal Staff	Other
Top 20% ...	40.5	47.4	51.2	70.9	40.4	49.2	47.6
Next 21–60%	46.8	46.0	45.1	27.8	51.9	42.4	28.6
Bottom 40%	12.7	6.6	3.7	1.3	7.7	8.5	23.8
	100%	100%	100%	100%	100%	100%	100%
	(N = 79)	(N = 137)	(N = 82)	(N = 79)	(N = 52)	(N = 59)	(N = 21)

$$\chi^2 = 33.6; \ p < 0.001$$

TABLE 5.10
Private Practice Contexts by Class Standing

Class Standing	Solo	Small Firm	Medium Firm	Large Firm
Top 20%	40.5%	47.4%	51.2%	70.9%
Below top 20%	59.5	52.5	48.8	29.1
	100%	100%	100%	100%
	(N = 79)	(N = 137)	(N = 82)	(N = 79)

$$\chi^2 = 16.6; \ p < 0.001$$

Somers' D = .21347 (asymmetric with
kind of practice dependent)

negatively correlated with being a solo practitioner (1968, p. 25). Both our study and Wilson's are consistent with a 1964 study of UCLA law school students that found that students expecting to practice in a firm were significantly more likely to have a higher class standing than those expecting to be solo practitioners.[24] Again, however, the solo/firm dichotomy hides the more important distinction among firms of different size. Just as large law firms are most likely to attract, and perhaps recruit, the graduates of particular law schools, they are significantly more likely to be composed of lawyers who graduated in the top echelons of their law school classes than are smaller firms or any other kind of practice for that matter.

Law school class standings are also predictive of the prestige of an attorney's specialty, with specialties at the high end of the prestige continuum having significantly more attorneys who graduated in the top 20 percent of their law school class than do lower prestige specialties ($\chi^2 = 14.7$, $p < .001$). But that relationship is due to the correlation between the size of practice context and specialty prestige. In other words, the relationship between class standing and specialty prestige disappears

24. The study, an unpublished doctoral dissertation, was based on a mailed questionnaire from UCLA law students (Schultz, 1969, table 38, p. 167).

if we control for the practice context. Thus the recruitment of graduates with high class standing by large law firms skews the range of specialties practiced since, as discussed previously, the larger firms tend to be engaged in higher status specialties.[25]

As Warkov (1965) has shown with respect to entrance into law school, academic performance does make a significant difference in the future careers of law school graduates. The question remains just how much of a difference. The same inquiry of course is equally applicable to the earlier discussion of the relationships among career in the law and social background and one's law school. These questions are examined in the next section of this chapter.

Background and Academic Factors as Predictors of Legal Career

The preceding analysis has been limited to an examination of selected factors or pairs of factors as they influence the subsequent careers of legal practitioners. The next step is to determine the aggregate impact of social background, law school attended, and academic performance on the distribution of lawyers with respect to both practice context and prestige of specialty. A multiple regression analysis will be employed to determine the relative contribution of each of these factors to the structure of the bar; this will allow us to analyze the impact of each factor while controlling for the effects of the other factors being considered.[26] The regressions are limited to private practitioners because size of pri-

25. No particular pattern emerges from cross tabulations of class standing with specialty prestige or with size of private practice context controlling for the nine law schools.

26. Multiple regression is a statistical technique for analyzing the relationship between a dependent variable and a number of independent variables. We have used it to decompose the variance in a dependent variable which is explained by a set of independent variables, and to analyze the impact of a specific independent variable on a dependent variable while controlling for the effects of the other independent variables. Each of the independent variables employed as predictors of the organizational context of practice and intrabar rating of specialty prestige is, at best, ordinal in nature. Although multiple regression analysis typically requires data more linear in nature, it is possible to use dummy variable regressions to avoid the statistical problems that would otherwise emerge. We have used hierarchical entry of the independent variables (or sets of dummy variables) determined by temporal sequence. Father's occupation variables were entered in the first step, law school attended variables were entered in the second step, and law school class standing variables were entered in the third step. Thus the proportion of the variance explained by a particular variable is the *additional* variance explained by that variable, controlling for the variables entered previously. Any variance shared by two or more independent variables and the dependent variable will be attributed to the variable(s) entered into the equation earlier. Analogously, the regression coefficient (beta) is a measure of the independent effect of each variable on the dependent variable, controlling for the effects of variables already entered into the equation. For further discussion of regression analysis see: Norman Richard Draper and H. Smith, *Applied Regression Analysis* (New York: John Wiley & Sons, Inc., 1966), and Frederick Nichols Kerlinger and Elazar J. Pedhazer, *Multiple Regression in Behavioral Research* (New York: Holt, Rinehart & Winston, 1973).

To avoid the multicolinearity problem in dummy variable regressions with polytomous variables representing father's occupation and class standing, one dummy variable must be dropped from each regression. By repeating the analysis alternating the excluded variable we were able to conclude that the results were unaffected by those choices.

vate-practice context has been at the core of discussions of stratification of the legal profession and because of the requirements of the statistical technique.[27]

Figure 5.1 and table 5.11 display the results of the regression analyses.

TABLE 5.11
Regression of Father's Occupation, Law School Attended, and Class Standing by Size of Private Practice Context and Prestige of Specialty

Dependent Variable[a]	Independent Variable	Simple R	Beta	R^{2}[b]
	Father's Occupation			*.018*
	Professional	.092	.082	
	Managerial, administrative, technical	.053	.094	
Size of Private Practice Context	Blue collar	−.088	.011	
	Law School			*.120*
	National	.360	.380	
	Class Standing			*.078*
	Top 1–10%	.158	.332	
	11–20%	.076	.208	
	21–40%	−.046	.118	
	41–60%	−.154	.027	
		multiple R^{2} =		.216
	Father's Occupation			*.010*
	Professional	−.015	−.037	
	Managerial, administrative, technical	.087	.061	
Prestige of Specialty	Blue collar	−.073	−.026	
	Law School			*.051*
	National	.228	.242	
	Class Standing			*.027*
	Top 1–10%	.036	.167	
	11–20%	.122	.190	
	21–40%	−.057	.054	
	41–60%	−.073	.012	
		multiple R^{2} =		.088

[a]The correlation between the two dependent variables is .2943, which is the equivalent of R^{2} = .87 (i.e., 87% of the variance explained).
[b]Each of the R^{2} figures applies only to the adjacent group of dummy variables.

These data show quite clearly that the nature of the law school attended is the most important of the predictors of both the size of organizational context of practice and the prestige of the specialty practiced. Attendance at a national law school explains 12 percent of the variance in the distribution of lawyers in offices of different sizes.[28] As shown in figure 5.1, this 12 percent constitutes 55.6 percent of the explained variance. From table 5.11 it can be seen that social background as indicated by father's occupation explains less than 2 percent of the total variance. Academic standing falls somewhere between the other two factors, explaining 7.8 percent of the variance in office size. One who graduates

27. The multiple regression analysis requires that the dependent variable be in interval form.

28. R^{2} in table 5.11 is the equivalent of the percent of the variance in the distribution of the dependent variable which is explained by a given independent variable.

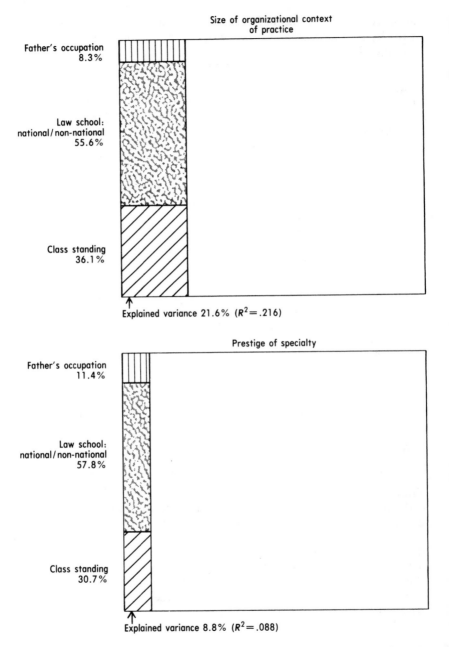

Figure 5.1 Variance in size of organizational context of practice and in prestige of specialty explained by father's occupation, type of law school, and class standing.

near or at the top of the class is significantly more likely to practice in a larger firm context than are other graduates.

The same general patterns were observed for predicting the prestige of the specialty practiced. The law school attended accounts for 5.1 percent of the total variance, or 57.8 percent of the explained variance. Overall, however, background and academic factors operated with less force in explaining specialty prestige. Only about 9 percent of the variance in prestige was explained by the three variables in comparison with approximately 22 percent of the variance in firm practice.[29]

With law school attended being the most important predictor of status and context of law practice, it is worth determining just how much more explanatory power law schools, taken individually, have for the determination of legal career than the dichotomous national/non-national categories employed heretofore. Therefore, the multiple regressions with both size of organizational context of practice and prestige of specialty were repeated with the law schools that train the predominant proportion of the Chicago bar entered as independent variables.[30] As with other parts of the analysis reported earlier, individual law schools do make a difference.[31] The results are presented in figure 5.2 and table 5.12.

Not surprisingly, there is no substantial difference in the explanatory power of either father's occupation or class standing when the analysis is limited to the law schools that train most of the Chicago bar. But individual law schools do make a difference, although that difference is much greater with respect to the size of the organizational context of private practice than to prestige of specialty. In both cases the *order* of influence of the individual law school is generally consistent with the prestige ordering of law schools presented in chapter 3. That is, with minor exceptions the law schools that were selected by students for their prestige value were the strongest predictors (i.e., had the largest betas)[32]

29. In predicting both size of organizational context of practice and prestige of specialty, the independent variables are virtually unrelated. That is, each is acting independently of the others and is not merely a secondary reflection of one of the other variables. The lack of multicolinearity was discovered by running separate regressions for the three sets of independent variables (father's occupation, law school, and class standing) for each of the dependent variables. The amount of variance explained for both independent variables when calculated by adding the results of the separate regressions is virtually the same (less than 1 percent difference) as that in the regression reported in table 5.11.

30. The sample for these regressions is by definition limited to graduates of the relevant law schools. Loyola was not included because of the necessity of dropping one category to avoid a multicolinearity problem that would otherwise arise in dummy variable regression with polytomous variables.

31. See for example the findings shown in tables 5.2, 5.4, and 5.7 as compared with tables 5.1, 5.3, and 5.6, respectively.

32. *Beta* is the standardized regression coefficient when both X and Y are standardized to have unit variance. Beta is then the most reasonable way to compare the relative effects of each independent variable on the dependent variable. In the case in point it is the means of comparing the relative influence that attendance at a particular law school has had on graduates' subsequent careers in the law.

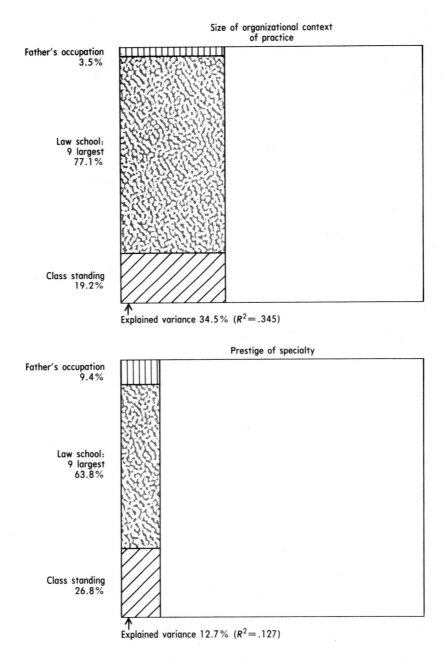

Fig. 5.2   Variance in size of organizational context of practice and in prestige of specialty explained by father's occupation, type of law school, and class standing.

TABLE 5.12
Regression of Father's Occupation, Type of Law School Attended, and Class Standing by Size of Private Practice Context and Prestige of Specialty

Dependent Variable	Independent Variable	Simple R	Beta	R^2
	Father's Occupation			*.012*
	Professional	.072	.084	
	Managerial, administrative, technical	.052	.109	
	Blue collar	− .058	.086	
	Law School			*.266*
	Harvard	.264	.328	
Size	Michigan	.216	.276	
of	Chicago	.221	.283	
Private	Northwestern	.042	.148	
Practice	Illinois	.097	.151	
Context	IIT-Chicago Kent	− .134	− .027	
	DePaul	− .271	− .093	
	John Marshall	− .190	− .096	
	Class Standing			*.066*
	Top 1–10%	.166	.298	
	11–20%	.050	.144	
	21–40%	− .016	.088	
	41–60%	− .171	− .043	
		multiple R^2 =		*.345*
	Father's Occupation			*.012*
	Professional	− .009	− .031	
	Managerial, administrative, technical	.090	.071	
	Blue collar	− .092	− .025	
	Law School			*.081*
	Harvard	.151	.170	
	Michigan	.142	.151	
Prestige	Chicago	.117	.107	
of	Northwestern	.011	.050	
Specialty	Illinois	.017	.037	
	IIT-Chicago Kent	− .119	− .079	
	DePaul	− .096	− .041	
	John Marshall	− .119	− .088	
	Class Standing			*.034*
	Top 1–10%	.052	.193	
	11–20%	.139	.266	
	21–40%	− .065	.066	
	41–60%	− .080	.042	
		multiple R^2 =		*.127*

of both size of practice context and prestige of specialty.[33] Furthermore, beyond being the best predictors, Harvard, Michigan, and Chicago are, as expected, quite similar in their likelihood of training future large-firm practitioners. Northwestern, on the other hand, at least in this regard, looks much more like the University of Illinois.

33. When undergraduate school attended is added to the regression analysis, much of the variance in career settings explained by law school can be predicted prior to the entry of law school into the equation. Adding individual law school attended after the undergraduate school still adds substantially to the explained variance (4.96 percent in the case of specialty prestige and 12.18 percent in the case of size of practice context). Yet it is not possible to actually differentiate the effects of law school from undergraduate school because of the distributions in the sample. For those schools with a sufficient number of graduates to make the analysis of undergraduate school reasonable, too many students at-

A comparison of figures 5.1 and 5.2 makes clear the substantial increase in the variance explained in both context of practice and prestige of specialty when individual law schools are included. The total explained variance in size of organizational context of practice goes from 21.6 percent to 34.5 percent; the comparable figures for prestige of specialty practiced are 8.8 percent to 12.7 percent. In part, this is due to the greater variation in the individual law school prestige measure than in the national/non-national dichotomy previously employed. However, together with the findings of the earlier cross tabulations of law school prestige with other variables (tables 5.2, 5.4, and 5.7), these regressions reveal the importance of the reputation of *individual* law schools in the careers of their graduates. In addition, it makes clear the limits of characterizing legal education in broad categories and prompts us to urge future research on professional education to avoid oversimplification.

The relatively smaller proportion of the variance in specialty prestige explained by the variables analyzed again raises the question of what influences practice in one or another area of the law. Consistent with our notion of drift into specialties and the considerable degree of stability in the specialties practiced by urban attorneys, it is not surprising that the proportion of the explained variance in the prestige of specialty practiced dramatically increases if the prestige of specialty practiced in the first job after law school is added to the regression equation.[34] An additional 23.7 percent explained (R^2 change = .0237) gives a total of 31.9 percent of the variance in specialty prestige explained using the dichotomous law school categories.[35] That amounts to close to a 200 percent increase in the explanatory power of the equation for those out of law school more than three years. Thus specialty practiced in the initial law job explains almost three times as much of the variance in the prestige of the specialty currently practiced as do family background, law school

---

tended the same institution for both undergraduate and law school education to permit us to differentiate their effects. For example, of the 36 respondents who attended the Northwestern University School of Law, 23 had also received their undergraduate education at Northwestern. Comparable figures for some of the other schools are 20 of the 31 DePaul University College of Law graduates and 18 of the 25 University of Chicago Law School graduates had received their undergraduate degrees from the same universities. Although it is important to note the stability of local educational setting, it makes the desired analysis impossible.

34. To avoid a bias toward those still in their first job, for these particular regressions the sample has been limited to respondents who have been out of law school three years or more. This is similar to the restriction placed on the sample for the analysis of stability in the practice of law discussed in chapter 4.

35. This is the result of adding the R^2 change = .237 to R^2 = .081, the multiple R^2 for father's occupation, law school, and class standing for those out of law school three years or more. That figure varies only very slightly from the multiple R^2 = .088 reported in table 5.12 for the entire sample. An analogous figure cannot be computed for office size because those data are not available for the first job. However, even using only the more crude distinctions of solo, firm, government, and business legal staff, knowing the organizational context of the first law job after law school graduation explains an additional 3.1 percent of the variance, with virtually all of that (3 percent) attributable to firm practice.

attended, and scholastic performance in law school combined. If the prestige of the second-ranked specialty in the first job (for those who mentioned more than one) is added, another 7.8 percent of the variance in current specialty prestige is explained. This is of course perfectly consistent with the earlier discussion of the nonrandom distribution of specialties that are practiced together. The same analysis was repeated for those out of law school three years or more who graduated from one of the nine predominant law schools. An additional 24.9 percent of the variance in specialty prestige is similarly explained by addition of the first job specialty to this equation.

To insure that these results did not simply reflect the original independent variables operating at an earlier stage in the career, further multiple regressions were calculated with the prestige of the first specialty practiced as the dependent variable. The original three independent variables (family background, nature of law school attended, and academic performance in law school) explain about the same amount of the first specialty practiced as they do of the current specialty. For private practitioners from all law schools $R^2 = 0.093$, with 6.6 percent out of this 9.3 percent of the variance explained by nature of the law school attended; father's occupation is again not a significant factor, and academic performance explains only 1.7 percent. As previously, if the analysis is limited to the graduates of the nine largest law schools, the variance explained increases to 15.1 percent with law school attended accounting for the increased explanatory power.

Context of practice and specialty have both been explored as indicators of stratification within the legal profession. Earlier studies (Carlin, 1962a, 1962b; Ladinsky, 1963a, 1963b) stressed the solo/firm context distinction; more recently (Lauman & Heinz, 1977) specialty has been characterized as the central element in professional stratification. In some cases the two variables have been used, at least by implication, as though they were interchangeable indicators of the same underlying dimension (Erlanger, 1980). In our opinion there is more likely an interactive effect between specialty and context which influences intraoccupational status. While that effect needs further elaboration,[36] several factors favor concentrating on size of private-practice context as the more fruitful line of inquiry: the results of the regression analysis of the two dependent variables (i.e., the relative strength of the predictions), the evidence that the path to a specialty is largely via recruitment to a practice context, and the indications (elaborated in chapter 4) that legally defined specialty categories often represent quite heterogeneous practices. Accordingly, the associations among the variables that provided the most productive regression model have been represented by a causal scheme in a path analysis (fig. 5.3). While there are naturally no star-

36. We attempted to create a variable that would represent this phenomenon, but the available data did not provide sufficient indicators of the appropriate weight to be assigned the two dimensions.

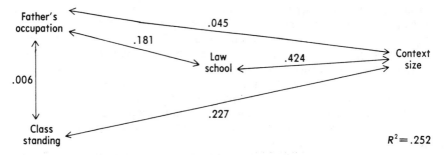

Note: The sample for this analysis is limited to the graduates of the nine law schools that train the bulk of the Chicago bar.

Fig. 5.3 Path analysis of legal practice

tling surprises, the relative influence of each variable is visually more clear. Although background has some impact on law school attended, by itself it is virtually meaningless in determining the ultimate career in the law. Just as clearly, it is academic credentials that provide the path to career contexts, and while class standing has some impact, the individual law school attended is the critical factor in predicting legal career.

A comparison of the results of the path analysis with the comparable regression model confirms the importance of individual law school in the structure of the legal profession. The path analysis has approximately 50 percent less predictive power than the regression analysis, explaining only 25.2 percent of the variance as compared with 34.5 percent shown in table 5.12. The law school variable is the source of this difference. In order to meet the requirements of the path analysis, the nine law schools entered individually as dummy variables in the regression were transformed to a linear prestige variable consistent with the ordering established by the practitioners. The diminished ability of the linear variable to predict outcomes as compared with the discrete law schools is consistent with a theme to which we continue to return. Law school reputations and the professional careers of their graduates are school specific and locally based. Attempts, therefore, to establish rankings of law schools nationwide are thus destined to be of limited validity, no matter how reliable (that is, subject to easy replication of the results). While law academics who do such ratings may have some basis for ranking law schools, it is practicing lawyers who hire new lawyers and largely determine their distribution within the bar. With the exception of perhaps the half-dozen schools typically designated as the "elite," the lawyer market takes little cognizance of "national" reputations. Rather there appears to be a well-established reputational hierarchy relevant to the local area with rather fine distinctions drawn among those law schools from which local lawyers are traditionally hired.

The larger firms are of course most able to actively recruit law students at whatever schools they choose, partly because of economies of scale. Large firms that can afford to interview at law schools and, where appropriate, to pay for students' travel expenses to visit the firm have a distinct advantage in hiring. They are attracted to the same law schools for hiring recruits that practitioners selected to attend because of the prestige accorded the law school. Given the positive correlation ($r = .29$, $p < 0.001$) between size of practice context and prestige of specialty, prestigious law schools' feeding of larger firms also ushers students into higher prestige specialties that do not serve the legal needs of individual citizens. Such recruitment practices may thus have the effect of drawing the best students from the prestigious law schools away from fulfilling those needs. While there is no direct evidence that such graduates would do otherwise were it not for recruitment practices in major law schools, these practices clearly constitute an advantage to large firms.

Conclusion

Just as Jencks (1972) discovered that "schooling seems to be important in and of itself, not as a proxy for cognitive skills or family background" (p. 191), so does a higher status law degree influence one's place in the profession apart from the influences of family background and academic achievement. Family background, which has been labeled in the limited literature on the legal profession as a central factor in ultimate professional status, simply does not explain much in a large urban center for this generation of lawyers.[37] While law school attended does have substantial explanatory power, it is much more likely to predict the size of the context of practice than the substance. The implication of this for legal education is not entirely clear since we have found that it is the substantive specialty practiced that is the key to understanding the importance of particular skills and the perceived value of law school training to the actual practice of law.

To the extent that we know anything about the route to law work that is accorded high status, the selection of a law school is the most important factor. Out of the 35 percent of the variance in practice context explained by the independent variables, 27 percent is attributable to law school attended. The comparable figures for the prestige of specialty practiced are 13 percent explained, of which 8 percent is determined by law school attended. In fact only law school attended and high class standing are even significantly related to the nature of one's law practice. The central importance of individual law school in the distribution of lawyers within the profession refutes the notion that law schools can be validly rated on a nationwide basis. Lawyer markets are relatively localized, and so apparently are the credentialing effects of the law schools. It was therefore eminently sensible for the practitioners to have

---

37. For examples of the literature stressing the importance of family background to legal career see Auerbach (1976), Carlin (1962b, 1966), Ladinsky (1963b), and Smigel (1964).

selected law schools in part because of their desire to practice law in the same community or state.

There are, however, several caveats that need to be mentioned. First, there is an assumption implicit in the whole credentialing notion that anyone who could would prefer to practice a high-status specialty in the context of a large firm. It may well be that many lawyers from high-status backgrounds with both high class standing and degrees from prestigious law schools do not aspire to jobs in large law firms or to practice in a substantive specialty that the rest of the bar views as highly prestigious.[38] Were such aspirations known, we might well discover that among lawyers who seek such jobs, those with the proper credentials are even more likely to succeed in obtaining them than is already indicated by the regression and path analyses. The difficulties faced by the University of Texas graduate mentioned above would be consistent with such a view.

Second, while his data support the primacy of schools as "selection and certification agencies" (1972, p. 135), Jencks concludes that schools are only secondarily socializing agents. While he may be correct that the actual talents of the schools' products are not attributable to their schooling, both aspirations and conceptions of appropriate work settings might be, particularly schools whose primary role is career training. With long traditions of alumni heading for particular kinds of practice, and with active recruitment efforts by the large law firms at selected schools, students are no doubt strongly influenced in their perceptions of acceptable work settings as well as realistic alternatives. Whether orientations to such jobs are brought with entering law students or developed during their three years in law school has only recently been the subject of systematic investigation (Erlanger & Klegon, 1978; Hedegard, 1979; Pipkin, research in progress on Law Student Activity Patterns; Levine, Erlanger, & Barry, in preparation). What is already known with some assurance is that the reputation of one's law school and, to a lesser extent, one's achievements therein are important influences on the shape of careers in the law.

Although the amount of variance explained by the law school attended and academic performance is not overwhelming, the importance

---

38. There is some anecdotal evidence that the limits of large-firm practice are increasingly being recognized. Although the large firm is perceived by practitioners as providing important training, the restrictions on independence are often quite severe. One of the advantages of doing litigation (as opposed to other tasks) in a large law firm is said to be the opportunity to make independent decisions in the courtroom without following the office practice of first consulting with a more established member of the firm. There also seems to be more movement among law firms than was previously the case. Some of this has been attributed to the internal organizational structure of the firms, with those more democratic in their decision-making structures being more attractive to younger lawyers than those with substantially more hierarchical structures. Yet because associates generate much more income (based on billing rates) than they cost to maintain, larger firms are able to provide higher income to partners. This remains an important attraction to large-firm practice, with new recruits aspiring to higher paying partnerships. It also continues to encourage the growth of ever larger law firms.

of these factors is substantial. For purposes of this analysis all other factors were assumed to be either unimportant or uniformly distributed throughout the law school graduate population. However, neither of these assumptions is likely to be true. First, individual aspirations affecting choice of work setting, where choices are open, have been ignored. Second, the personality characteristics that make some law school graduates more attractive employees or associates in particular settings have not been considered. And third, the personal connections that provide an entrée into some sectors of the job market have been neglected. This last consideration may be particularly important for a profession in which a full 14 percent of the practitioners are children of lawyers who can be assumed to have well-established connections in the legal community, even in the largest urban settings. It is likely that each of the three above-mentioned factors plays an important role in the distribution of law graduates among legal career settings. Therefore, given both the importance and the expected variability in these factors, the proportion of variance explained by law school and class standing is all the more impressive. As credentials, the source of the law degree and the academic standing therein are important signals in the recruitment and allocation of new lawyers.

These current patterns in the practice of law have important implications. More than fifteen years ago it was noted that "legal talent from quality law schools [had] flowed heavily into the large firms for many years," followed by "extensive elaboration of legal procedures to handle the problems of corporate enterprises as opposed to those to care for the problems of private citizens" (Ladinsky, 1963b, p. 142). Surely this is true today. Yet we think the picture is not quite that simple. As long as recruitment is tied to the context of practice, with large firms having a decided advantage, then attention to corporate clientele will continue. With such trends likely to continue, and with the documented stability in legal practice, those interested in broadening the base of service provided by the legal profession need to direct their efforts to providing *new* lawyers with job settings that are likely to provide training and experience for broader service.

In addition, and equally important to the nature of the profession, the initial allocation of lawyers into practice contexts will determine the colleagues who are so central to the continuing socialization of the bar. New lawyers actively seek colleagueship to acquire the skills and expertise they deem requisite to practice. We shall see in chapter 6 that office colleagues are given substantial credit for the training of lawyers. Whether by choice or default, a lawyer's job context also provides what Hughes identifies as the reference group in his discussion of the socialization of doctors—the people on whose good opinion one stakes one's reputation and to whom attention is paid. The reference group not only influences skills training but also, as we shall see in chapter 7, the conceptualization of lawyers' obligations as professionals. With the growth

in firm positions as first law jobs, coupled with the stability of law practice context, the central role of today's firm lawyers in shaping the future
of the bar is increasing. For the making of legal professionals, job context is critical in developing lawyering skills and expertise, in affecting
the portion of the public that will benefit, and in molding a sense of professional responsibility and how it is translated into behavior. Through
their influence on job setting, law schools affect the making of the legal
profession well beyond their direct influence in the schooling process.

Chapter 6

PREPARATION FOR THE PRACTICE OF LAW

Introduction

Along with a common identity and control over access derived from public acceptance of its authority and contribution to the public good, a profession is distinguished by the special knowledge and skills of its members. With formal legal education maintaining a virtual monopoly over preparation for entry into the legal profession, it is assumed that law schools are or ought to be the primary source of the skills and knowledge requisite to the practice of law. Actually very little is known about the skills and knowledge that lawyers find important and useful in the practice of law, and still less about how and where they are acquired.[1] In an attempt to understand the making of the legal profession, in this chapter we will identify the skills and areas of knowledge considered important to the practice of law and examine the sources from which lawyers believe they have been acquired. Particular attention will be given to the actual and potential role of law schools as compared with personal experience and law firms in the preparation of future lawyers. We shall see that while there is substantial variance among lawyers as to the competencies they think are most important in the practice of law, there is considerable agreement on the contributions made by law schools.

Knowledge and Skills Important to the Practice of Law

The literature on the legal profession has devoted little, if any, attention to what lawyers actually do. While the recent debate over lawyer

1. A few attempts have been made to determine the skills considered important to the practicing bar, such as Benthall-Nietzel (1975) and Schwartz (1973). Comparisons with our findings are severely restricted by differences in the precise skills included as well as in the methodologies and research designs.

competence may imply a consensus about the skills important to the practice of law, no systematic evidence has been available. Little progress has been made since Llewellyn characterized what was wrong with "so-called" legal education in 1935:

> Meantime, what pictures should we of today be making about the actual workings of "the" heterogeneous Bar?
>
> *Not rules, but doing, is what we seek to train men for.* Rules our men need. Rules do in part control or shape, do in still greater part set limits to, their doing. But the thing remains the doing.
>
> What *is* this doing of lawyers? Whither are we to head our students? We do not know (p. 654).

We begin this chapter by investigating the competencies that practicing lawyers consider important to the lawyering enterprise.

A list of selected skills and areas of knowledge thought to be potentially useful in the practice of law was presented to the respondents for their evaluation.[2] Table 6.1 presents the mean "importance" score, the percent "important," and the percent "extremely important" for 21 different skills and areas of knowledge.[3] As is apparent, many of the skills considered most important to legal practice (e.g., "instilling others' confidence in you") are not traditionally part of law school curricula. Close to half of the items are considered important by more than two-thirds of the lawyers in practice, with only the last several items important to less than half of the practitioners. These data indicate the range of competencies employed in the actual practice of law.

With so many items rated "important" by so much of the sample, the "extremely important" ranking provides a more sensitive measure. While the ordering of items does not vary much from the original list, the increased variance provides further information. Of particular interest is the extent to which "fact gathering" stands alone as the skill that almost 70 percent of practicing lawyers consider "extremely important"

2. The list of items included was developed in pretests of the questionnaire. A number of items are similar to those in Stevens's consideration of law schools' emphases (1973, tables A.20–A.26, pp. 699–701). Lawyers' activities can also be characterized and evaluated in broader terms, such as the "rapport-building" and "advice and consultation" discussed in DeCotiis and Steele (1977, pp. 486, 488).

It should be noted again that in all cases our inquiry has been phrased to elicit a respondent's opinion based on personal experience in the practice of law. When aggregated, these individual views will, we think, provide the most accurate picture of the practicing bar's view of law schools' contribution to practice. The most obvious alternative to this method would have been to ask each respondent to speak about law schools' contributions to the practice of law in general. However, since each attorney's experience is limited, the results have greater validity when respondents are asked to provide information about what they know best. The actual question on which the knowledge and skills data are based is on p. 11 of the questionnaire (pt. III, Q. 1, appendix 1).

3. The questionnaire (pt. III, Q. 1, p. 11) shows the 5-point scale of importance presented to the survey respondents. With the mean or average of the responses as the basis for the importance ranking, the rankings of all the respondents are given equal weight. Since it is possible, however, for the same average responses to represent different distributions, table 6.1 includes the percentage of respondents who have ranked the skill important (including ranks 1 or 2 out of five possible ranks). The order of importance of the various categories of knowledge and skills varies hardly at all regardless of the ranking scheme employed.

TABLE 6.1
Relative Importance[a] of Selected Skills and Areas of Knowledge

Skill or Area of Knowledge	Importance Score[b]	% Rating Important[c]	% Rating Extremely Important[d]
Fact gathering	72 (1.39)	93.0	69.7
Capacity to marshal facts and order them so that concepts can be applied	70 (1.52)	91.6	57.8
Instilling others' confidence in you .	68 (1.60)	88.6	53.9
Effective oral expression	67 (1.64)	87.4	51.3
Ability to understand and interpret opinions, regulations, and statutes	67 (1.66)	86.6	50.0
Knowledge of the substantive law . .	66 (1.69)	90.1	42.3
Legal research	64 (1.81)	80.6	44.5
Negotiating	63 (1.84)	78.9	44.0
Drafting legal documents	61 (1.94)	74.2	40.8
Understanding the viewpoint of others to deal more effectively with them	61 (1.96)	76.4	33.6
Ability to synthesize law	56 (2.22)	64.4	22.6
Getting along with other lawyers . . .	55 (2.27)	63.2	19.2
Knowledge of theory underlying law	54 (2.28)	61.1	23.0
Letter writing	54 (2.32)	61.3	18.1
Knowledge of procedural law	54 (2.32)	62.9	24.4
Financial sense	52 (2.42)	59.2	18.5
Interviewing	51 (2.43)	58.1	22.8
Writing briefs	46 (2.68)	49.1	19.8
Opinion writing	44 (2.80)	44.7	13.5
Knowledge of political science, psychology, economics, sociology	40 (3.01)	35.9	9.7
Accounting skills	35 (3.24)	23.6	5.5

[a]The rankings are based on standardized scores calculated from the mean of the responses for each skill. With five possible scores from a high of 1 to a low of 5, the mean for each skill was subtracted from 5 and multiplied by 20 to get the standardized score. These skills were then ranked in order from the highest (the most important) to the lowest score. The Ns on which all figures in the table are based range from 523 (ability to synthesize law) to 541 (fact gathering, legal research, getting along with other lawyers). Throughout the tables in the rest of this chapter, unless otherwise indicated, these skills are listed in this order of importance.
[b]Numbers in parentheses are mean responses.
[c]Percentage important includes responses of "extremely important" or "important," meaning ranks 1 or 2 on a 5-point scale of importance.
[d]Percentage of responses ranking skill extremely important, or 1 on a 5-point scale.

to their practice.[4] We recall that Louis Brandeis reminded himself to "know thoroughly each fact" in a memorandum on "What the practice of the law includes" (quoted in Hurst, 1950, p. 339). Judge Jerome Frank castigated the bar, the bench, and legal education for neglecting the critical role of facts in the resolution of legal disputes (Frank, 1950,

4. The importance of facts to the practice of law has been documented elsewhere. In an alumni survey of the 1966–69 graduates of the University of Toledo College of Law, Stern (1972) finds "dealing with facts" to be the single most important skill in practicing law (p. 30). In her survey of the Kentucky State Bar Association, Benthall-Nietzel (1975) reports that "organizing facts" is the skill ranked third in importance (p. 384). Based on a skill

ch. 3). The nearly 60 percent of the sample who rate the second item in table 6.1 as "extremely important" seem to be echoing Frank's sentiments that legal concepts become effective only as they are applied to fact situations.

Perhaps most revealing is the fact that the four skills seen as important by the largest proportion of legal practitioners—"fact gathering," "capacity to marshal facts and order them so that concepts can be applied," "instilling others' confidence in you," and "effective oral expression"—are not peculiar to the legal profession. Although lawyers may need to master these skills to be effective attorneys, these skills are equally appropriate to other occupations. It is not until the items ranked 5, 6, and 7 that skills and knowledge peculiar to the legal profession appear. And two of the skills that most typify the work of lawyers in the popular view—"writing briefs" and "opinion writing"—are rated quite low in importance as compared with other items, with only 19.8 percent and 13.5 percent of the sample ranking them as "extremely important" to their practices. To some extent the declining percentages in the "extremely important" column reflect the variance in the importance of various items to different kinds of law practice. Still the first six items are rated "important" by about 90 percent of the practitioners and are about equally divided between skills peculiar to lawyering and more generally applicable skills.

Interestingly, evaluations of the various skills and knowledge important to the practice of law are not randomly distributed among lawyers. A correlation analysis reveals that the various competencies cluster with respect to their importance in the actual practice of law.[5] Figure 6.1 represents only those correlation coefficients of 0.3 or better.[6] When the correlations are displayed graphically, two groupings emerge.[7] On the right side of figure 6.1 are the more purely analytic skills, what might be characterized as the core tasks of the lawyering process. Indeed these are the tasks that are tied most exclusively to the law and thus distinguish the legal profession. It is here we find the referents for much of the arcane knowledge and specialized skills said to characterize a profession.[8]

list different from ours but similarly employing a 5-point Likert scale, the mean derived was 1.71, somewhat higher (less important) than the 1.52 we found for the comparable "capacity to marshal facts and order them so that concepts can be applied."

5. See chapter 5, note 23, for a description of correlation analysis.

6. The coefficients range from 0.3026 to 0.4817. "Knowledge of political science, psychology, economics, sociology," and "accounting skills" have been omitted from the figure as the least important items (the mean importance of each is greater than 3 on a 5-point scale, i.e., very low). "Financial sense" not surprisingly correlates with "accounting skills" and so was also excluded. In addition, "understanding the viewpoint of others to deal more effectively with them" was omitted by virtue of its correlating in an unsystematic fashion (as a quasi-universal skill) with 10 of the 21 items.

7. A factor analysis of skill importance yielded three factors that did not give dramatic results. Two of the factors closely matched the two groupings in figure 6.1.

8. These analytic skills, central to the arcane knowledge and specialized skills that characterize a profession, are unrelated to another core characteristic of a profession, the contribution to the public good. See chapter 7 for a discussion of this issue.

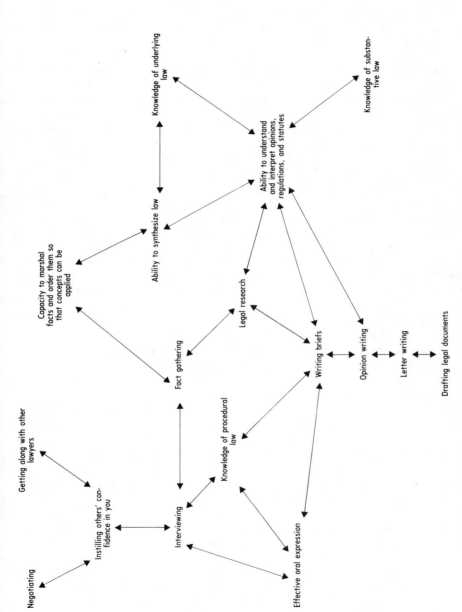

Fig. 6.1. Interrelationships among skills and knowledge important to the practice of law

If these skills constitute the core image of the professional role, then it should not be surprising that college seniors planning careers in the law do not highly value "working with people" (Davis, 1965, pp. 173-74, 183).[9] For despite the reality, the ideal-type tasks of the lawyer's work have little to do with interpersonal relations.

On the left side of figure 6.1, and again interrelated, are the interpersonal tasks so central to the actual practice of law but rarely characterized by observers as core, or ideal-type, tasks that lend definition to the role of lawyers in practice. This cluster includes more generalizable skills applicable to a number of endeavors. They are neither exclusive to the practice of law nor more important to it than to many other occupations. While as indicated in table 6.1 both kinds of tasks are equally important to lawyers in practice, the separate clusterings indicate that the two are not thought equally important by the same lawyers. That is, there are some lawyers for whom the package of interpersonal skills is central to their practice and some for whom the same is true for the more purely analytic skills. These two groupings of correlated competencies do meet in the center of figure 6.1 in skills and knowledge requisite to litigation. It appears that in litigation both the more purely analytic and the interpersonal skills play important parts. Not surprisingly "fact gathering"—ranked most important of the competencies—is centrally placed in figure 6.1, involving both the analytic skills central to the image of a lawyer's work and the interpersonal skills also important to the actual lawyering process.

In sum, the correlation analysis shows that certain competencies important to the practice of law are indeed interrelated. That is, a legal practice in which some interpersonal skills are particularly important is also likely to entail other interpersonal skills as well. The same is true for the more purely analytic competencies: they are seen as important to practice in tandem with other similar skills. Although the analytic skills may be characterized as the "core" tasks of the legal profession, it is important to note that in litigation, which most typifies, though hardly characterizes, the work of lawyers, we find a meshing of the two sets of competencies. To say that some skills are similarly ranked in importance to practice is another way of saying that some lawyers are more likely to find certain sets of skills useful than are other lawyers. The inquiry that follows is an attempt to determine the impact of both the substance and the organizational context of law practice on these evaluations of the competencies important to the practice of law.

9. In a later publication (1965) based on the same NORC survey data, Davis reports "a faintly surprising negative finding" that of all the predictor value items, "only 'people' shows no relationship to choice of a legal career." Davis observes that "a case could be made that the lawyer, much more than the physician, is involved in interpersonal relations as part of his job, but among the students it is the doctor, not the lawyer, who wants to work with people" (p. 140).

Relationship of Legal Practice to the Importance of
Skills and Knowledge

An urban attorney's legal practice is typically defined by two criteria: the substantive area of legal specialization[10] and the organizational context. As discussed previously, specialty and organizational context of practice are closely related to one another—that is, some specialties are significantly more likely than others to be practiced in selected organizational contexts. Yet when it comes to evaluations of skills and areas of knowledge as important to the actual practice of law, it is the predominant substantive specialty of the practice that is the best predictor of importance ratings. Virtually all the significant relationships found between skill evaluation and organizational context of practice disappear when the substantive specialty is held constant. Beyond the competencies that are of relatively equal importance to all lawyers, most of the remaining skills and areas of knowledge are evaluated differently by lawyers according to the different legal specialties in which their practices are concentrated.[11]

The magnitude and nature of the differences between specialties were assessed by an analysis of variance of the seven specialties practiced by at least 5 percent of the Chicago bar.[12] This technique calculates the differences in evaluation within groups as compared with the differences between groups. Where it is shown that the differences between the groupings is significantly greater than the differences within the groupings, we can conclude that the established groupings are informative with respect to the variable in question. In this case we are interested in learning whether those specializing in different areas of the law differ in their ratings of various skills and areas of knowledge and if so, how.

From table 6.2 it is clear that specialists in certain areas of the law evaluate the importance of skills differently and, further, that those differences fall into patterns. For example, tax lawyers and criminal lawyers are most likely to evaluate the importance of skills to their practices differently; they differ not only from each other but also from specialists in other areas.[13] Criminal lawyers' ratings of 9 of the 12 items differ

10. For our operational definition of specialization see chapter 4.

11. It should be noted that the differences that emerge from this analysis understate the actual diversity in the practice of law as a result of the very broad brush of the specialty categories. See the section "Relationships Among Specialties" in chapter 4 for a discussion of these limits.

12. We used the Scheffe test (0.05 level) to ascertain the difference between means. A two-way analysis of variance including both substantive specialty and organizational context of practice was also done. No interaction effects were revealed between the two variables.

13. One way of measuring the degree of specialization among specialties is to compare the number of areas of the law in which attorneys in each specialty spend a significant amount of their time. Considering the mean number of areas of concentration of attorneys who list different specialties as the area in which they spend the greatest proportion of their time, tax lawyers and criminal lawyers are the most specialized. That is, among

TABLE 6.2
One-Way Analysis of Variance of Importance of Selected Skills and
Areas of Knowledge by Legal Specialty[a]

Skill or Area of Knowledge[b]	Significantly Different Specialties[c]	
Effective oral expression	Criminal[d] (1.3333)[e] Personal injury (1.3750) Family (1.4000)	Real estate (1.9219) Trusts and estates (2.0000)
Ability to understand and interpret opinions, regulations, and statutes	Tax (1.1765)	Personal injury (2.0175)
Legal research	Tax (1.2941)	Real estate (2.2344)
Negotiating	Family (1.4000) Personal injury (1.7193) Corporate (1.7320) Real estate (1.7424)	Trusts and estates (2.3171)
Drafting legal documents	Trusts and estates (1.5238) Corporate (1.5500) Real estate (1.6667)	Personal injury (2.5636) Criminal (2.7742)
Letter writing.................	Corporate (2.0800) Real estate (2.1846) Trusts and estates (2.2143) Family (2.2800) Tax (2.4412) Personal injury (2.4727)	Criminal (3.0625)
Procedural law	Criminal (1.6875) Personal injury (1.7679)	Tax (2.8485)
Financial sense................	Tax (1.9091) Corporate (2.0400) Real estate (2.2031)	Criminal (3.1875)
Interviewing..................	Family (1.7200) Criminal (1.7273)	Trusts and estates (2.4524) Real estate (2.5313) Corporate (2.6970) Tax (2.8485)
Writing briefs	Criminal (2.2727)	Real estate (3.2581)
Opinion writing...............	Tax (2.2647)	Family (3.3600) Criminal (3.3750)
Accounting...................	Tax (2.2353)	Criminal (3.8387) Personal injury (3.9630)

Corporate (2.7347)
Trusts and estates (2.8605)

[a]Includes only those seven specialties that are each practiced as the primary specialty by at least 25 lawyers (approximately 5 percent) of the sample.

[b]Although listed in the same order of aggregate importance as in table 1, only those 12 skills that vary significantly in importance to the practice of different substantive specialties are included here. The skills that are evaluated differently by specialists in various fields do not cluster in terms of aggregate importance; they are distributed throughout the importance listing from a fourth to a twenty-first ranking.

[c]The groupings indicate significant ($p \leq 0.05$) differences between the mean responses of lawyers concentrating in different legal specialties. Those specialties not mentioned for a particular skill are those that are not significantly different in substance from the specialties in one or the others, but not all, of the groupings listed. This does not necessarily mean that the excluded specialties are related to each other with respect to skill importance. The Student-Newman-Keuls procedure was employed (see chapter 3, table 3.18, note a, for an explanation of this procedure).

[d]Specialties are listed from low (very important) to high (not very important) in the order of the mean importance of each skill.

[e]Mean importance of skill for those specializing in each area based on a 5-point scale rating. A mean of 1.0 (low) would indicate that all practitioners who spend the predominant amount of their time in each specialty consider that skill extremely important to their practice; a mean of 5.0 would indicate that every practitioner considers it not at all important.

significantly from ratings by specialists in some other area of the law, and tax lawyers' ratings differ on 8 of the skills. Further, tax lawyers and criminal lawyers are significantly different from each other whenever the skills ratings by both of them differ from those in the other areas of specialization. The tax lawyers are more likely to rate analytic and business skills as particularly important to their practice, the criminal lawyers more likely to emphasize interpersonal and procedural skills.

As table 6.2 shows, the other specialties also fall into a pattern. Corporate law, trusts and estates law, and real estate law seem to demand certain skills but are significantly less likely to require others. Thus drafting legal documents and letter writing are particularly important to these specialties, and interviewing relatively unimportant. Of skills that are selectively important to only one or more of the seven predominant specialties, interpersonal skills like negotiating and interviewing as well as knowledge of procedural law and writing briefs for litigation are significantly more likely to be important to lawyers concentrating in specialties considered relatively low in prestige by the practicing bar in general: criminal law, family law, and personal injury law.[14] On the other hand, the ability to understand and interpret opinions, regulations, and statutes, drafting legal documents, letter writing, and financial sense are significantly more likely to be considered important to the practice of those concentrating in higher prestige specialties.[15] Apparently the ac-

---

the seven specialties practiced by the largest number of attorneys in Chicago, those concentrating in tax law or criminal law have the lowest mean number of areas of concentration. As groups, then, tax lawyers and criminal lawyers are relatively "pure" specialists.

14. See chapter 5 for a discussion of intrabar prestige ratings of substantive specialties in the law.

15. This conclusion is supported further by the distribution of some of the specialties that do not appear in table 6.4. For the competencies appearing in the table below there

Analysis of Variance[a] of Importance of Selected Skills by Current Specialty, Rank 1

Skills	Corporate Law	Criminal Law	Family Law	Personal Injury	Tax Law	Trusts & Estates	Real Estate
Ability to understand and interpret opinions, regulations, and statutes	1.4950 (3:1,3)[b]	1.6970 (3:1)	1.8000 (3:1)	2.0175 (3:1,2)	1.1765 (3:2,3)	1.8810 (3:1)	1.7969 (3:1)
Accounting skills ..	2.7347 (5:1,3,4,5)	3.8387 (5:1,2,3)	3.1200 (5:1,4,5)	3.9630 (5:1,2,3,4)	2.2353 (5:2,3,4)	2.8605 (5:1,2,3,4)	3.1270 (5:1,4,5)
Financial sense	2.0400 (3:2,3)	3.1875 (3:1,2)	2.3600 (3:3)	2.8182 (3:1)	1.9091 (3:2,3)	2.3902 (3:3)	2.2031 (3:2,3)
	(N = 103)	(N = 33)	(N = 25)	(N = 57)	(N = 34)	(N = 44)	(N = 67)

[a]The Student-Newman-Keuls (SNK) test was used to analyze the variance. For a description of this procedure see note a in table 3.18.

[b]The first number in the parentheses is the number of homogeneous subsets. Numbers following the colon indicate the subsets from which the group is excluded.

are additional specialties significantly different from one or more of the specialties appearing in the analysis of variance results illustrated in table 6.2. All three skills are signif-

tual competencies requisite to practice differ to some extent according to the prestige level of the specialty.

To verify our interpretation we added to the analysis those respondents whose specialties were not among the seven largest but had been rated according to the same prestige scale. The results of the previous analysis based on individual specialty are supported by the data reported in table 6.3. Of the 12 competencies for which the importance varies significantly by individual specialty practice, 10 vary significantly according to the prestige of the specialty within the bar. As is usually the case when such categories are established, the extreme groups (here low- and high-prestige specialties) are not consistently different from one another. With the exception of writing briefs the importance ratings are (or approach being) linear. The higher the prestige, the more important are the ability to understand and interpret opinions, regulations, and statutes, drafting legal documents, letter writing, financial sense, opinion writing, and accounting skills. The lower the specialty prestige, the more important are effective oral expression, knowledge of procedural law, and interviewing. The lower prestige specialties seem to involve more interpersonal skills, while the higher prestige specialties are more likely to rate more purely "analytic" skills as important to their practice.[16] This indicates that specialties receiving higher intrabar prestige ratings are those for which the analytic skills are more likely to be important. That is, they may be rated highly because the work involved more nearly meets the ideal-type tasks of the profession which set it apart from and contribute to its prestige in the larger society. These are the same areas of specialized knowledge and expertise which support the profession's claims to self-regulation.

Acquisition of Skills and Knowledge Important to the Practice of Law

Although formal law school training is the virtually universal prereq-

---

icantly more likely to be valued by those specializing in corporate law than by those specializing in criminal and/or personal injury law. In addition, in their valuing of "financial sense," personal injury specialists are also significantly different from the high-prestige corporate and tax attorneys. In fact the threefold prestige categories for different specialties is reflected rather nicely with real estate and trusts and estates specialties, defined earlier as having middle-level prestige within the bar, falling midway in the analysis of variance with respect to skill importance. That is, they are the groups that overlap the subsets most frequently.

16. Given the differences in the kinds of competencies important to the practice of different specialties, it would be interesting to know whether lawyers who choose to enter different specialties differ in terms of personality characteristics and/or values. Although Davis found that on their scale of values college seniors planning careers in law rank "people" low and "money" very high as compared with those planning careers in other professions (1964, pp. 173–74, 183; 1965, pp. 140–52), we have no such information about actual practitioners in general or in particular specialties. Were that information available, we would want to compare the extent to which values influence the specialty selected and the extent to which representation of a particular side in a substantive field generates and reinforces beliefs consistent with the position advocated.

TABLE 6.3
Skills and Areas of Knowledge Important to the Practice of Law by
Prestige of Specialty

Skill or Area of Knowledge	% Rating Extremely Important		
	Low Prestige[a]	Medium Prestige[b]	High Prestige[c]
Fact gathering	. . .	. . .	. . .
Capacity to marshal facts and order them so that concepts can be applied	. . .	. . .	. . .
Instilling others' confidence in you .	. . .	. . .	. . .
Effective oral expression*	65.3	44.8	50.0
Ability to understand and interpret opinions, regulations, and statutes	38.5	44.6	62.1
Knowledge of the substantive law . .	. . .	. . .	. . .
Legal research	. . .	. . .	. . .
Negotiating	. . .	. . .	. . .
Drafting legal documents	18.8	44.1	50.8
Understanding the viewpoint of others to deal more effectively with them	. . .	. . .	. . .
Ability to synthesize law	. . .	. . .	. . .
Getting along with other lawyers . . .	. . .	. . .	. . .
Knowledge of theory underlying law	. . .	. . .	. . .
Letter writing*	12.6	17.9	21.2
Knowledge of procedural law	39.2	17.7	20.0
Financial sense	10.1	18.1	24.1
Interviewing	41.3	18.0	16.1
Writing briefs*	15.4	13.7	24.2
Opinion writing	5.0	10.5	21.1
Knowledge of political science, psychology, economics, sociology	. . .	. . .	. . .
Accounting skills	2.6	2.6	10.3

*$p \leqslant 0.05$; for all others $p \leqslant 0.0005$
NOTE: Each row of the table corresponds to a separate contingency table. Percentages
are cited only when $p \leqslant .05$.
[a]Percentages based on Ns ranging from 116 to 122.
[b]Percentages based on Ns ranging from 190 to 196.
[c]Percentages based on Ns ranging from 185 to 190.

uisite for admission to the bar, it is an open question just how much and
in what ways it prepares its graduates for practice. Indeed much of the
criticism aimed at legal education focuses on this very issue.[17] Law
schools of course do not constitute the sole source of attorneys' skills
and knowledge relevant to practice. Many of these competencies are
equally important to other enterprises and may be developed in other
contexts. The same may also be true of some of the more analytic skills
such as capacity to marshal facts and order them so that concepts can be
applied. A developmental approach to socialization suggests that what is
learned in law school both builds upon previous experiences and in-

17. See chapter 1, note 12, for examples.

fluences and is enhanced by subsequent experience and socialization.[18] To examine the acquisition of selected skills and knowledge important in the practice of law we will consider lawyers' evaluations of the various contributions made by their own experience and study,[19] by law school education, and by the influence of other attorneys.

Experience as Professional Training

Practicing attorneys are most likely to credit their own experience with providing the competencies important to practice. Indeed, lawyers' own experience is, on the whole, perceived to be the most important contributor to the development of skills and knowledge important to the practice of law.[20] As can be seen in table 6.4, only for knowledge of theory underlying law do less than 35 percent of the sample credit their own experience with making a major contribution to their competence. From table 6.4 it is also evident that more than two-thirds of the respondents rank their own experience as the first or second most important influence on 11 of the 21 competencies evaluated. Included among these are the 4 skills most important to the bar as a whole: fact gathering (76.2 percent), capacity to marshal and order facts to apply concepts (68.2 percent), instilling confidence (86.9 percent), and effective oral expression (76.0 percent).[21] We shall see later that these and other competencies developed primarily through personal experience are those for which most lawyers give law schools very little credit.

The important role played by lawyers' own experience, whether prior or subsequent to law school, will be worth remembering as we turn to the contributions attributed to law school in the development of selected skills and areas of knowledge relevant to the practice of law. With personal experience having such a prominent place in the development of lawyers' expertise, for both competencies covered in law school and those neglected, the nature of law practice—both substantive and organizational—is quite important. Indeed to the extent that, as we have documented, attendance at particular law schools increases the likelihood of (and in some cases almost dictates) entry into certain types of

18. See the discussion of the developmental approach to socialization in chapter 1, note 25. For an application of this approach to legal socialization see Tapp and Levine (1974).

19. The question about the contributions of experience did not specify the time sequence (questionnaire, pt. III, Q. 2, pp. 12–13). Later in the analysis, by comparing the competencies expected to be brought to the first job and the contributions of law school, it will be possible to ascertain the contributions of pre–law school experience.

20. The perceived importance of experience varies with the amount of experience (i.e., years since law school graduation) for only a few competencies. For both negotiating and interviewing, the greater the number of years in practice, the more likely respondents are to credit experience as an important contributor to skill development. The exception is that those out of law school more than 35 years are least likely to credit experience for these and the other competencies evaluated.

21. The percentages for each item are based on the number of respondents ranking any source for that item. For example, 76.2 percent of the 429 respondents who ranked any source as making a "substantial contribution" to the development of fact-gathering skills ranked "own repeated experience" as rank 1 or 2.

TABLE 6.4
Importance of Experience in the Development of
Selected Skills and Areas of Knowledge

Skill or Area of Knowledge	% Rating Experience Important[a]	N[b]
Fact gathering	76.2	429
Capacity to marshal facts and order them so that concepts can be applied	68.2	412
Instilling others' confidence in you .	86.9	413
Effective oral expression	76.0	413
Ability to understand and interpret opinions, regulations, and statutes	43.4	417
Knowledge of the substantive law . .	35.3	436
Legal research	42.4	439
Negotiating	78.3	415
Drafting legal documents	69.0	422
Understanding the viewpoint of others to deal more effectively with them	85.4	403
Ability to synthesize law	49.6	403
Getting along with other lawyers . . .	84.1	396
Knowledge of theory underlying law	20.1	408
Letter writing	86.9	404
Knowledge of procedural law	49.8	408
Financial sense	77.8	370
Interviewing	83.9	391
Writing briefs	51.1	409
Opinion writing	57.7	388
Knowledge of political science, psychology, economics, sociology	48.8	369
Accounting skills	51.1	354

[a]Includes respondents ranking own experience 1 or 2.

[b]Ns represent the number of respondents ranking any source as contributing substantially to the development of each competency. For example, of the 429 respondents ranking something as contributing substantially to the development of fact-gathering skills, 76.2 percent ranked "own experience" 1 or 2 of a possible 8 rankings.

law practice, it also indirectly influences the content and nature of post–law school experiences that shape the development of expertise and the perceptions of the competencies important to the practice of law.

Law Schools' Contribution to the Development of Skills and Areas of Knowledge Important to the Practice of Law

Keeping in mind the relative importance assigned by Chicago lawyers to skills and areas of knowledge useful to practice, and the credit given to personal experience, what is the perceived contribution of law schools to the development of these competencies? Table 6.5 shows the bar's evaluation of their law schools' contributions to specific skills and knowledge they consider important to the practice of law. The items are again listed

TABLE 6.5
Law School's Contribution to and Employers' Expectations of
Skills and Areas of Knowledge Important to the Practice of Law

Skill or Area of Knowledge	% Respondents Who Learned Essentially in Law School[a]	% Evaluators[b] Expecting New Lawyers to Bring Ability with Them
Fact gathering	16	31[c]
Capacity to marshal facts and order them so that concepts can be applied	44	63
Instilling others' confidence in you	4	20
Effective oral expression	15	57
Ability to understand and interpret opinions, regulations, and statutes	77	90
Knowledge of the substantive law	79	78
Legal research	75	91
Negotiating	2	3
Drafting legal documents	11	31
Understanding the viewpoint of others to deal more effectively with them	10	36
Ability to synthesize law	62	78
Getting along with other lawyers	4	35
Knowledge of theory underlying law	84	92
Letter writing	3	32
Knowledge of procedural law	50	54
Financial sense	4	26
Interviewing	2	8
Writing briefs	42	56
Opinion writing	28	39
Knowledge of political science, psychology, economics, sociology	6	61
Accounting skills	13	50

[a]Percentages based on Ns ranging from 488 (ability to synthesize law) to 511 (legal research).

[b]Attorneys who have evaluated new lawyers as prospective associates or employees.

[c]Percentages based on Ns ranging from 307 (accounting skills) to 334 (legal research).

in order of importance to facilitate comparisons with previous tables. Respondents' evaluations of their law schools' contributions to their skills and knowledge are not related to their evaluation of the importance of the same competencies to their practices or to their class standing in law school.[22] In addition, graduates of national and of non-national law schools differ in their evaluation of their law schools' contributions on

22. The sole exception is for the evaluation of the contribution of law school to writing briefs, for which a greater proportion of those ranking below than within the top 20 percent credit law schools ($\chi^2 = 3.98$, $p < 0.005$).

only three items when nature of practice is held constant.[23] Given the substantial similarity in law school curricula this is not surprising.[24]

The first column of figures in table 6.5 reveals the extent of the variance in the perceived contributions of law schools to the skills that lawyers consider important to their practices. From this table it is apparent that legal theory, substantive law, ability to understand and interpret opinions, regulations, and statutes, and legal research are seen as most likely to be learned in law school. These all fall into the cluster of analytic skills illustrated in figure 6.1. Although several are considered important to the practice of law (as illustrated in table 6.1, their means range from 1.66 to 2.28), no one skill is considered extremely important by more than half of the practicing bar. The skills rated as the *most* important to the practice of law were apparently learned *outside* law school. Only for the capacity to marshal and order facts to apply concepts do the law schools receive substantial credit (44 percent). The other three skills most important to the practice of law—fact gathering, instilling confidence, and effective oral expression—were learned in law school by only very small proportions of the bar. As indicated in table 6.4, lawyers largely attribute these same three skills to their own experiences. A comparison of tables 6.4 and 6.5 reveals that law school education is similarly given quite low rankings by most lawyers for a number of the other competencies for which personal experience has been very important. These include, in order of their importance: negotiating, drafting legal documents, understanding the viewpoint of others to deal more effectively with them, getting along with other lawyers, letter writing, financial sense, and interviewing. The five competencies in table 6.5 which the largest proportions of the sample learned essentially in law school are all among the more purely analytic skills employed in the practice of law. Not a single one of the interpersonal skills, irrespective of aggregate importance, was seen by much of the sample to have been developed in law school.[25]

Comparing the two columns in table 6.5 we can see that the five competencies that most lawyers who had been evaluating new lawyers as prospective associates or employees (78–92 percent) expected new lawyers to bring with them to their first job are the same five that the largest proportion of lawyers (62–84 percent) saw as essentially learned in law school: ability to understand and interpret opinions, regulations,

23. A similar analysis for the graduates of each of the nine law schools would not yield reliable tests of significance because of the reduced N and the skew in the distribution of graduates in practice contexts. In any case, no observable patterns emerge from the cross tabulations for each skill item.

24. Pipkin (1977) discusses the extent of the similarity in curricula.

25. An evaluation of the extent to which participation on law review contributed to the acquisition of competencies for practice revealed a special perceived contribution to two particular skills: writing briefs and opinion writing. The other competencies for which law review is given substantial credit by its participants are the same for which law school in general is rated highly.

and statutes, knowledge of the substantive law, legal research, ability to synthesize the law, and knowledge of theory underlying law.[26] Additionally, some skills, particularly negotiating and interviewing but also instilling confidence, are being learned only after certification.[27] The data suggest that these interpersonal skills, which are considered central to the practice of law, are thought to be developed outside formal professional education. In addition, recall that on-the-job experience is perceived to play an important role in the development of a number of the competencies rated important by most (76.4–93 percent) of the bar (e.g., fact gathering, instilling confidence, effective oral expression, drafting legal documents, understanding the viewpoint of others, and financial sense). The experience to which these and other competencies are attributed is, of course, substantially delimited by the nature of one's law practice, including organizational context and size of practice, substantive area of specialization, and clientele served.

The evaluations of law schools' performance in educating their students do not differ between older and more recent law school graduates.[28] Furthermore, that portion of the practicing bar that has evaluated new law graduates as prospective associates thinks that they have generally the same skills and knowledge as earlier graduates. On a 5-point scale new graduates were rated as "much better," "somewhat better," "about the same," "somewhat worse," or "much worse" than their predecessors in terms of their preparation in each of the 21 competencies (questionnaire, pt. III, Q. 4h, p. 17). The similarity in the evaluations of the skills and knowledge of recent and of earlier law school graduates remains constant through a number of different analyses of the data. The means and medians are all within a few tenths of a point of each other on all items, with new graduates ranking ever so slightly *better* than their predecessors on two-thirds of them.[29] Although 65.5

26. Although the figures as they appear in the two columns of table 6.5 are based on different populations, the comparison is appropriate because the figures do not vary more than a few percentage points when calculated for comparable populations.

27. Table 6.5 also shows that some competencies (e.g., effective oral expression, knowledge of social sciences, and accounting skills) are expected to be brought to the first law job but are not learned in law school. These are apparently assumed to be learned before entry to law school.

28. Based on cross tabulations, the only exceptions are writing briefs, for which the more recent law school graduates give more credit to the law schools, and opinion writing, for which those out of law school more than 35 years are less likely to credit law school training than are more recent graduates. In addition, although a correlation reveals that more recent law school graduates are less likely than their predecessors to consider most of the listed items important to their practices, the correlations are quite low (the highest is 0.16), explaining only insignificant proportions of the variance.

29. In fact, new graduates are rated lower than their predecessors on only three skills: negotiating, letter writing, and financial sense, for each of which the mean response is 3.1—only one-tenth of a point below a response of "about the same." The stability of the quality of new lawyers' abilities over the years is further illustrated by the modal response for each item: in *every* case the mode, or most popular response, is that new graduates are "about the same" as their predecessors with respect to skills and knowledge important to the practice of law.

percent of the evaluators think that new graduates have only a fair or poor notion of what the practice of law actually entails, in the memory of the current bar (all of whom received their own formal legal training within law schools) other new attorneys apparently had the same shortcomings.

Limits of Law School Training

In every occupation there are probably important competencies that are not best acquired in a formal school environment. Indeed, many of the items cited by only a few attorneys as learned in law school are the very ones that large proportions of the bar do not think can be taught there effectively (questionnaire, pt. III, Q. 3, pp. 14–15).[30] For example, while instilling confidence is rated the third most important item, only 4 percent of the respondents have learned this skill essentially in law school (see table 6.5). Moreover, only 17 percent of the bar believe that this skill *can* be taught effectively in law school (see table 6.6). The same pattern is found for the ability to get along with other lawyers. Further, the discrepancies between table 6.5 (first column) and table 6.6 (second column) provide an opportunity to compare the proportions of the practicing bar who learned certain competencies in law school with those who think that these same competencies could be taught there effectively. Law schools are commonly perceived of as capable of effectively teaching a number of skills but as failing to have done so. Fact-gathering, effective oral expression, drafting legal documents, opinion writing, and accounting skills are all generally considered to be within the capacity of law schools to teach, but they are viewed by only very small proportions of the respondents as having actually been learned there. As indicated in table 6.6, the attention given by law schools to these same areas is generally viewed as insufficient.

It should also be noted that many lawyers feel that law schools should give more attention even to some skills for which they are seen as having only limited potential effectiveness. Examples include negotiating and interviewing, which only 35 percent and 48 percent of the bar think can

---

30. There is no relationship between the belief that law schools *can* teach particular competencies and their importance to one's own legal practice. There is also no relationship between attorneys' opinions about the ability of law schools to teach skills effectively and the kind of practice in which they are engaged. This is particularly interesting in light of what we will see later: that whether skills have been learned in law school is frequently dependent upon the nature of the practice in which the respondents are engaged. This is of course consistent with the finding that the importance of the skill does not predict the evaluation of the law schools' ability to teach it. There is, however, a highly significant relationship between having learned a skill in law school and believing that it can be taught there effectively. It would be surprising if it were otherwise. The significance level is < 0.005 for 18 of the items, and < 0.01 for another one. The relationship between learned "essentially in law school" and "can . . . be taught effectively in law school" cannot be established for the two remaining items, negotiating and interviewing. For these statistics compare variations in distributions, and in both cases there is virtually universal agreement that the skills were not learned in law school; therefore, there is no variation in the "learned essentially in law school" variable.

TABLE 6.6
Law School's Attention to and Capacity for Teaching Skills
and Areas of Knowledge

Skill or Area of Knowledge	% Indicating	
	Insufficient Attention[a] in Law School[b]	Can be Taught Effectively in Law School[c]
Fact gathering	65	66
Capacity to marshal facts and order them so that concepts can be applied	. . .	87
Instilling others' confidence in you .	72	17
Effective oral expression	64	74
Ability to understand and interpret opinions, regulations, and statutes	. . .	96
Knowledge of the substantive law ..	. . .	95
Legal research	. . .	98
Negotiating	84	35
Drafting legal documents	79	84
Understanding the viewpoint of others to deal more effectively with them	62	42
Ability to synthesize law	. . .	89
Getting along with other lawyers ...	68	16
Knowledge of theory underlying law	. . .	98
Letter writing	74	50
Knowledge of procedural law	. . .	91
Financial sense	72	32
Interviewing	78	48
Writing briefs	. . .	93
Opinion writing	57	84
Knowledge of political science, psychology, economics, sociology	59	32
Accounting skills	65	71

[a]Includes data only for those skills and areas of knowledge that more than 50 percent of the bar think received insufficient attention in law school.
[b]Percentages based on Ns ranging from 492 (interviewing, accounting skills) to 517 (fact gathering).
[c]Percentages based on Ns ranging from 437 (ability to synthesize law) to 488 (drafting legal documents).

be taught effectively in law school but which 84 percent and 78 percent, respectively, still think are given insufficient attention in school. In fact, more than half of the practicing bar think insufficient attention was devoted to the 13 items entered in the first column in table 6.6.[31] However, only small proportions of the sample think insufficient attention was

31. The importance of the skills to the respondents does not affect their evaluation of the law schools' sufficiency of attention to them. Opinions about the adequacy of attention given by law schools to competencies important to the practice of law are also unaffected by the respondents' class standing. Again, we will see later that the nature of one's law practice does affect the evaluation of law schools' contribution to skills and knowledge important to practice.

given to the 6 skills in table 6.5 for which law schools are most likely to receive credit (learned essentially in law school by at least 50 percent).[32] These include ability to understand and interpret opinions, regulations, and statutes, knowledge of the substantive law, legal research, ability to synthesize law, knowledge of theory underlying law, and knowledge of procedural law. Again, these are the more analytic skills and those that are relatively unique but not most important to the practice of law.

Law Schools' Projected Image of Competencies Important to the Practice of Law

In our earliest pretests involving discussions among small groups of lawyers, there was general agreement that not all competencies important to the practice of law are most appropriately or even possibly learned very well in a school setting. Nevertheless, there was substantial criticism of law schools' failure even to make their students *aware* of the importance of some of these competencies to the actual practice of law. The attorneys believed that as a result their expectations of the nature of practice upon graduation were more unrealistic than necessary.

The most prominent examples of this attitude relate to giving clients advice as to their legal rights and how best to pursue them. Unlike the law school setting, where alternatives are distilled from a multitude of perspectives, there is a point in the actual practice of law when closure is necessary, when the practicing attorneys must finally give the educated and considered opinions for which they have been hired. A corollary of this is the unsuspecting new graduates' realization, after entry into practice, that the "best" legal advice in a given instance is dependent upon the client's capability to wait for resolution and to pay the fees involved. Although to think otherwise may seem an extremely naive view of the practice of law, our pretest respondents believed that many new lawyers come to practice unaware of these constraints.

These discussions made us wonder whether law students become aware of the potential value of the competencies that will be important to their practices but that law schools do not consider within their province. Accordingly, we asked: "Did law school training indicate the potential value of this [each skill and area of knowledge considered] to the practice

___

32. Graduates of different law schools do differ in their evaluations of the adequacy of their law school training on a few of the items covered. Irrespective of the nature of their legal practice, graduates of national law schools are significantly more likely than graduates of non-national law schools to believe that their law schools paid sufficient attention to the following skills and areas of knowledge: legal research, negotiating, effective oral expression, and knowledge of theory underlying law.

We also inquired whether or not the bar thinks that too much attention was given to any of these skills and areas of knowledge, but no skill was seen that way by more than 12 percent of the attorneys. That "insufficient attention" was cited by so many and "too much attention" by so few strongly indicates that the practicing bar wants law school to do more rather than different things. This implication will be considered later in our discussion of specific suggestions concerning lawyers' views about curriculum and the idea of a two-year law school.

of law?'' As shown in table 6.7 there is substantial variability in the proportions of the bar crediting law schools with acknowledging the role of various competencies in the practice of law. With the skills and areas of knowledge in table 6.7 ordered by importance, it is again clear that

TABLE 6.7
Law School's Indication of Potential Value of Skills and Areas of Knowledge to the Practice of Law

Skill or Area of Knowledge	% Crediting School With Indicating Value[a]
Fact gathering	58
Capacity to marshal facts and order them so that concepts can be applied	79
Instilling others' confidence in you	16
Effective oral expression	64
Ability to understand and interpret opinions, regulations, and statutes	95
Knowledge of the substantive law	98
Legal research	89
Negotiating	12
Drafting legal documents	50
Understanding the viewpoint of others to deal more effectively with them	26
Ability to synthesize law	81
Getting along with other lawyers	16
Knowledge of theory underlying law	93
Letter writing	9
Knowledge of procedural law	81
Financial sense	12
Interviewing	11
Writing briefs	75
Opinion writing	51
Knowledge of political science, psychology, economics, sociology	26
Accounting skills	31

[a]Percentages based on Ns ranging from 454 (financial sense) to 480 (legal research).

law schools' emphasis on particular competencies is not directly related to the prominence of their place in the practice of law generally. Nor are respondents' appraisals of their law schools' indication of the potential value of various skills and areas of knowledge related to the importance of those competencies to their own practices. The particular law school attended does make a difference. On 7 of the 21 items graduates of national law schools are significantly more likely than graduates of non-national law schools to agree that the law schools indicated their potential value. However, in no case is the difference sufficient to affect the general picture; law schools, regardless of their geographic scope or reputation, are highly likely to emphasize the potential value of the more analytic skills.

In addition to successfully developing the four competencies that were actually learned in law schools (as indicated on table 6.5 these are: ability to understand and interpret opinions, regulations, and statutes, knowledge of the substantive law, legal research, and knowledge of theory underlying law), law schools are also likely to indicate the potential value of the capacity to marshal and order facts to apply concepts, ability to synthesize law, knowledge of procedural law, and writing briefs. Although not all purely intellective competencies, they relate closely to the core image of the profession. Indeed, the law schools are overemphasizing the potential value of the litigation-related competencies of knowledge of procedural law and writing briefs, while in contrast they are less likely to present as potentially valuable an office skill such as drafting legal documents, which is both peculiar to the practice of law and considered important by three-quarters of the bar. None of the skills and areas of knowledge likely to have been presented by law schools as valuable falls within the cluster of interpersonal competencies displayed in figure 6.1. With the exception of effective oral expression (which is also tied closely to litigation), law schools omit from their panoply of competencies relevant to the legal professional the interpersonal facilities (as well as substantive skills such as accounting and social science knowledge) that are not at the core of their self-perceived mission.

To fail to indicate the potential value of important competencies is to provide an unrealistic impression of the professional task.[33] It is not that law schools are providing knowledge and skills irrelevant to the practice of law—the data clearly indicate that quite the contrary is the case. Nevertheless, there are areas where practitioners believe that law schools can and should do more.[34] The contribution of lawyers' own repeated

---

33. This criticism of professional education is not restricted to law. A similar point was made by a graduate of the University of Chicago business school. Interestingly the failure is similarly in the area of interpersonal skills.

> It seems to me the most important thing needed for success in business is personal magnetism. I can't understand why no one mentioned that to me in school. Without excellent skills in getting along with people you really can't get anywhere. What I learned in school is that you need to prove something with your credentials. I don't know if schools can teach you how to have a forceful personality, but they should at least mention it (interview by Andrea Frey with Judy Thornber, Chicago Business Year in Review 1977–1978 (Graduate School of Business, University of Chicago), p. 9).

34. A new bar exam experiment in California, if institutionalized, might have some impact on law school coverage of these competencies. In February and July 1980 new California bar examinees were given an "alternative assessment" test in selected competencies (e.g., legal research, client counseling and interviewing, and advocacy or negotiation). While the experimental section will not affect success on the exam, it is the belief of its supporters that such an approach, if accepted, would contribute to a more accurate measure of an applicant's competence to practice law. See Slonim (1980).

experience and their own study to so many of the skills and areas of knowledge needed in the practice of law does not in and of itself diminish the role of law schools in preparing attorneys for practice. Rather it demonstrates the continuing socialization of the profession to the capabilities requisite to practice.

In some areas, such as knowledge of theory underlying law, the proportionate role of law schools is quite large; in others it is quite small. Indeed, formal schooling in general may be important but not sufficient to education. In some respects law schools may contribute the expertise not easily or likely gained elsewhere, partly because certain skills are peculiar to the law, thus precluding their development prior to law school, and partly because the constraints and pressures of practice do not allow for abstract contemplation. While practitioners give law schools great credit for their legal education, they fault them for giving insufficient attention to some areas and for failing to present a realistic picture of the nature of the practice of law by neglecting to even mention the potential importance of some competencies excluded from law school curricula.

Law School Curriculum

Law school curricula are universally organized around substantive areas of the law. Although such curricular organization does not necessarily exclude consideration of the competencies necessary to practice within those areas of the law, we have seen that law school graduates apparently believe that such exclusion occurs for a substantial proportion of those considered important, and in many cases without good cause. Yet the curriculum currently packaged around substantive areas of law receives a great deal of support from the respondents. More than half (57.3 percent) cite at least three courses that have been particularly helpful to their careers (questionnaire, pt. I, Q. 7, p. 4).[35]

In contrast to the very large numbers who cite law school courses as helpful to their careers, only 31.5 percent would "eliminate or drastically shorten" any areas of the curriculum (Q. 8, p. 4). Further, among these respondents there is little agreement as to which courses should be eliminated or shortened, with only future interests, common law pleadings/practice, and property generating much negative response. Of all the courses cited for elimination or shortening, these three accounted for 12.7 percent, 10.8 percent, and 8.4 percent, respectively. Actually even these figures overstate the objections of the practicing bar, for when asked why they would shorten or eliminate the courses mentioned, 24.2 percent of the respondents merely suggested that the course be changed from a requirement to an elective.[36]

35. At least one course is cited by 87.8 percent and, at least two by 79.2 percent. Since there is no way to distinguish between those who did not cite any courses because none have been particularly helpful to their careers and those who simply skipped this question, these figures, based on the total sample, underestimate the proportion of the bar who find some law school courses particularly helpful to their careers.

36. Two other responses each accounted for more than 20 percent of the reasons cited

The basic point is clear: only a limited proportion of the practicing bar would restrict the areas currently covered by law school curricula, the most prominent recommendation being simply not to force all of it on all law students. Thus, in light of our findings that lawyers continually cite insufficient treatment of important competencies on the one hand but rarely indicate excess attention to any competencies on the other, it again appears that law school graduates do not want less from their formal legal education and that in many instances they want more.

That observation is supported by the practicing bar's view of the two-year law school.[37] Only 12.3 percent of the sample ($N = 538$) think that the law school curriculum should be shortened to two years. Indeed some of the respondents, consistent with the call for greater law school contributions, prefer expanding the curriculum to four years. With law school attention considered sufficient by more than 75 percent of the respondents for only three competencies (knowledge of the substantive law, knowledge of theory underlying law, and ability to understand and interpret opinions, regulations, and statutes), it should not be surprising that so few favor a shortened period of instruction. Those who do favor the two-year curriculum are not randomly distributed among the bar. They are significantly more likely to be the most recent graduates ($p < 0.001$), to have had a lower class standing ($p < 0.05$), and to have more negative views about their law school experiences. Also they are more likely to wish that the goals of their law schools had been different ($p < 0.001$) and less likely to have maintained any relationship with their schools after graduation ($p < 0.05$).[38] Although they are significantly more likely ($p < .05$) to have attended a national rather than a non-national law school, that difference disappears if we look only at the graduates of the nine law schools that train most of the Chicago bar. Michigan and Chicago graduates are most likely (20 percent and 21 percent re-

---

for shortening or eliminating parts of the curriculum: that the course was "a waste of time" and that the course was "outdated." The latter seems particularly applicable to common law pleadings/practice and future interests, both of which are thought by many to be of more historical than practical interest.

37. The Packer and Ehrlich study *New Directions in Legal Education* (1972), prepared for the Carnegie Commission on Higher Education, agreed with the Carrington Committee's time recommendations and proposed optional three-year prelaw and two-year law school time periods. They believed that legal education must make one of two choices today: "either (a) diversify the three years so that the student acquires the rudiments of an understanding . . . of the interrelations of social knowledge with the law or (b) reduce the minimum time-serving requirement to two years with a resulting emphasis on doctrinal analysis" (p. 80). Although they hedged on whether all schools should immediately adopt a two-year option for all students, the authors were nonetheless "convinced that the case has been made for the bar to reduce its three-year standard to a two-year standard (p. 82).

38. Interestingly, those favoring a shortened curriculum are no more likely to wish they had attended another law school. These relationships are particularly noteworthy because of the skew in the responses to all of these items. They are, however, consistent with the general satisfaction of the bar discussed in chapter 1 in note 22 and the related text.

The recommendation to limit course requirements may also reflect specialization within the bar, an interpretation supported later by our analysis of the courses most likely to be considered helpful to the practice of law and the variance in that evaluation according to specialty practiced.

spectively) to favor the shorter curriculum, and Harvard graduates least likely (3 percent).

Law school training covers a broad range of substantive areas within the law and is meant to provide a basic legal education. As one law school dean put it, "the importance of the lawyer is that he is a generalist. Thus, there is no reason to change our basic goals and curriculum. Regardless of a lawyer's ultimate career, he must still have a broad basic education in Contracts, Torts, Public Law, and Property" (Kelso, 1972, p. 61; Ehrlich & Hazard, 1975, p. 112). Indeed these courses along with civil procedure (practice) typically constitute the required and usually first-year law school courses. The curricular message, if one can speak in those terms, is that these are the "basic" courses, the areas of the law most central to its practice and the foundation for more specialized courses.[39]

While table 6.8 confirms that those courses are among those con-

TABLE 6.8
Courses Particularly Helpful to Career

Course[a]	% Rating Helpful[b]
Contracts	50.3
Property[c]	25.2
Torts	23.5
Evidence	17.3
Civil procedure/practice	16.4
Constitutional law	16.0
Corporations[d]	15.6
Taxation	14.1
Trusts and estates[e]	10.4

[a]Includes only those courses cited by a minimum of 10 percent of the bar.
[b]Percentage based on N (481) of respondents citing at least one course as particularly helpful to their careers.
[c]Includes real and personal property and real estate.
[d]Includes partnership, agency, and securities.
[e]Includes wills.

sidered most helpful to the practice of law, it is perhaps surprising that only one course—contracts—is mentioned by a majority of the bar, with the others cited by no more than one-fourth (questionnaire, pt. I, Q. 7, p. 4). Contracts is also the course most likely to be considered helpful because its content underlies most legal issues. Of those who cite contracts as particularly helpful to their practice, 45 percent attribute its

39. The American Bar Foundation–sponsored study Law Student Activity Patterns, under the direction of Ronald M. Pipkin, has yielded some interesting data on law school curricula from the students' perspectives. The three courses cited most frequently by practitioners as particularly helpful to their practice are also rated by students as above average in terms of enjoyment, interest, and value of time spent on the course. Students' evaluations of law school courses as potentially helpful for passing bar examinations are also telling. Only 13 of 44 courses considered in the study received above-average ratings for their anticipated helpfulness on bar exams. The 9 courses practicing lawyers consider most helpful to practice are all included among these 13 (Pipkin, 1977).

benefits to the fact that its content underlies most legal issues. The percentages of those respondents citing other courses as particularly helpful because the area underlies most legal issues range from a low of 2.0 percent for trusts and estates to a high of 33.8 percent for constitutional law. Contracts is apparently *the* single basic law course, with the perception of its importance generally increasing the longer the years in practice ($\chi^2 = 14.55$, $p < .005$).

Like competencies important to practice, law school courses are by and large perceived as helpful by virtue of their contribution to particular specialties. Indeed the aggregate selections of courses as most helpful, the area of practice of the lawyers who select them, and the reasons given for their usefulness all relate to specialization within the practice of law.

The aggregate distributions are of course themselves affected by the specialties that predominate within the Chicago bar. Thus, for example, a course in labor law, even if mentioned by every attorney whose primary area of specialization is labor law, would not be included in the list of those courses receiving a minimum of 10 percent of the sample's mentions of helpful courses unless a rather substantial proportion of attorneys who never deal in labor law in their practice for some reason cited a course in the area as helpful to their careers. That is, of course, a highly unlikely prospect. The obverse is also easily illustrated. With 12 percent of the sample spending the largest proportion of their time in real estate law, and another 12.4 percent practicing in this area as a second area of concentration, it would be rather surprising if a listing of courses helpful to the careers of the Chicago bar did not include property.

Table 6.9 shows the relationship between the courses mentioned as

TABLE 6.9
Courses Particularly Helpful to 'Career by Specialty

Course	% Ranking Helpful to Primary Specialty[a]	
	Most Likely	Second Most Likely
Contracts*	Corporate law 59.6	Real estate/family law 54.2
Property**	Real estate...........52.5	Trust and estates 28.6
Torts**	Personal injury.......52.7	Family law 33.3
Evidence*	Criminal law.........34.6	Personal injury.......34.5
Civil procedure/ practice*	Personal injury.......32.7	Family law 25.0
Constitutional law* ..	Criminal law.........46.2	Tax law 20.0
Corporations**	Corporate law 33.0	Tax law 20.0
Taxation**	Tax law 63.3	Trusts and estates 22.9
Trusts and estates** ..	Trusts and estates 48.6	Real estate...........20.3

*$p < 0.005$
**$p < 0.001$

NOTE: Each line in the table represents a cross tabulation between the course cited as particularly helpful to practice and the first-ranked specialties of the respondents.

[a]Percentages are based on the number of attorneys in the specific specialty who answered the question. The Ns range from 24 (family law) to 94 (corporate law). Thus, percentages corresponding to a specific specialty are all based on the same N, while percentages corresponding to different specialties are based on different Ns.

particularly helpful to practice and the primary substantive specialty of the respondents. This relationship is significant for all of the nine courses considered particularly helpful to the practice of at least 50 of the 548 respondents. The middle column of the table, indicating the specialists most likely to rank each course as particularly helpful to their practice, holds not a single surprise. Nevertheless, there is considerable variation in the proportions of specialists in a particular area who positively evaluate courses related to that specialty. For example, 63.3 percent of the tax lawyers rate their course in tax as particularly helpful to their practice, while only 33.0 percent of the corporate lawyers rate corporations similarly.

Although the specialty most likely to rate each course as helpful is rather obvious, the specialty that is second most likely to do so is not always as clear. There are a number of reasons explaining the observed pattern. Taking the most obvious items first, the specialties listed for both evidence and constitutional law are perfectly reasonable. Attorneys who spend the greatest part of their time on criminal and personal injury matters are also likely to be actual or potential courtroom advocates, a role requiring a working knowledge of the rules of evidence. Although criminal lawyers and tax lawyers may appear dissimilar on most measures of legal practice, they practice in areas of the law that are the most "public" in the sense that they deal with the direct relationship between citizen and government in which the tenets of constitutional law apply.[40]

The ratings for the other courses, save contracts, reflect a somewhat different phenomenon. We have been speaking of specialists in selected areas of the law as those who spend more of their time in a given substantive area than in any other area of the law. This means of course that many of these "specialists" practice in other areas of the law as well. As we noted in chapter 4, different substantive specialties are not combined in practice at random. That is, certain combinations of specialties are likely to be practiced by the same individuals. The specialties second most likely to appear in connection with a "helpful" rating of property, torts, civil procedure/practice, corporations, taxation, and trusts and estates are in every case very likely to be practiced in tandem with the specialties most associated with first rankings of these courses and also most obviously related in substance.

To take one example, we found it somewhat peculiar that attorneys specializing in family law were, after personal injury specialists, the most likely to cite torts as a particularly helpful course. The relationship no longer appears strange once it is realized that those whose first-

40. Constitutional law is the single course whose evaluation is not significantly related to the prestige of the specialty practiced by the respondent. This is of course predictable from the distribution of individual specialties, with tax first and criminal second—two specialties close to the opposite ends of the legal specialty prestige continuum. See chapter 4 for a discussion of specialty prestige.

ranked specialty is family law are most likely to spend the next largest share of their time in the area of personal injury. Thus it seems likely that the importance of torts to attorneys in family law is a function of the time they spend on personal injury cases. In some cases, of course, as with tax attorneys and corporations, there is also a direct relationship between the substance of the second-ranked specialty and the substance of the course itself.

The pattern of responses for contracts again differs from that for other courses helpful to practice. Although the evaluation of its helpfulness is also significantly related to the specialty of the evaluator, the distribution of the responses of specialists in different areas of the law is unique among the nine most important courses. With the single exception of attorneys specializing in criminal law, contracts is relatively important to *all* of the largest specialties practiced by the Chicago bar. In addition to the specialties listed next to contracts on table 6.9, from 34.5 percent to 48.6 percent of the practitioners in each of the unlisted specialties (except criminal law) cite contracts as particularly helpful to their practices. The 34.5 percent figure, representing the specialty from which contracts receives its second lowest rating, is in fact higher than the extent to which some courses (corporations, for example) are deemed helpful by "specialists" in the field to which the course is most applicable. This adds further evidence that to the practicing bar, contracts stands quite apart from other courses as basic to the practice of law.

Although the evaluation of courses helpful to practice is related to the specialty practiced, if we look at the stated reasons for citing particular courses we find that some more than others are likely to be cited as useful precisely because of their contribution to the respondent's specialty. As table 6.10 shows, three courses in particular—corporations, taxation, and trusts and estates—are most likely to be cited as useful to the practice of one's specialty. Law schools typically treat these courses as more specialized undertakings to be studied after a basic grounding has been established in the first year.

Lortie, in his study (1959) of newly graduated lawyers, reflects the prevailing view that the formal apparatus of training pays little attention to the specialization that prevails among the urban bar. Our data imply otherwise. The curricular basics include courses that are significantly more likely to be important to specialists in selected areas of the law. As discussed in chapter 4, we have little direct evidence of the factors that influence lawyers to select one specialty over another. It may be that the bar's positive evaluation of the traditional law school curriculum as helpful to their practice is a result of the influence that this curriculum has had on their selection of particular specialties. To the extent to which that is the case, queries of the practicing bar about curricular reform are destined to be somewhat circular and to result in relatively positive evaluations of the standard curriculum. If the message of our law

TABLE 6.10
Courses Particularly Helpful to Career Because
Useful to Practice of Specialty

Course[a]	% Giving Specialty As Reason Course Helpful[b]	N
Contracts	14.0	242
Property	32.2	121
Torts	23.0	113
Evidence	21.7	83
Civil procedure/practice	16.5	79
Constitutional law	11.7	77
Corporations	48.0	75
Taxation	41.2	68
Trusts and estates	46.0	50

[a]Courses are listed in order of their usefulness to the bar in general.

[b]Many additional respondents mentioned "useful to my practice" as the reason for the course's relevance to their practice. It is not possible to determine which of these responses may also refer to specialty (see questionnaire pt. I, Q. 7, p. 4, appendix 1). To the extent that some of those responses do refer to specialty, then, the above figures are a conservative estimate of the bar's evaluation of courses useful to specialties practiced. The figures, however, are reasonably accurate reflections of the *relative* importance of specialty practiced to the evaluation of different courses.

schools is that these are the "basic" areas of the law, with others less central or less important, then we would expect graduates to reflect that in the areas of specialization within which they choose to concentrate. Students are, of course, mindful of both the bar examinations and the job market that they must face, and it is perfectly rational for them to wish to prepare themselves accordingly.

Law Practice as Contributor to Legal Expertise

In discussions with law students on the job market and recent law school graduates it is not at all unusual to hear complaints over self-admitted incompetence to practice law despite three years spent in formal legal training. Although some of these complaints relate to such easily acquired information as how to file a complaint, many reflect more serious concerns. Knowledge of the legal principles of trusts and estates but ignorance of how to write a will for a client; knowledge of tort law but little or no idea of how to negotiate a settlement for a client who needs and wants some payment for damages without waiting for a trial; understanding of real property but ignorance of how to search a title—such are the worries often expressed by the graduates of even the most prestigious law schools.[41]

41. A humorous and perhaps extreme example of the discrepancy between formal training and its application in the practice of law is provided by the following anecdote related to us by a member of the Indiana State Bar Association who participated in an ear-

It is said that new graduates often attempt to overcome these difficulties by seeking jobs with established law firms immediately following law school.[42] There is in fact a statistically significant ($p < 0.005$) relationship between mentioning the opportunity to learn practice from other attorneys as a reason for selecting the first law-related job after law school and the nature of that job. Those whose first experience is in either a judicial clerkship or a law firm are most likely to have considered the educational advantages of their first jobs. Further, our initial analysis indicates that the most telling distinction among evaluations of law schools and alternative skill-development sources is not between those in firms and those not practicing in firms. Instead, as with the relationship between law school attended and legal practice and as with the stability of legal practice, the most informative distinctions are among attorneys practicing in firms of different sizes.[43]

Our precise question was the extent to which, if at all, lawyers practicing alone and in firms of different sizes evaluate their law school training differently. For the following 6 (of the 21) skills and areas of knowledge there is a generally linear relationship between the size of practice and evaluation of law school:

fact gathering ($p < 0.005$)

---

ly pretest for this study; he described an experience he had while sitting as a special judge in a case involving a bailment for hire where the plaintiff sued for $614.

> When the clerk laid the file on the desk, it was at least two inches thick. In looking through the file, there were motions to dismiss . . ., there were requests for admissions 11 pages long, there were 200 and some interrogatories submitted by the plaintiff to the defendant, and there had been all sorts of hearings, at least six on various pleading matters. And the defendant had not satisfactorily answered some of the interrogatories, and this motion was to—there had already been a motion to compel discovery by answering some 60 of these interrogatories, and this was on a motion for sanction for the reason that the defendant had not complied with the court's order compelling discovery. In discussing the matter, I asked the plaintiff's attorney who had been out of law school 18 months how much he wanted. I said, "The prayer in your complaint here is for $614. Let's get down to the nitty-gritty. What would you take?" And he said, "Until I get the answers to these interrogatories, I can't advise my client as to what he should take." I said to the defendant's attorney, "What would you pay?" He said, "We have twice offered him $614, the amount of the prayer" (Indianapolis, 5/30/75).

Not surprisingly this little vignette generated a good deal of laughter from the other lawyers in the group. The speaker was, however, trying to make a very serious point. "Here's a fellow," he went on, "who has learned all about requests for admissions, all about interrogatories and procedure, he's learned what they were, he's learned what is required and all of this and that, and yet he has spent hours and hours and hours when the defendant has twice offered him the amount of his case." Whether apocryphal or not, this anecdote makes an important point regarding experienced lawyers' perceptions of more recent law graduates' abilities to translate legal rules into practice.

42. Many law students also seek summer and part-time employment with law firms before graduation to gain this kind of experience. The impact that selection of a first job has on future career development was considered in chapter 4.

43. For a discussion of the derivation of the size parameters employed see chapter 4, note 9. The points of division would certainly be different in smaller cities. Since the data on size of firm are available only for current employment, the results provide a conservative picture of the contributions of firms of different sizes to the development of legal skills.

instilling others' confidence in you ($p < 0.08$)*
knowledge of the substantive law ($p < 0.001$)
drafting legal documents ($p < 0.06$)*
writing briefs ($p < 0.06$)*
opinion writing ($p < 0.005$)
(*indicates relationship approaches but does not meet
probability level of 0.05)

The smaller the context within which one practices, the more likely the lawyer is to believe that the competency was learned in law school. For example, for knowledge of the substantive law—for which law school receives so much credit in the aggregate—attribution to law school declines from 93.4 percent for solo practitioners, to 79.4 percent for those in small firms, to 73.9 percent for those in medium-sized firms, to 62.5 percent for those practicing in large-firm contexts. This implies of course that those practicing in larger firm contexts are adding to these same competencies outside law school, most probably within their own firms.

The statistically significant relationships for both knowledge of the substantive law and fact gathering are of particular interest, for they are among the competencies most important to the practice of law (90.1 percent and 93.0 percent, respectively) and their importance does not vary by the nature of practice. That is, the overwhelming majority of practicing lawyers consider these important to the practice of law, irrespective of the substantive specialties in which they are engaged.

The perceived value of formal legal training to the development of skills and knowledge is therefore substantially dependent upon the opportunities for education after graduation from law school. Further, those opportunities are directly related to the size of firm within which one practices law. This becomes particularly important if we recognize that the skills for which post–law school training is important are in most cases skills the bar as a whole did *not* learn in law school. Where and how do other attorneys develop these skills, some of which are considered extremely important to the practice of law? The answers provided by the respondents indicate that lawyers' own experience and own study are mentioned most frequently as contributing to the development of all competencies except knowledge of theory underlying law, knowledge of the substantive law, and the ability to understand and interpret opinions, regulations, and statutes, the three skills for which law school receives most credit (see table 6.5). Does the observed relationship indicate that lawyers practicing in firms of different size actually credit their law firm experience with contributing to the development of their legal skills? To answer this question we concentrate on the members of the bar who have had some experience practicing with other lawyers.

Law Firms as Legal Educators

Many of the competencies considered important to the practice of law can be acquired in many settings. Even some of the most important skills, such as instilling confidence and effective oral expression, are perhaps most typically acquired outside law school and are hardly restricted to practicing attorneys. In trying to ascertain the sources of selected skills and areas of knowledge, we gave particular attention to four sources outside formal legal training: "observation of or advice from other lawyers in your law office," "observation of or advice from other lawyers *not* in your law office," "your own repeated experience," and "your own study of the area" (questionnaire, pt. III, Q. 2, pp. 12–13). Although not all lawyers have had other attorneys in their own offices, we can determine the relative likelihood of attorneys in a given kind of practice citing observation of or advice from other lawyers in their own office as an important contributor to the development of their skills and knowledge.[44] This part of the analysis includes all members of the sample whose current job is with a law firm or the government, that is, those with the opportunity to learn legal skills from other attorneys in the same office.[45] Since we have information for only first and current jobs, the results provide conservative estimates of the actual attribution of skill development to lawyers in the same law office.

Table 6.11 presents these data.[46] For approximately half of the competencies evaluated, there is a significant difference in the extent to which their development is attributed to attorneys in one's own office. Large firms are, by and large, the most likely to be so credited. For development of skills in fact gathering, negotiating, drafting legal documents, and opinion writing, two-thirds or more of those practicing in large law firms rate other attorneys in their own offices as very important. From the perspective of those who have had the opportunity, there is, for certain skills, a distinct advantage in working in an office

44. We have not presented extensive data on the influence of attorneys outside one's own office because our survey revealed that they are given very little credit for the development of competencies. They are mentioned as a source of skill development by more than 100 respondents on only six items: negotiating, drafting legal documents, instilling confidence, effective oral expression, getting along with other lawyers, and understanding the viewpoint of others. Of these six skills, only for negotiating do attorneys outside one's law office receive more than 15 or 21 percent, respectively, of the ranks 1 or 2 for contributing to a particular competency.

Credit attributed to attorneys outside one's own office does not vary significantly by practice context for any of the items evaluated. Although it might have been expected that those in solo practice in particular would be more likely to learn from attorneys outside their own offices, the data do not support that view. And with respect to negotiating specifically, it is lawyers in large firms who are most likely (28.6 percent as opposed to an average of 21.1 percent for all respondents) to credit attorneys outside their own offices as a source of their own skill development.

45. By excluding those who worked in the same office in other than the current job, the data provide a conservative picture of the differences in attribution of skill development to office colleagues. A similar analysis of those whose first job was with a firm or the government yields parallel but less informative results because we do not have data on first-job firm size. Lawyers who did or do work as counsel on the staff of a business firm are not included because we cannot determine whether other attorneys worked in the same office.

46. Lawyers in own office was counted as an important source of a skill if it was ranked first or second most important among the sources ranked.

TABLE 6.11
Attorneys in Own Office as Source of Skill Development by Kind
of Practice

| Skills[a] | % Ranking Attorneys in Own Office Important[b] | | | |
	Govern-ment	Small Firm	Medium Firm	Large Firm
Fact gathering*	31.9	42.9	53.3	64.1
Instilling others' confidence in you*	30.4	33.3	53.3	62.1
Effective oral expression**	27.7	15.3	19.2	35.5
Negotiating**	53.5	50.9	56.0	73.0
Drafting legal documents*	47.7	50.8	63.9	76.9
Understanding the viewpoint of others to deal more effectively with them**	37.2	27.4	45.8	45.2
Ability to synthesize law**	13.6	9.3	26.4	21.3
Letter writing**	36.6	34.8	47.2	54.8
Opinion writing*	40.0	24.8	46.4	75.0

*$p < 0.005$
**$p < 0.05$.

[a]Includes only those skills for which there is a statistically significant difference in the attribution to attorneys in own office by the size and nature of the office. Writing briefs approaches statistical significance ($p \leqslant 0.06$), with large firms credited most frequently (50 percent), medium firms and government next (40 percent), and small firms least (30 percent).

[b]Percent is based on number of lawyers in each kind of practice who rank "attorneys in own office" first or second among sources contributing to the development of each competency.

with other attorneys. While the competencies to which firm experience is most likely to contribute cover a broad range in their importance to practice, none of them are likely to be developed in law school.

As we have seen earlier, not all firm experiences are equal with respect to their educational advantages. The benefits increase with the size of the firm, with government offices generally perceived to be similar to small firms in educational advantages. There are a number of possible explanations for this pattern, not the least likely of which is that large law firms are better able to sustain the costs involved in training new lawyers. For our purposes what is most interesting is that, again, the solo-firm dichotomy so popular in the literature on the legal profession masks important differences among firms of different sizes.[47] In addition, it is the skills to which experiences in the medium-sized and large law firms are contributing substantially for which the law schools receive limited credit.

The growing prevalence of firm practice, however, may not necessarily be sufficient for covering the needed skills and areas of knowledge excluded from formal training in the law. First, the large firms given most credit for contributing to skill development tend to specialize in particular areas of the law and consequently serve particular segments of the society. Those portions of the society served by lawyers who have not

47. With the present data we cannot determine whether the same is true for the first job after law school.

had the opportunity for this post–law school training may be providing the "practice" cases for attorneys just out of law school. Another possibility is that the growing proportion of lawyers in the society may not be absorbed by the traditional lawyer market. To the extent that this means more individual and small-firm practitioners, particularly outside urban areas, dependence on the law firms for skill training may be unrealistic. Those without experience in a firm of reasonable size will, for the development of some of the competencies considered most important to the practice of law, be left to their own experience and study.

Alternatives for the Development of Selected Skills and Areas of Knowledge

Where do lawyers develop competencies requisite to practice but not sufficiently covered within the law school curriculum? While the data indicate that a number of other sources provide assistance, they are not uniformly available to all lawyers. Although there is no lack of criticism, there has as yet been no systematic effort to evaluate the competence of practicing attorneys. The data indicate, however, that whatever level of competence is eventually achieved, practicing lawyers believe that much of their expertise developed long after they were licensed to practice. Thus if their views are to be given consideration, simply replacing parts of the current curricula with others will not remedy the situation. It is not so much that what law students are receiving is inapplicable to practice but rather that in the view of practitioners more is necessary for the development of the competencies requisite to the practice of law. There are a number of possible alternatives to develop these competencies both within and outside the law school setting.

Since each and every competency considered important to the practice of law is used in conjunction with work in some substantive area of the law, a pervasive method of skill instruction would be not only possible but perhaps most practical. This approach would require that within the context of a substantive area of the law, some attention would be given to the practical skills necessary to translate the legal principle into legal practice—for example, recognition and discussion of, and instruction in, negotiating techniques as part of a course in torts, or drafting a will and relating its provisions in layman's language as part of a course on trusts and estates. Such an approach would, of course, be severely limited if law schools continue to rely exclusively on appellate court opinions as the subject of analysis. For example, neither the nuances of negotiating nor the complexity of fact gathering can be examined without substantially broadening the materials of legal instruction to include the details of case development from the point of initial attorney-client contact. At a minimum it would be possible for instructors to make brief references in various courses to the necessity, *in practice,* of understanding and using legal rules and techniques within the context of the case at hand and the circumstances of the litigants involved.[48] The major stumbling block to such a curricular proposal might be law faculties themselves, for whom both interest and capability may militate against such curricular reform.

The addition of practice-oriented law school courses has also been recommended, and in many cases instituted. The most popular among these fall under the rubric of clinical education. Clinical education takes many forms, thus making systematic comparisons among programs very difficult if not impossible.[49] In addition, clinical education has been widely available to law students only since the infusion of support by the Ford Foundation's Council on Legal Education for Professional Responsibility (CLEPR)[50] beginning in 1969. A further difficulty in characterizing clinical education emanates from the multiple, and not always consistent, goals it is used to serve.[51] Besides the development of practice-oriented skills, these include the enhancement of professional responsibility, development of an understanding of the legal system in operation, and direct provision of legal services to the poor. In particular, as acknowledged in the description in a leading text in the field, "because most clinical programs work with indigents faced with legal crises [there is a tilt] toward lawyer problems in conflict situations" (Bellow & Moulton, 1978). This emphasis on advocacy and adversariness in most clinical programs leaves relatively untouched the bulk of

48. An example can be found in Richard Danzig's contracts textbook entitled *The Capability Problem in Contract Law: Further Readings on Well-Known Cases* (Mineola, N.Y.: Foundation Press, Inc., 1978). The readings concentrate on well-known contract cases with an emphasis on the practical problems involved in pursuing real cases up to and beyond judgment. A curious response to this approach is reflected in a recent review of Danzig's book. While the reviewer has no quarrel with the author's objectives, he worries "that the student not be demoralized completely," noting that "no rehabilitation of student morale is provided" by the book (Oldham, 1978–79, p. 951).

49. For a listing and general description of current clinical programs see *Survey and Directory of Clinical Legal Education, 1978–1979* (New York: Council on Legal Education for Professional Responsibility, Inc., 1979). For each program the directory provides information on the fields of law, the clinical model or format, and the physical location (table 1), enrollment status and credit given (table 2), funding sources and budget (table 3), grading procedures (table 4), forms of clinical training experiences (such as interviewing, fact gathering, and investigation) (table 5), academic status of staff or faculty who supervise clinical programs (table 6), and student practice rules in state and federal jurisdictions (table 7).

50. CLEPR was given a funding commitment of approximately $12 million over a 10-year period by the Ford Foundation in 1968. For a brief survey of the growth of clinical education in both numbers and substantive breadth of programs, as well as limitations of their success, see *Council on Legal Education for Professional Responsibility, Inc.: Fifth Biennial Report 1977–1978* (New York: Council on Legal Education for Professional Responsibility, n.d.). For descriptions of clinical legal education in England and Australia, respectively, see Smith (1979) and Nash (1979).

It should be noted that the idea for clinical education within law school curricula is not new. Jerome Frank suggested a clinical approach to legal education in his 1933 article "Why Not a Clinical-Lawyer School?"

51. See Kitch (1970) for a collection of materials from a conference on clinical education, held shortly after CLEPR's initial funding in 1969. The discussion includes the goals and the perceived advantages and disadvantages of clinical legal education.

practice and requisite skills that lie between advocacy and the intellective analysis at the heart of the traditional law school curriculum.[52]

A final possibility within law school training—and this was suggested by some members of our sample—is simply lengthening the law school curriculum to four years. In an era when the costs of law school are escalating and a serious campaign is being waged for the two-year law school, such a possibility seems dim indeed. The remaining and perhaps more likely alternatives involve training outside the halls of the law schools, and the data indicate that this is already occurring.

Education relevant to the practice of law, but outside law school, may precede, follow, or chronologically coincide with one's law school experience. Suggestions to require some of the less specialized skills important to the practice of law (e.g., instilling confidence, effective oral expression, letter writing, financial sense) as prerequisites of law school admission are not well received since expanding rather than restricting access to legal education is the stated goal of most law schools. Some skill training, however, already takes place prior to law school through personal experience, some of it within the context of employment. In fact almost half (48.7 percent) of practicing lawyers credit employment held prior to or during law school with contributing significantly to their careers (questionnaire, pt. II, Q. 2, p. 6). Close to two-thirds (63.4 percent) of those who responded positively to this inquiry mentioned jobs that were specifically law-related.[53]

Most responses to a query about the specific contribution made by each job to the practitioner's career in the law (see questionnaire, pt. II, Q. 1, p. 6) were related to learning (or becoming interested in) a specific type of law (17.9 percent), learning one's way around the courthouse (17.6 percent), and learning how to deal with people (13.4 percent). "Learning one's way around the courthouse" serves as a catchall phrase for the acquisition of information requisite to the practice of law in any community. Beginning with the location of the courthouse, this includes the "where's" and "how's" of such things as filing briefs and other documents, posting bond, and so forth. Information of this variety is easily acquired, and its dissemination is not seriously suggested as an appropriate task of the law school.

The other two most prominent job contributions mentioned are directly related to some of the skills and areas of knowledge considered important to the practice of law. The "learning how to deal with people" rubric covers a number of the more specific interpersonal skills examined earlier in the discussion of the clusters in figure 6.1. In addition, at least with respect to selected areas of the law, there is some

52. As indicated above, clinical education is relatively new and variable. Thus its potential for covering the competencies that the practitioners consider so important may not have been fully realized to date.

53. Since some respondents mentioned more than one job, the law-related proportion of *all* jobs is lower (40 percent). Still, including all jobs, the law-related ones account for the largest and only substantial proportion.

learning of the substantive law that occurs in jobs held before admission to the bar, as would be expected since most of the jobs mentioned are directly law related. It is interesting that of all those who cited any job as contributing significantly to their careers, 86.6 percent held that job *during* law school.[54]

Many of the serious suggestions that have been proposed as either alternatives or additions to current educational practice concentrate on post–law school studies. Training after completion of formal schooling is neither new nor unique to the legal profession. In fact, continuing education is often cited as one of the hallmarks of a profession as distinguished from other occupational pursuits. Some clerkship, apprenticeship, clinical experience, or specialized skills training is actually required before practice in four states (Delaware, New Jersey, Rhode Island, and Vermont). New Jersey, in fact, provides a skills and methods course for this purpose (Klein, Leleiko, & Mavity, 1978, p. 20). A similar program currently operates in Australia. The Australian bar has created special schools where the so-called practical skills are learned over a period of many months of intensive training only after graduation from law school (or the equivalent) but prior to certification for practice.[55] Other common law countries have developed their own brands of postgraduate education. The British articling and pupilage and the Canadian articling systems both require the continual cooperation of the practicing bar. A suggestion by a participant, in a group session in the Indiana pretest, that articles are the equivalent of the training of new lawyers in large law firms in the United States met with an immediate and sharp denial. Other participants noted that the economics of law practice mean that the cost of a new lawyer including salary, insurance, office space, secretary, and clerical support amounts to a $20,000 to $25,000 package.[56] The pretest informants neglected to point out that a first-year law-

54. Because some respondents mentioned more than one job, the percentage of jobs held during law school is lower but still more than a majority (54.2 percent). Although we do not know precisely when within one's law school career these jobs were held, it is likely that most of those that were directly law related were summer jobs in law offices. Obtaining summer jobs is a practice that is apparently increasing (Thorne, 1973, p. 136). Among the sample, of those who mentioned pregraduation jobs as contributing to their careers, the proportion of those jobs that are law related has increased the more recent the law school graduation. These jobs are akin to the old apprentice system not only because of the precertification training in the law that they provide but also because they are often recruitment devices for future associates. See chapter 5 for a discussion of the attractions to a first job and chapter 4 for consideration of the importance of first law job to future career patterns.

55. For a description of the program of the College of Law established by the Law Society of New South Wales as part of the preparation of a fully qualified solicitor see Stewart (1979).

56. These figures are already out of date. The actual costs are dependent largely on the salaries of starting lawyers, which vary by location. Recent figures are available in the latest survey published by *Student Lawyer*, the publication of the American Bar Association Law Student Division. The average starting salaries for new lawyers in nonpatent law firms are generally about $17,000, with New York ($21,000) and Washington, D.C. ($22,000) having the highest average starting salaries. To the salary figures must be added

yer may bill as much as $50,000–$80,000 in the same period, more than covering costs even if a greater proportion of time were devoted to training. In addition, it would of course be possible to develop a program for substantially less money *if* such experience were requisite to practice, thus eliminating the competition of the marketplace which currently operates in determining the costs of new legal talent. Were that to occur, the cooperation between the practicing bar and legal educators would have to increase enormously. In addition, given their increasing numbers, the problem of placing all law graduates in suitable training programs would be an enormous task, even recognizing the possibility of excluding law graduates who did not intend to practice.

Another idea that does get occasional consideration is the internship based on the medical model. Michael Sovern, former dean and now president of Columbia Law School, has suggested something along this line in his recommendation that law students "spend a year in practice after their second year of law school, provided that they return to school for a final year of formal instruction after their year in the wilderness" (1975, p. 29). Sovern goes on to pose a rhetorical question that is perhaps more telling than he intended: he wonders out loud "if the institutional law firms will, if asked, agree to share the cost of educating their young" (p. 75). Reference to "institutional law firms" reflects the lack of a legal institution comparable to the medical profession's hospitals. Regardless of the willingness of law firms, which may indeed be problematic given the costs involved, there remains the question of whether or not that is the required training we wish all lawyers to receive, recognizing as we must the substantial diversity in the practice of law. While the state of a population's health may be correlated with its financial well-being, the same problems do occur across socioeconomic strata. Thus training that depends on the treatment of charity patients can in most cases be readily transferred to the patients the average doctor typically encounters in private practice. The same cannot be said with respect to the law; the legal problems of the rich and of the poor, and most particularly of businesses and of individuals, differ in kind, often requiring strikingly different skills and expertise from legal counsel.

There is, then, a critical question relating to the nature and structure, within legal education, of any program based on the internship model. As we have demonstrated, the larger law firms, which are most likely to be willing and able to support interns, are very likely to be engaged in legal work that is considered high in prestige within the practicing bar. Laumann and Heinz (1977) find a very high negative correlation between the prestige of specialties and the percentage of blue-collar clients served (table 2, pp. 169–71, 177–79, although they observe that this apparent effect of client type on prestige may be in part "an effect of peer

---

the costs of office space and support staff. See Kilmer's "The Fifth Annual Salary Survey" (1979) for more complete figures.

opinions of the intellectual demands of the different sorts of practice" (pp. 203, 213–55). As currently conceived, then, post–law school internship training would likely be restricted to the areas of the law serving quite limited segments of the population. Law schools themselves have already been criticized for skewing their curricula in that very direction, and thereby influencing the distribution of legal services away from portions of the population that are underrepresented in relationship to their legal needs.[57] Any apprenticeship, internship, continuing education courses, or any other program that depends on large law firms for its institutional base will focus on selected areas of the law. Made cognizant by the analysis of the importance of first law-related jobs to ultimate legal career, as reported in chapter 4, we are concerned about the concentration of early career training in areas of the law that serve almost exclusively corporate entities and individuals in high economic strata. The effect will likely be to further influence new lawyers to begin and to continue serving selected segments of the population.[58] It does not therefore seem likely that such programs will receive much support from those critics of legal education most interested in its reform who by and large believe that law schools are already influencing their graduates too far in that direction.

The most widely discussed and most popular form of legal training outside law school is commonly termed "continuing legal education." It appears in many forms and is one of the most rapidly growing areas in legal education.[59] Within the Chicago bar 79 percent have participated in continuing legal education programs, and 80.9 percent of that group do so at least annually.[60] The vast proportion of these programs are held outside the law school environment; only half of Chicago's six law schools even offer programs.

The seriousness of the continuing legal education enterprise is reflected in the rules recently adopted by the highest courts of nine states. The active practice of law in Colorado, Idaho, Iowa, Minnesota, North Dakota, South Carolina (effective July 1981), Washington, Wisconsin, and Wyoming is now contingent upon annual participation in continuing legal education.[61] In addition, three other states (Califor-

---

57. For an example of this view see Cahn and Cahn (1970). The related issues of law schools' influence on professional and social responsibility will be considered in chapter 7.

58. The extent to which early legal experience serving the needs of the poor can affect later legal practice is illustrated in Erlanger (1977).

59. The rise of continuing education is not restricted to the law. With declining birth rates it is the single largest growth area in the entire field of education. See Fred Harvey Harrington, *The Future of Adult Education: New Responsibilities of Colleges and Universities* (San Francisco: Jossey-Bass, 1977).

60. There are no statistically significant relationships between participation in continuing legal education and any of the following: legal specialty, organizational context of legal practice, law school attended, class standing in law school, self-evaluation of legal skills, or self-evaluation of success.

61. Although the specific rules and regulations vary among the nine states they all follow the same pattern. From 10 to 15 hours of continuing education is required annually in a program subject to the approval of a state board or commission established for the pur-

nia, Texas, and Florida) accredit continuing legal education programs as part of their certification of legal specialties.[62] Although it has been suggested that continuing legal education could bridge the gap between ap-

pose of administering the newly promulgated rules governing continuing legal education. Enforcement operates through the required filing of an annual report by every active attorney certifying compliance with the rules. Finally, each state has more or less elaborate hearing and appeals procedures for noncompliance, with suspension from practice the ultimate sanction. For further information on the details of the requirements in the nine states see the following: Rule 260, "Mandatory Continuing Legal and Judicial Education," adopted by the Colorado Supreme Court August 14, 1978, effective January 1, 1979, in *Colorado Revised Statutes 1973,* vol. 7A, *Court Rules,* 1979 Cumulative Supplement, pp. 54–71 (Denver, Colo.: Bradford-Robinson Printing Co., 1977); Supreme Court of the State of Idaho Order (Final Proposed Draft) "Amending the Rules of the Supreme Court and the Board of Commissioners of the Idaho State Bar by Adding Rules 130 to 141 inclusive to Provide for Mandatory Continuing Legal Education for Licensed Attorneys and Amending Other Rules to Conform with this Requirement," November 1978, effective January 1, 1979, in section on "Bar Commission Rules," *The Idaho State Bar Desk Book* (published periodically by the Idaho State Bar Association, with limited distribution to attorneys); Rules Governing Admission to the Bar, Rule 123, "Continuing Legal Education of the Members of the Bar of Iowa," adopted April 9, 1975, in *Iowa Code Annotated,* vol. 40, *Social Justice, Trial Court,* 1980–81 Cumulative Supplement, pp. 81–84 (St. Paul, Minn.: West Publishing Co., 1975; "Rules of the Supreme Court for Continuing Legal Education of Members of the Bar," adopted and effective April 3, 1975, in *Minnesota Statutes Annotated,* vol. 52, *Court Rules,* pp. 589–94 (St. Paul, Minn.: West Publishing Co., 1980); "Rules of the State Bar Association for Continuing Professional Education of the Members of the Bar," approved by Supreme Court of North Dakota, July 27, 1977, in Rules of Supreme Court of North Dakota, vol. 4, *Rules of Professional and Judicial Conduct* (looseleaf); Rules 35, "[Continuing Legal Education of the Judiciary]," adopted December 8, 1976, effective January 1, 1977, and "Rules for the Examination and Admission of Persons to Practice Law in South Carolina," Rules 5A–5B, effective July 1981, in *Code of Laws of South Carolina,* vol. 22, *Court Rules,* 1979 Cumulative Supplement pp. 118–21, 163–68 (Rochester, N.Y.: Lawyers Co-Operative Publishing Co., 1977); Admission to Practice Rules, Rule 11, "Continuing Legal Education," adopted November 29, 1976, effective January 1, 1977, in *Washington Court Rules Annotated,* pt. I, pp. 92–94 San Francisco: Bancroft-Whitney Co., 1977); Supreme Court Rules 30.01–31.13, effective January 1, 1977, in *Wisconsin Court Rules and Procedure 1980,* pp. 640–41 (St. Paul, Minn.: West Publishing Co., 1980); "Rules of the Supreme Court for the Continuing Legal Education of Members of the Wyoming State Bar," Rules 1–8, adopted December 6, 1977, in *Wyoming Court Rules Annotated,* pp. 475–78 (Charlottesville, Va.: Michie Co., 1979).

62. As of June 1977 California and Texas each certified only three legal specialties: respectively, criminal law, workmen's compensation, and taxation; and family law, labor law, and criminal law. Florida covers a much more extensive list, including registered general practice. Participation in continuing legal education is requisite only if the lawyer wishes to present him- or herself as a specialist in the selected fields, but thus far it has not been requisite to the practice itself.

The recent amendments to Canon 2 of the Code of Professional Responsibility, approved by the ABA House of Delegates in February 1976, will likely affect the trend toward certification. This amendment was promulgated in response to the United States Supreme Court decision in *Bates v. State Bar of Arizona* (433 U.S. 350 (1977)), which characterized state enforcement of bar association prohibition on advertising as a violation of the First Amendment's free speech provision as applied to the states through the due process clause of the Fourteenth Amendment. Part of the American Bar Association amendment to the code now allows lawyers to publish the following information: "one or more fields of law in which the lawyer or law firm concentrates[;] a statement that practice is limited to one or more fields of law[;] *or* a statement that the lawyer or law firm specializes in a particular field of law or law practice" (DR 2-102(A)(6), amended, 1976, p. 299). The discussion draft of "Model Rules of Professional Conduct," to be considered for adoption by

prenticeship and law school to improve preparation in the practice of law, established programs tend to concentrate on changing areas of the law (consistent with the annual requirements of the bars of several states) or on training in highly specialized or technical areas of the law. Only rarely do they provide training in competencies that are not covered in law school but are requisite to the practice of law.[63]

While some form of post-law school training may be the most popular reform that could be instituted in legal education, several factors bear consideration before it can be viewed as a remedy for most of the shortcomings with which legal education has been charged. First, suggestions that continuing legal education is the best and most obvious means of developing skills important to the practice of law indicate some misunderstanding of continuing legal education as it is currently constituted. Programs would require substantial redevelopment before they would begin to be appropriate to this task. Second, since so little attempt has yet been made to formalize training in many of these skills, the feasibility of the entire endeavor still remains questionable. Third, continuing legal education needs to be critically evaluated before its role in the training of lawyers is expanded.[64] As the data make clear, the legal profession is extremely diverse, and continuing legal education, particularly where mandatory, must be accommodated to that reality. Finally, the notion that participation in continuing legal education will somehow be able to succeed where the practicing bar thinks law schools have failed is not yet persuasive. And further, if post-law school training can succeed in teaching skills and knowledge particularly important to the practice of law, it can be argued that such training should precede licensure so that certification to serve the legal needs of the public will be withheld until competencies important to practice are inculcated.

Conclusion

An examination of both the knowledge and skills lawyers consider important to the practice of law and the contributions of law school and

---

the ABA to replace the current Code of Professional Responsibility, states that ''A lawyer may communicate the fact that the lawyer will accept employment in specified areas of practice. A lawyer whose practice is limited to specified areas of practice may communicate that fact.'' Certification or designation as a specialist is limited to those admitted to practice before the U.S. Patent and Trademark Office and those so designated by provisions of state rules.

63. A possible variation in legal education would be to rely on continuing legal education programs to provide training in more specialized areas of the law which are valuable in practice only for a very limited segment of the bar. The NITA program does that currently for trial advocacy skills. Other examples might include labor law, admiralty law, corporate finance, and the like. This would then allow law schools to cover some important skills to which they currently devote insufficient attention, without increasing the prepractice training period.

64. See, for example, the 1976 article by Charles C. Bingaman, associate director of the Institute of Legal Education of the Illinois State Bar Association, in which he reflects on a number of shortcomings of continuing legal education and suggests a bit of caution lest mandatory CLE be expanded before its effectiveness is known.

experience to their development does not reveal a simple or uniform relationship. Indeed there is substantial variance in the respondents' views, and not necessarily along the dimensions deemed predictable. Some competencies are perceived to be significantly more important than others to the practice of law. Further, the importance of each varies according to practice in different legal specialties. It must be recognized, therefore, that the legal profession is differentiated not only by the context, substance, and clientele of practice but also by the actual competencies requisite to the tasks performed. In particular it means that the focus of formal legal education on selected skills provides proportionately more preparation for practicing some legal specialties than others, even though, as discussed in chapter 4, the specialty categories are overly broad and thus provide a conservative picture of diversity in the practice of law. Similarly, curriculum evaluations are also related to the specialty practiced by the evaluator.

Although formal legal education contributes greatly to the development of the skills and knowledge requisite to the practice of law, the contribution is not directly proportional to the usefulness of the competence either to the aggregate bar or to practitioners of individual specialties. Neglected by law schools are the interpersonal skills so important to the client-oriented problem solving that is the task of the legal professional. The more analytic skills may constitute the ideal symbolic work of the legal profession, but very often they are not deemed to be as useful as interpersonal competencies in the actual practice of law.[65]

As we showed in chapter 5, individual law schools make a significant difference in the distribution of lawyers within the profession; yet the particular law school attended does not predict the evaluation of law school as a source of knowledge and skills important to the practice of law.[66] Despite great variability in reputation for quality and orientation of the education provided, including graduates' perceptions of their school's goals (as reported in chapter 3, tables 3.15 and 3.16), practitioners have a remarkably uniform view of the actual training provided by their formal legal education. While practitioners view law schools' neglect of some skills simply as a reflection of the inappropriateness of formal schooling to such training, that explanation is not sufficient. Many of the competencies considered most important and believed to be potentially subject to successful law school instruction have nonetheless

65. Cognizant of both the importance of the nonanalytic skills and the failure of law schools to deal with them, the ABA Task Force on Lawyer Competency recently recommended that in admissions decisions "law schools should consider a full range of the qualities and skills important to professional competence." In particular the task force report encourages giving greater weight to "such factors as writing ability, ability in oral communication, work habits, interpersonal skills, dependability, and conscientiousness" (*Lawyer Competency,* 1979, Recommendation 1, p. 3).

66. To the extent that the law school attended and the nature of practice are related, as discussed in chapter 5, there is a statistical connection between school attended and evaluation of schools' contributions to skills important to practice. However, once the nature and context of practice is held constant, the effect of law school loses its significance.

been left to be acquired elsewhere. For those with the appropriate opportunities, some competencies are developed in the employ of sizable law firms. For other attorneys, and to some extent for all attorneys, the areas of knowledge and skills most important to the practice of law are learned by experience, possibly at the expense of the quality of service to initial clientele.

Although disagreements over the training in lawyering competencies are rampant, there seems to be some agreement that it would be preferable if many of these skills were acquired before licensure. Legal education receives a rather good report from its consumers, but there is substantial support for a more complete job in a number of skills viewed as very important to the practice of law. For those competencies that can be taught within the current curricular model, a new emphasis may be all that is required. However, when accompanied by only limited suggestions for eliminating or shortening areas of the curriculum, requests for additional attention to skill development raise practical problems if the three-year law school is to be retained.

The data clearly indicate that preparation for the practice of law has always extended well beyond formal training (both before and after law school) and that both the defenders and critics of legal education have overestimated its role to date, even with respect to the tasks most closely identified with the legal profession. The practicing bar credits law schools in precisely those areas in which they have chosen to concentrate their attention. It is the neglect of competencies outside the law schools' self-defined mission with which practitioners find most fault. That mission is based on an image of the profession not reflected in the data, for in many cases what is neglected is the very competencies that practitioners find most important to the actual practice of law.

Chapter 7

SOCIALIZATION TO PROFESSIONAL RESPONSIBILITY

Introduction

The powers of self-regulation that the state grants to a profession rest on the assumption that it will develop appropriate ethical standards and behave according to those standards, even when it is not possible to compel compliance. Codes of professional responsibility or professional ethics are formal mechanisms announcing publicly that the profession in question is self-regulated and is therefore to be trusted with the autonomy granted to it by the state. Such ethical standards of behavior and codes of self-regulation are said to set the profession apart from the norms of the general society. The standards of behavior of the legal profession are of special concern because lawyers are in peculiar positions of trust and at the same time have, in the aggregate, substantial autonomous power over the direction of the legal and social order.

In a letter urging renewal of ABA membership, then ABA President William B. Spann, Jr., listed "protection of the right of the profession to self-regulation" as one of the major priorities of the organization (Sims, 1978, p. 2). There is, however, no "right" to self-regulation. As Llewellyn noted decades ago, "the ground for monopoly is that it makes possible better service . . . . The condition of monopoly is that it serve" (1933, p. 190).[1] States grant monopoly powers to professional groups ostensibly both to facilitate better service for their clientele and to better serve the public good. At a minimum this would seem to require consideration of how one's actions affect the larger society.[2] This

---

1. Llewellyn (1933) goes on to say that the latter "does *not* hold of the bar" (p. 190). The extent to which the legal profession serves the society and particularly the part that legal education can and does play in generating such service will be discussed later in this chapter.
2. It is that kind of very generalized sense of responsibility that is now being urged

professional responsibility of the bar to the public is partially reflected in the denotation of lawyers as "officers of the court." In that role lawyers are said to serve not only their clients but also the court or system of justice and the society as a whole. "The symbol of the profession . . . portrays a group whose members have altruistic motivations and whose professional activities are governed by a code of ethics which heavily emphasizes devotion to service and the good of the client and condemns misuses of professional skills for selfish purposes" (Becker, 1962, pp. 36–37).[3] Those concerns are reflected in at least eight of the nine canons[4] of the Code of Professional Responsibility[5] promulgated by the American Bar Association and adopted in some variant in every state. State and local bar association grievance committees are thereby charged with enforcing the Code of Professional Responsibility by investigating possible violations and recommending action to the appropriate state body.[6]

---

upon business corporations. See Christopher Stone, *Where the Law Ends* (New York: Harper & Row, 1975).

3. It should perhaps be noted that Becker goes on to state that such codes are "sternly enforced by appropriate disciplinary bodies" (1962, p. 37). While that may be the symbol, it is certainly not the reality, at least not with respect to the legal profession. The actual enforcement of the Code of Professional Responsibility will be discussed later.

4. Those eight canons (1978, pp. iii–iv) are as follows:

Canon 1. A lawyer should assist in maintaining the integrity and competence of the legal profession.
Canon 2. A lawyer should assist the legal profession in fulfilling its duty to make legal counsel available.
Canon 4. A lawyer should preserve the confidences and secrets of a client.
Canon 5. A lawyer should exercise independent professional judgment on behalf of a client.
Canon 6. A lawyer should represent a client competently.
Canon 7. A lawyer should represent a client zealously within the bounds of the law.
Canon 8. A lawyer should assist in improving the legal system.
Canon 9. A lawyer should avoid even the appearance of professional impropriety.

However, the disciplinary rules subsumed under these canons do not necessarily act to translate the symbol to reality (see note 14 *infra*). Canon 3, which states that "a lawyer should assist in preventing the unauthorized practice of law" (p. 19), is more protectionist than altruistic, even symbolically. It could be argued, however, that prevention of "unauthorized" practice is intended first and foremost to protect an unsuspecting and insufficiently knowledgeable public.

5. The Code of Professional Responsibility was adopted in 1969 by the House of Delegates of the American Bar Association upon the recommendation of the Special Committee on Evaluation of Ethical Standards, created at the request of then ABA president Lewis F. Powell, Jr. (currently associate justice of the United States Supreme Court). Although it includes substantial revisions, the 1969 Code relies heavily upon the 32 Canons of Professional Ethics originally adopted by the American Bar Association in 1908. Those canons in turn were based principally on the Code of Ethics of the Alabama State Bar Association written in 1887 but borrowed substantially from Judge George Sharswood's lectures, published in 1854 under the title of *Professional Ethics* (Preface, *Code of Professional Responsibility and Code of Judicial Conduct*, as amended 1978, p. i). The extent of the parallel between the Canons of Professional Ethics and the Code of Professional Responsibility is clearly delineated in *Parallel Tables Between the ABA Canons of Professional Ethics and the ABA Code of Professional Responsibility* (1970), compiled by Olavi Maru of the American Bar Foundation.

6. The extent to which the ABA Code has been adopted and is enforceable nationally

Despite the promulgation of rules and establishment of enforcement mechanisms to ensure high standards of behavior by American lawyers, there is substantial unease, in some cases outright indignation, with the actual behavior of lawyers. Part of the public discomfort with lawyers' behavior is probably as old as the profession itself and relates not in small measure to the power and control it exerts. Well-known examples include Swift's reference to lawyers in *Gulliver's Travels* as "a society of men among us, bred up from their youth in the art of proving by words multiplied for the purpose, that white is black, and black is white, according as they are paid" (pt. IV, ch. 5). More contemporary and perhaps more familiar is the refrain from Carl Sandburg's poem "The Lawyers Know Too Much"—"tell me why a hearse horse snickers hauling a lawyer's bones" (from *Smoke and Steel*, 1920). John Dean's testimony before Senate hearings describing his realization that lawyers predominated among the Watergate conspirators only served to substantiate a negative public image of lawyers. Modern pollsters have now documented the general public's skepticism about the legal profession. A 1978 Harris survey inquired into public confidence in selected institutions; for the three years of surveys reported (1976–78), law firms rank near the bottom: they are joined in that glory by the United States Congress, organized labor, and advertising agencies.[7]

The bar itself has expressed continuing concern over standards of professional responsibility, and particularly over how they can be inculcated.[8] The recent Supreme Court decision (*Bates v. State Bar of Arizona,* 433 U.S. 350 (1977)) that effectively lifted the Code of Professional Responsibility's ban on lawyer advertising as a violation of constitutionally guaranteed free speech has generated a new wave of concern over the relevance and appropriateness of the rest of the Code and the standards by which lawyers are expected to behave. An ABA Commission on Evaluation of Professional Standards was subsequently appointed to

---

was among the contested issues in recent antitrust litigation: *United States v. American Bar Association*, United States District Court for the Northern District of Illinois Docket #76 C 3475. The case was ended upon the government's motion to dismiss, August 30, 1978. In addition to state bodies, every federal court constitutes a separate disciplinary jurisdiction.

7. Survey reported in Louis Harris, "Confidence in America is Rising," *Chicago Tribune*, January 5, 1978, sec. 3, p. 4.

8. Professional responsibility was the topic for consideration at the 1956 Boulder Conference on the Education of Lawyers for Their Public Responsibilities, sponsored by the AALS Committee on Education for Professional Responsibility, and by a similar meeting in 1968, the National Conference on Education in the Professional Responsibilities of the Lawyer, sponsored by AALS under a grant from the Council on Education in Professional Responsibility (proceedings in Weckstein, 1970). The second conference, "Boulder II," followed the formation of the ABA Special Committee on Evaluation of Disciplinary Enforcement chaired by former Supreme Court justice Tom C. Clark. The "Clark Committee" itself was a response to state and local bar association support for a study of lawyer discipline. The "Clark Report," *Problems and Recommendations in Disciplinary Enforcement*, was published in 1970. For an extended critical evaluation of the Code of Professional Responsibility, see Morgan (1977). For recent brief critiques, see Cowger (1978), Lieberman (1978a, 1978b), and Schnapper (1978).

evaluate the Code of Professional Responsibility. It recently circulated a discussion draft of *Model Rules of Professional Conduct* (January 30, 1980) to supersede the Code.[9]

At the same time that the Code and its enforcement have been under scrutiny, there has been growing discussion of the education of lawyers to desirable standards of behavior.[10] Virtually all proposals to expand efforts to socialize attorneys to preferred standards of behavior have focused on formal training in law school despite continuing skepticism over its potential impact.[11] Indeed, the American Bar Association now requires schools that it accredits to offer "instruction in the duties and the responsibilities of the legal profession" and to ensure that all degree candidates take it.[12] Since graduation from an ABA-approved law school is, in all but five states, a prerequisite to sitting for the bar examination that is necessary for admission to the bar, the standard has almost universal applicability.

At the same time that requirements in the teaching of professional responsibility are being added to law school curricula, there are continuous claims that ethical or responsible behavior cannot be taught in school, certainly not at the age when students begin their formal training in the law. Others argue that it is simply not the role of law school to inculcate ethical standards, that law professors are supposed to teach technical skills and present materials in an objective manner, a stance inappropriate to ethical questions. Law teachers have traditionally accorded low status to the subject of professional responsibility, and there is now evidence (Pipkin, 1979) that law students also give a low rating to courses in professional responsibility and the legal profession.

9. A final version is to be submitted to the House of Delegates of the ABA at its February 1981 meeting.

10. The American Bar Association has prepared and produced materials to educate the practicing attorney in appropriate standards of behavior. The ABA Consortium for Professional Education has published *Professional Responsibility: A Guide for Attorneys* (Chicago: American Bar Association, 1977); in addition, it has prepared and distributes a six-part videotaped program (with printed discussion guides) called *Dilemmas in Legal Ethics* (Chicago: American Bar Association, 1977) (described in 1979 catalog *Video Law Seminars*). Both rely heavily on the provisions of the current Code of Professional Responsibility. The ABA Standing Committee on Professional Discipline and the Center for Professional Discipline of the ABA have published (1975) a pamphlet, *Professional Responsibility and the Lawyer: Avoiding Unintentional Grievances,* dealing with the issues most likely to be contained in complaints against lawyers. The difference between the issues of complaints and those dealt with by the Code will be discussed later in this chapter.

11. Despite explicit attacks on legal education during the 1960s, which charged that the process transformed socially concerned students into hardened, cynical, profit-motivated hired guns (to consolidate a few of the more popular phrases), there is as yet little real evidence that any such inclinations develop, or that if such changes do occur, that the law school itself has played a major role. In an effort to test the assumption that "during the course of their education, law students tend to relinquish more public-oriented views in favor of those endorsed by the law school," Erlanger and Klegon (1978, p. 14) evaluated the views of one class at the University of Wisconsin law school and concluded that there were no significant changes while in law school. For additional examples of attempts to relate law school training to changes in ethical standards see Quarantelli, Helfrich, and Yutsy (1964), Thielens (1969), and Katz and Denbeaux (1976).

12. Standard 302 of the 1973 ABA standards, in *Approval of Law Schools* (1977).

Despite the ABA accreditation requirement, a survey in 1977 revealed that 15 percent of ABA-approved law schools do not require the instruction offered in professional responsibility.[13] Among these are the law schools of the University of Chicago, University of Michigan, Stanford University, and Yale University. It is of course possible that the vocal support for the teaching of professional responsibility is simply rhetoric intended to present an image of concern, a kind of defense mechanism in the face of public criticism and recently dismissed litigation threatening the status of the profession's powers of self-regulation.[14]

The topic of this chapter is the professional responsibility message projected by law schools to their consumers. In particular we will focus on the perceived role that legal education has played in the development of the professional responsibility of legal practitioners. An examination of this issue is quite complex because of the different meanings and usage of this term, ranging in the lawyers' views from an almost technical role-specific rule obedience to a broad value orientation. Our goal is to concentrate on lawyers' perceptions of the impact of law school on professional responsibility, as compared with pre–law school and post–law school development. In doing so we will reveal, in the lawyers' views themselves, a basic ambiguity and tension regarding what professional responsibility is and can be and, accordingly, what the role of legal education is and should be.

As professional responsibility is discussed and evaluated we must be aware that standards of professional responsibility are like any scheme of preferred behavior. Accordingly they may be exclusively oriented toward the establishment of minimal standards below which none should fall and for which some form of sanction is likely to follow, or (although these types are not necessarily mutually exclusive) they can be stated as goals toward which all ought to aspire. In Lon Fuller's terms, in the former case we are speaking of a "morality of duty" and in the latter case a "morality of aspiration" (1969, p. 5).

A morality of duty

> lays down the basic rules without which an ordered society is impossible, or without which an ordered society directed toward certain specific goals must fail of its mark. . . . It does not condemn men for failing to embrace opportunities for the fullest realization of their powers. Instead, it condemns them for failing to respect the basic requirements of social living (Fuller, 1969, pp. 5–6).

The attorneys who adhere to this positivist view focus on violations of the disciplinary rules which can lead to censure. They want the law

13. The survey was undertaken by the Section on Professional Responsibility of the Association of American Law Schools in conjunction with the National Conference on Teaching Professional Responsibility held at the University of Detroit Law School in the fall of 1977. Of the 162 ABA-approved law schools, 96 percent responded to the inquiry. For more detailed results see Goldberg (1979).

14. See note 6 *supra* on the dismissed case of *United States v. American Bar Association*.

schools to provide them with a more sensitive awareness of the pitfalls of practice so that they can avoid violations of the rules. They look to the Code of Professional Responsibility and to the cases decided by the grievance committee of the local bar association and the state courts. Such a perspective is not at all inconsistent with the orientation of legal education around cases and rules, and the fit of rules to fact situations.

A morality of aspiration, on the other hand,

> is the morality . . . of excellence, of the fullest realization of human powers. . . . [I]nstead of ideas of right and wrong, of moral claim and moral duty, we have rather the conception of proper and fitting conduct, conduct such as beseems a human being functioning at his best (Fuller, 1969, p. 5).

In terms of a lawyer's professional responsibility, we find practitioners seeking "professional" conduct, responsibility to people, integrity, and honesty—all goals not meaningfully translated into minimal criteria measurable for enforcement purposes. It is from this more aspirational perspective that a substantial proportion of the practicing bar conceptualize professional responsibility. They find law school coverage of the Code of Professional Responsibility too limiting and suggest that law schools orient themselves toward encouraging their students to uphold standards above those enforceable through a code, standards that take cognizance of a lawyer's and the legal system's role in achieving justice.[15]

As we consider the various dimensions of professional responsibility we would do well to keep in mind the duality inherent in a standard such as professional responsibility, regardless of the dimension. This duality will be particularly germane when we attempt to evaluate the role and the potential of law schools and other socializing contexts in inculcating standards of professional responsibility.

We turn now to an examination of the nature of professional responsibility as conceptualized by practicing lawyers and their perceptions of the influences on the development of their own standards of professional responsibility. We shall see that lawyers vary in the extent to which they view professional responsibility as essentially a morality of

15. The Code of Professional Responsibility, itself divided between "Ethical Considerations" and "Disciplinary Rules," reflects these dual moralities. The Ethical Considerations, like the nine Canons that constitute the major sections of the Code, do not fit the morality of duty model. These portions of the Code reflect a much more aspirational view of professional responsibility—what lawyers *ought* to do. In contrast, the Disciplinary Rules tell attorneys what they *must* do if they are to avoid possible sanction. Yet attempts to inculcate norms and mold the behavior of the bar emphasize the latter. While the disciplinary rules are supposedly intended to promote the Ethical Considerations in the Code, the reality may be quite different. Indeed there are those who argue that concentration on the Disciplinary Rules has often had the effect of obviating the more aspirational goals of the Ethical Considerations. The most prominent example is the recently invalidated traditional restriction on advertising embodied in the Disciplinary Rules that constitute part of the Canon that obligates the lawyer to "assist the legal profession in fulfilling its duty to make legal counsel available" (Canon 2, Code of Professional Responsibility 1978, p. 5).

duty, that is, of rules whose negative consequences are to be avoided, or as a morality of aspiration, which ought to set the profession apart from the rest of society in reaching toward a behavioral goal that will enhance the operation of the legal system and benefit society as a whole. We begin with an inquiry into the attribution of influence to legal education as compared with other sources and the implications that these evaluations have for the nature of the legal profession.

Socialization to Professional Responsibility

The multidimensionality of professional responsibility makes socialization to it necessarily complex. Most discussions of socialization, even those concerned with later stages in what is a developmental process, credit early experiences as most important.[16] According to the developmental approach to socialization underlying our research, as we discussed in chapter 1, early learning establishes the boundaries for later experiences. In this view role-specific socialization does not occur in a vacuum; rather, professional norms are inculcated through a filter of prior, more basic standards of behavior.[17] In evaluating the relative impact of various sources on their own professional behavior, practicing lawyers seem to confirm the view that "the aspects of behavior that dictate how a person shall behave professionally derive from the internalized values that the person has incorporated from prior experience with other people" (Watson, 1963, p. 4). Despite a question phrased to elicit role-based responses expected to yield references to peculiarly role-oriented socialization (such as law school or observations of other lawyers), lawyers consider their general upbringing as the most important source of their own *professional* behavior.

Like many of the skills important to the practice of law, early socialization is credited by the overwhelming majority of the bar as making the greatest contribution to the resolution of questions of professional responsibility which arise in the practice of law. Table 7.1 clearly shows the relative importance lawyers attribute to various sources as influences on the ethics of their practice. All other sources combined are no match for general upbringing. If we add to the 61.6 percent of the respondents who rank general upbringing as number 1, those who are listed in the "other" category who cite moral standards or religious training, the figure rises to 63.5 percent. Combining that figure with those ranking the item as second most important, more than 80 percent of the practicing bar consider their general upbringing to have been very important in the resolution of problems of professional responsibility in their practice. The high ranking of general upbringing does not vary by law school attended or by years since graduation from

16. For a discussion of the prominence of the family in general socialization see Elkin (1960).

17. See Tapp and Levine (1974) for an application of a developmental theory of socialization to the concept of law.

TABLE 7.1
Rank Order of Sources Contributing to the Resolution of
Questions of Professional Responsibility
Arising in Practice

	% Ranking	
Source[a]	Most Important	Second Most Important
General upbringing	61.6	17.5
Observation of or advice from other attorneys in your law office	21.5	37.4
Law school consideration of these topics	11.0	19.6
Observation of or advice from other attorneys *not* in your law office . . .	1.7	14.6
Advice from persons other than attorneys	0	4.9
Other	4.1	6.0
	99.9	100
	(N = 534)	(N = 514)[b]

[a]Items listed in the order of the percentage of respondents ranking it as the most important source contributing to the resolution of questions of legal ethics and/or professional responsibility that have arisen in practice (questionnaire, pt. IV, Q. 3, p. 19, appendix 1).
[b]The lower N for rank 2 is due to those respondents who limited themselves to ranking a single item. The discrepancy is small, however, and so the rankings are relatively comparable.

law school. Nor is it affected by the nature or size of practice context or the substance or prestige of the specialty practiced.

These findings lead us to make two related points. First, taken with comments such as "you don't need the Code to tell you right from wrong," these practicing lawyers are implicitly questioning the assumption that legal ethics and professional responsibility are peculiar to the practice of law. Put another way, they recognize the direct relationship between professional responsibility as they conceptualize it and more general ethical standards. Second, they are aware of the important influence of early development on later behavior in general, whether or not it has been oriented specifically to law practice.

Time and again one hears disclaimers from the organized bar that legal ethics and professional responsibility have very precise meanings appropriate to the practice of law and applicable only within that context. These professional standards are not, it is often stated, equivalent to or necessarily even related to general ethics or moral standards. Indeed, according to one law school dean "much . . . of the historic and current hostility toward lawyers derives . . . from the clash of values between the basic professional ethic . . . and common notions of morality and fairness" (Schwartz, 1974, p. 20, col. 3). Lawyers are thus said to be obligated to act in their professional role in a way that they would not necessarily act in another context. In fact, notes Wasserstrom (1975), it is in the very

> nature of role-differentiated behavior that it often makes it both appropriate and desirable for the person in a particular role to put to one

side considerations of various sorts—and especially various moral considerations—that would otherwise be relevant if not decisive (p. 3).

While role differentiation may at times demand behavior that would be considered inappropriate in another context, it is too simple, and the data indicate that it would be incorrect, to characterize within-role responsibility as totally distinct from personal and social responsibility more generally. That many in the legal profession compartmentalize in such a way that they define the issue of professional responsibility solely in role-specific terms reveals the implicit socialization model they endorse or prefer to endorse.

The Professional Environment as Socializer to Professional Responsibility

The literature on the sociology of professions indicates that much professional socialization is effected outside the professional schools, particularly in direct observation of professionals themselves rather than in academic discussions about professional responsibilities (Becker, 1961, 1962; Carlin, 1962a, 1966). The professional environment most likely to affect the attorney's understandings of professional responsibility, and presumably his or her behavior as well, is that professional environment most closely tied to one's own practice. That was Carlin's point in his evaluation of the professional behavior of lawyers in New York City (1966), and substantiated by Handler's findings in a smaller town (1967). Such references to the professional environment, however, fail to distinguish the peculiar role of lawyers within the same firm in influencing the professional behavior of their associates. Looking back to table 7.1, we see that after general upbringing, the source given the greatest credit for learning professional responsibility is the "observation of or advice from other attorneys in your own law office."

Close to 60 percent of the practicing bar rank lawyers in their own offices as among the two most important sources that have contributed to the resolution of questions of professional responsibility in the practice of law. That figure actually underestimates the importance of lawyers in the same office since it is calculated on the entire sample, which includes solo practitioners for whom this response choice is irrelevant. Table 7.2 indicates that those with experience in law firms, in either their first or current jobs, are quite likely to rate lawyers in their offices as among the two most important contributors to the resolution of problems of professional responsibility which have arisen in practice. The perceived influence, however, seems to vary by the kind of office. In both first and current jobs other lawyers in one's own office are more likely to be credited with assisting in the area of professional responsibility in a private firm, particularly in a large firm, than in a government office, even though other lawyers are available in both situations.

The greater credit that lawyers in larger firms give to other lawyers in their own offices as sources of instruction is not unique to the area of professional responsibility. We have shown in chapter 6 that the

TABLE 7.2
Evaluation of Lawyers in Own Office as Contributors to the Resolution of Questions of Professional Responsibility by First and Current Job Contexts

First Job[a]	% Rating Very Important[b]	% Not Rating Very Important	N
Firm	70.7	29.3	215
Government advocate..........	52.8	47.2	53
Other government	61.8	38.2	34

$$\chi^2 = 6.35; \ p \leqslant .05$$

Current Job	% Rating Very Important[b]	% Not Rating Very Important	N
Small firm (2–8)	58.6	41.4	140
Medium firm (9–49)	69.7	30.3	89
Large firm (50 or more)	81.0	19.0	79
Government advocate..........	52.8	47.2	53

$$\chi^2 = 11.68; \ p < .01$$

[a]First job means first law-related job after graduation from law school. Business legal staff is included in neither job category because we could not distinguish the single counsel for a business firm from those working among a large legal staff.
[b]Lawyers in one's own office are rated as very important if they are ranked as the first or second most important source contributing to the resolution of questions of legal ethics of professional responsibility that have arisen in practice.

members of larger law firms are significantly more likely than those in smaller firms to attribute the development of a number of their skills to other members of their firms. They include particularly the following skills: fact gathering, instilling confidence, negotiating, drafting legal documents, and opinion writing. Also the similarity in the source of development of these skills and of professional responsibility is striking in the low ratings given to law schools as contributors to their development. As with some of the skills considered most important to the practice of law, the large law firms are seen as providing training, if only by example, in the area of professional responsibility.[18]

To some extent there is a trade-off between law schools and law firms as perceived instructors in skills and behavior important to the practice of law. Table 7.3 reflects lawyers' evaluations of law schools' relative contribution to the resolution of problems of professional responsibility in practice by the organizational context of practice. The results are congruent with those in table 7.2. The larger the firm, the less likely a lawyer is to rate law school instruction as important in the resolution of problems of professional responsibility arising in practice, with solo practitioners twice as likely to credit law school instruction as are large firm lawyers. As indicated in table 7.4, the effect of practice context on the perceived importance of law school for learning professional responsibility is observed even when controlling for law school type. That is to

18. Like skills and areas of knowledge important to the practice of law, professional responsibility is not perceived by government lawyers to have been substantially influenced by other attorneys in their offices.

TABLE 7.3
Importance of Law School's Consideration of Topics in Contributing
to the Resolution of Questions of Professional Responsibility by
Nature of Practice

	% Rating Very Important[a]	% Not Rating Very Important	N
Solo	43.0	57.0	86
Small firm (2–8)	29.3	70.7	140
Medium firm (9–49)	24.7	75.3	89
Large firm (50 or more)	17.7	82.3	79
Government lawyer	30.2	69.8	53
Business legal staff	36.1	63.9	61
Other	28.6	71.4	21

$$\chi^2 = 14.96; \ p < 0.05$$

[a]Law school's consideration of topics is rated as very important if it is ranked as the
first or second most important source contributing to the resolution of questions of legal
ethics and/or professional responsibility that have arisen in practice.

TABLE 7.4
Importance of Law School in Contributing to the Resolution of Questions of
Professional Responsibility by Size of Private Practice Context and Type of
Law School

Private Context	National Law School[a] % Rating Important[b]	N[c]	Non-national Law School % Rating Important	N[d]
Solo	36.8	19	46.2	65
Small firm (2–8)	21.7	46	33.3	90
Medium firm (9–49)	16.7	42	31.9	47
Large firm (50 or more)	14.0	57	27.3	22
	Somers' $D = 0.093$ (asymmetric with importance of law school dependent)		Somers' $D = 0.096$ (asymmetric with importance of law school dependent)	

[a]The similarity in the strengths of relationship between the size of private practice context and the
law school's perceived contribution to the development of professional responsibility for graduates
of national and non-national law schools is clear from the asymmetric Somers' D shown above.
[b]See table 7.3, note a, on the construction of the importance variable.
[c]Ns in this column represent the number of national law school graduates in each practice
category answering the question. The corresponding percentage in each row is based on this N. For
example, of the 19 national law school graduates who are currently solo practitioners, 36.8 percent
cited law school's consideration of the topics as important in learning professional responsibility.
[d]Ns in this column represent the number of non-national law school graduates in each practice
category answering the question. The corresponding percentage in each row is based on this N and
interpreted as in the first column.

say, irrespective of attendance at a national law school, lawyers practicing within larger firms are least likely to attribute to their law schools
important contributions to professional responsibility.

The role of law school in the development of professional responsibility, like its role in developing many of the skills important to the practice of law, is perceived as less important by those who have had the opportunity to learn these things from other members of the same law of-

fice. Thus we see that apprentice-like training still to be found in the modern law office centers on selected areas, one of them being professional responsibility. By contrast, those without experience in a firm context rely more heavily on law school instruction. The substantive difference this might make in the professional behavior of lawyers is an intriguing but unanswered question and one for which there are, unfortunately, no available data.

Law School Instruction in Professional Responsibility

Irrespective of the context of one's practice, when practitioners are asked to evaluate the contribution that their law school training has had in matters of ethical concern which have arisen in their practices, law schools receive very little credit (questionnaire, pt. IV, Q. 1, p. 18, appendix 1). As seen in the ranking of possible sources in table 7.1, only 11 percent of the practicing bar rank law school as the most important in resolving such questions of professional responsibility (Q. 3, p. 19). Another 18.9 percent rank law school second.

When law school is evaluated on its own rather than in comparison with other sources, it fares only somewhat better. Only 42.3 percent of the practicing bar even credit law school training with some material assistance in the resolution of problems of professional responsibility,[19] despite the exposure of approximately 80 percent of the sample to instruction in professional responsibility in law school.[20]

What is of particular interest in these data is the extent to which different law schools are given special credit for the development of the professional responsibility of its graduates. As shown in table 7.5, in the *relative* evaluation of law schools' contribution as compared with other sources, national law schools are given less credit than non-national schools. Table 7.6 shows that in response to a simple inquiry not requiring comparison with other sources, graduates of national law schools are also significantly less likely than graduates of non-national law schools to credit law school with material assistance in the resolution of issues of professional responsibility in their practices. These findings are consistent with Stevens's conclusion that "in general, education in legal ethics has been stressed more heavily at the 'regional' than the 'national' schools" (1973, p. 597).

The pattern persists if we look only at the graduates of the nine law schools that train most (79.9 percent) of the practicing bar in Chicago.

---

19. Another 7.2 percent claimed that no such problems had ever occurred, making the question irrelevant to their experience. That still leaves 50.5 percent who had such experiences but for whom law school training provided no material assistance.

20. These data must raise questions about the efficacy of the American Bar Association requirement that schools it accredits ensure that all degree candidates receive "instruction in the duties and responsibilities of the legal profession" (Standard 302(a)(iii), in *Approval of Law Schools*, 1977). Most practicing lawyers have received instruction that would meet this requirement, and yet they give it very little credit for inculcating standards of professional responsibility.

TABLE 7.5
Importance of Law School in Contributing to the
Resolution of Questions of Professional Respon-
sibility by Type of Law School

Type of Law School	% Rating Important[a]	N
National	20.6	209
Non-national	36.5	312

$\chi^2 = 14.40$; $p < 0.001$

Somers' $D = -0.160$
(asymmetric with
importance of law
school dependent)

[a]See table 7.3, note a, on the construction of the importance
variable.

TABLE 7.6
Law School's Consideration of Topics as Materially Aiding
in the Resolution of Problems of Legal Ethics or Professional Responsibility by Type of Law School

Type of Law School	% Answering Yes	% Answering No	N
National	33.3	66.7	144
Non-national	52.5	47.5	244

$\chi^2 = 12.60$; $p < .001$
(Somers' $D = -0.191$ (asymmetric with law school aid
dependent)

As is clear from table 7.7, a larger proportion of the graduates of the
locally oriented law schools rank their schools' contributions to the development of professional responsibility higher (as compared with other
sources). Table 7.8 shows that they are also significantly more likely
than graduates of the national schools to perceive of their legal education as materially aiding in the resolution of problems of professional
responsibility in practice even without considering other possible
sources.

It is somewhat ironic that the very schools that pride themselves on
being *professional* rather than *trade* schools are in fact placing little or
no emphasis on the special obligations of professional responsibility.[21]
This apparent irony can be explained by the conceptualization of professional development which underlies law school curricula. Consistent
with the emphasis on highly analytic intellective skills documented in

21. The relationship Carlin (1966) found between attendance at more prestigious law
schools and compliance with the Code of Professional Responsibility is more a function
of the nature of practice and the appropriateness of established norms to practitioners in
selected kinds of practice than of any important role played by law school training in inculcating the virtues of the Code of the organized bar.

TABLE 7.7
Importance of Law School's Contribution to Professional Responsibility
by Law School Attended

Law School[a]	% Rating Law School Very Important[b]	% Rating Law School Very Important	N
Harvard	12.9	87.1	31
Michigan	19.2	80.8	26
Chicago	17.0	83.0	53
Northwestern	26.2	73.8	61
Illinois	30.3	69.7	33
Loyola	36.4	63.6	33
IIT-Chicago Kent	40.0	60.0	35
DePaul	26.3	73.7	95
John Marshall	54.9	45.1	51

$\chi^2 = 28.67$; $p < 0.001$
Somers' $D = -0.122$ (asymmetric with importance of law school dependent)

[a]The law schools are listed in decreasing order of ascribed prestige. See chapter 3, table 3.14, for an explanation of the basis of this ordering.
[b]See table 7.3, note a, on the construction of the importance variable.

TABLE 7.8
Law School Consideration as Materially Aiding in the Resolution of
Problems of Professional Responsibility by Law School Attended

Law School	% Answering Yes	% Answering No	N
Harvard	35.7	64.3	14
Michigan	13.6	86.4	22
Chicago	35.7	64.3	28
Northwestern	35.8	64.2	53
Illinois	41.7	58.3	24
Loyola	48.3	51.7	29
Kent	60.0	40.0	25
DePaul	41.9	58.1	74
John Marshall	67.5	32.5	40
	134	175	

$\chi^2 = 22.82$; $p < .005$
Somers' $D = -0.138$
(asymmetric with law school aid dependent)

chapter 6, law schools in general, and those considered the most prestigious in particular, are perceived to concentrate almost exclusively on only one part of the traditional definition of a profession—that related to the arcane knowledge and specialized skills of its members. Although not completely ignored, the other more prominent characteristic of a profession—its obligation of service to the public good—is given extremely low priority (Pipkin, 1979).

An alternative hypothesis—that the Code of Professional Responsi-

bility is particularly inattentive to the needs of national law school graduates who disproportionately practice in settings very different from the
solo practice with individual clients envisioned in the Code—simply does
not hold up under investigation. For as is clearly shown in table 7.4, irrespective of the practice context, national law schools are less likely
than non-national schools to be cited as important to the development
of the professional responsibility of their graduates.

As noted earlier, law schools are now required to offer instruction in
professional responsibility for ABA accreditation. The data indicate,
however, that the coverage is viewed to be rather superficial, with only
25 percent of the practitioners reporting considerable emphasis on this
topic in their law school experiences. Consistent with the emphasis on
legal rules, the typical coverage concentrated exclusively upon the
Canons of Professional Ethics or the Code of Professional Responsibility, whichever was applicable at the time, as well as cases and decisions
of disciplinary bodies. It is the rare attorney who tells us, as one respondent did, that his or her school dealt with the "broad significance of
[the attorney's] role in society." That is to say that where law schools
have attempted instruction in professional responsibility they are generally perceived to be treating the concept as a unidimensional morality
of duty directly represented in the Code.

In contrast, the responses of the practicing bar present a more complex multidimensional conceptualization of professional responsibility.
This view is, in part, reflected in suggestions for curricular change.
Despite the extremely limited contribution to professional responsibility
attributed to law school, 94.1 percent of the respondents still support
curricular consideration of the issue (Q. 2, p. 18).[22] Yet the reasons
given for this general opinion reveal both the perceived complexity of
professional responsibility and the inherent dichotomy between a morality of duty and a morality of aspiration. Close to 30 percent of the respondents support the teaching of professional responsibility in law
school because, in the words of one respondent, "lawyers often make
mistakes and need to be aware of these issues to avoid problems."
Another 22 percent emphasize a different aspect of professional responsibility, the need to maintain the integrity of the bar.[23] These differing
views are reflected in the following responses:

22. As indicated in part IV of the questionnaire (pp. 18–19, appendix 1), the terms
"legal ethics" and "professional responsibility" were both used throughout the study to
make the questions applicable to the entire sample, since prior to the adoption of the
Code of Professional Responsibility in 1969 the bar was guided by the Canons of Professional Ethics originally adopted by the ABA in 1908. Throughout the remainder of this
book all references to data on the teaching of professional responsibility should be taken
to include professional ethics for those respondents who graduated from law school
before 1970.

23. So as not to influence the responses, the question simply asked why law schools
should or should not teach professional responsibility. Without forced-choice responses
provided (Q. 2, p. 18) a coding scheme then had to be developed to classify responses. The
categories were created on the basis of the responses, with no efforts to fit them into pre-
determined niches. The actual codes into which the responses fell were: (30 percent) an-

> Law school can teach what rules are and that lawyers can get in trouble for violating them.
>
> Law schools have a responsibility to produce good lawyers who are not only good technicians but honest and ethical individuals.

These data should not be taken to imply that practicing lawyers necessarily have one conception of professional responsibility or another. For in addition to these and various individualized responses, many of the respondents indicate the importance of both role-specific and general ethics, and a dual morality. Thus, for example, one respondent indicates that professional responsibility should be taught because a lawyer must know how to meld obligation to client with sense of right and wrong. Another says that instruction both "reduces/eliminates chance of disbarment" and "upholds professional integrity." Still another states that

> apart from practical reasons of avoiding discipline and/or government regulation, and apart from the individual necessity of self-respect, the prestige of the profession requires and obligates its individual members to be persons of honesty, integrity, and respect.

Perception of the complexity of professional responsibility is not limited only to those who support law school instruction in the area. One respondent who recognizes the dual nature of professional responsibility rejects the idea of law school consideration of the topic on the dual grounds that

> ethical questions are most often answered by a person's own moral values [and] technical problems can be looked up in the Canons.

Not surprisingly, 61.9 percent of the respondents think that law school instruction in professional responsibility should be substantially broadened. It appears that the emergence of a strong sentiment that professional responsibility should extend substantially beyond the Code is, if anything, somewhat understated in the data. The question of whether law school instruction has materially aided in the resolution of problems in professional responsibility focuses on incidents rather than overall approaches to the practice of law. Despite that bias, however, the respondents have made clear and insightful distinctions.

In response to the question "What else would you include?" (in the teaching of professional responsibility) (Q. 2, p. 18), several quite different additions are mentioned: 41.3 percent suggest that practical applications of daily encounters with the Code be provided, another 30.6 percent stress establishing a "sense of social responsibility," including, but not exclusively, "general moral responsibility," "humanity," and standards "above the current morality of the marketplace"; another 5.3 percent want coverage of a general code of conduct, an interpersonal or

---

swers that suggest that lawyers lack awareness of problems or that many commit mistakes and (22 percent) answers to the effect that it is essential to maintain the integrity of the bar and/or profession. Of those who gave reasons, about 8 percent were reasons why *not* to offer instruction in professional responsibility.

"client relations" approach. The following are individual elaborations on these different perspectives. The code-oriented lawyer reflecting a morality of duty suggests "more case studies of lawyers who were disbarred or suspended" or information about the "malpractice risk." A morality of aspiration is inherent in the recommendations that law schools "teach [the] obligation to assist society to understand how to govern itself for its own best interest," or provide an "analysis of [the] role lawyers play in society and government as [a] basis for high standards of conduct," or "should go beyond codified rules to ethical bases for decision-making in practice."

Again not all lawyers can be easily classified along one dimension or another, for many respond with references to more than one facet of professional responsibility. Some even acknowledge the potential conflicts among its different dimensions. For example, in response to an inquiry into what should be included in formal instruction beyond the Code, one respondent mentions "the inherent conflict of advancing a client's position and being an officer of the court."

The interpretation of the variance in conceptualization is supported when we compare the sources to which development of professional responsibility is attributed with the suggestions for law school coverage of professional responsibility. As indicated in table 7.9, there is a statisti-

TABLE 7.9
Percent Distribution of Respondents Ranking General Upbringing Important in Development of Sense of Legal Ethics or Professional Responsibility by Suggested Additions to Curriculum ($N = 206$)

Contribution of General Upbringing	Suggested Additions to Cirriculum			
	Practical Application of Code ($N = 85$)[a]	Interpersonal Relations ($N = 11$)	Social Responsbility ($N = 63$)	Other ($N = 47$)
Rank 1 ($N = 128$)[b]	35.9	4.7	34.4	25.0
Rank 2 ($N = 35$)	37.1	14.3	22.9	25.7
Not important ($N = 43$)	60.5	0.0	25.6	14.0

$$\chi^2 = 16.02; \; p < 0.05$$

[a] The Ns under the column headings indicate the number of lawyers suggesting each type of addition.
[b] The Ns under the ranks represent the number of lawyers who ranked general upbringing first, second, or not very important in development of a sense of professional responsibility and who also suggested additions to the law school curriculum (questionnaire, pt. IV, Q. 2, p. 18, appendix 1). For example, of those ranking upbringing 1 who also suggested additions, 35.9 recommended a course in applying the Code.

cally significant relationship between crediting general upbringing with influencing professional responsibility in practice and recommendations for curricular change. About 35 percent of those who emphasize general upbringing (rank 1 or 2) suggest further applications of the Code, in contrast to 60 percent of those who do not think general upbringing is important. The conceptualization one holds of professional responsibility is thus similarly reflected in both perceptions of sources of influence and notions of the appropriate direction for law school instruction. In the aggregate the credit given to general upbringing along with suggestions for a broader curricular approach indicate that most of the practicing bar view professional responsibility as extending well beyond the Code and as substantially coinciding with general ethics.

While the inference may be drawn from the distribution depicted in table 7.1 that lawyers believe prior socialization to have the *most* important impact on later professional behavior, it does not necessarily follow that they do not consider subsequent experiences to have an effect. Indeed, it is telling that among attorneys who rate their general upbringing as most important to their professional behavior there is a clear call for further consideration of personal and social responsibility within the law school curriculum, presumably as they are manifested concretely in the practice of law.

Despite protestations to the contrary, then, many lawyers perceive a connection, although not an equivalency, between professional responsibility and personal ethics.[24] To some extent the confusion in the literature is a problem of semantics. Terms such as "ethics" and "responsibility," which in normal language are used to describe an individual's character, are given specialized and different definitions—for example, the extent to which one abides by rules set down as minimal standards of behavior to be practiced within one's occupational role.

Yet much of what lawyers do, and the basis of much of their image, has to do with interpersonal relationships not all that dissimilar from the kinds in which all persons engage. This was shown quite clearly in chapter 6 in the bar's estimation of the skills most important to the practice

---

24. Curiously, and despite explicit statements that professional responsibility is quite distinct from personal ethics, there has been a tendency to attribute low standards of personal character to those who violate the rules embodied in the Code of Professional Responsibility. This is particularly striking since some of the prohibited behavior would hardly constitute unethical behavior in the normal usage of that term. The slippery implied interchangeability between practice context and personal characteristics (as they influence professional behavior) found in the sociological literature can be traced to the work of Hughes (1958):

> A lawyer may be asked whether he and his client come into court with clean hands; when he answers, "yes," it may mean that someone else's hands are of necessity a bit grubby. For not only are some quarrels more respectable, more clean, than others; but also some of the kinds of work involved in the whole system (gathering evidence, getting clients, bringing people to court, enforcing judgments, making the compromises that keep cases out of court) are more respected and more removed from temptation and suspicion than others. In fact, the division of labor among lawyers is as much one of respectability (hence of self concept and role) as of specialized knowledge and skills. One might even call it a moral division of labor, if one keeps in mind that the term means not simply that some lawyers, or people in the various branches of law work, are more moral than others; but that the very demand for highly scrupulous and respectable lawyers depends in various ways upon the availability of less scrupulous people to attend to the less respectable legal problems of even the best people (p. 71).

The extent to which those attending to "less respectable legal problems" are themselves "less scrupulous people" is undocumented. Indeed it is possible to argue that the determination of what is "less respectable" legal work is itself a function of who determines the rules.

of law, among them instilling confidence, effective oral expression, and understanding the viewpoint of others. Despite the low marks law schools receive for developing these skills, most new lawyers are expected to bring these skills with them to their first law job. Indeed, these are skills that may be developed at an early age and are applicable in a number of occupational pursuits. The same can be said of many of the characteristics and much of the behavior of the professionally "responsible." That is to say, they are considerate of others with whom they deal, and they act honestly and with integrity. In the particular context of the lawyer role, they return clients' telephone calls, they keep clients abreast of the progress of their cases, they provide a reasonable amount of attention to them, and they do not procrastinate. They do their best to establish at the outset just what work will be done and how much it will cost. While these standards are not in any way unique to lawyering, they are essential to it because of the people centeredness of most law practice.[25]

The cases actually brought to bar disciplinary committees also reflect the centrality of general standards of personal responsibility in the lawyer-client relationship. For example, a study of complaints received by the disciplinary agency in Michigan reveals that more than half (52.7 percent) of the client complaints (with client complaints constituting three-quarters of all complaints) center on fees, delay, neglect, or inaction (Steele & Nimmer, 1976, p. 976). While some of these complaints may simply reflect dissatisfaction with the outcome of one's case, there is good reason to believe that a responsible person can do much to ease the likelihood that such dissatisfaction will be focused upon the attorney.

Recognition of the importance of these matters is also reflected in the 1975 pamphlet of the ABA Standing Committee on Professional Discipline and the Center for Professional Discipline of the ABA, *Professional Responsibility and the Lawyer: Avoiding Unintentional Grievances*. Among the items discussed that might be classified as personal rather than peculiarly professional responsibility are fee disputes, procrastination, and creating unreasonable expectations. What we are suggesting is that the lawyer's obligation to the client, indeed behavior that will enable members of the bar to fulfill their role to contribute to the administration and distribution of justice, requires personally responsible behavior that is in no way unique to the practice of law. Personally irresponsible behavior comes to constitute one dimension of professional irresponsibility when it occurs within the context of the practice of law. The following anecdote provides an apt example.

Another example of little tricks of the trade to build up a reputation to get

25. It should be noted that a number of these issues have been directly addressed in the discussion draft of the new Model Rules of Professional Conduct. See especially Rule 1.2 on "Promptness" (p. 10) and Rule 1.4 on "Adequate Communication" (p. 12). No action has yet been taken on these proposed rules (see note 10 *supra*).

> business and keep business is if I call up Joe Blow and say, "I've got $10,000 if you settle this suit right now." He says, "Okay, let me check with my client and get back with you." He calls the client now and says, "I've got $7,500. But if you let me work on this for a day or two, I think I can get you ten." He tells the client that and comes back and says, "We'll take your ten." You know, I've got that release and receipt already in my mind, a draft and release situation for dismissal, and I'm all set. And if we get it done and I see the client who happens to be a friend of mine, he says, "Boy, that guy, he just did me a hell of a job and he told me that I should tell everybody in the countryside what a good lawyer he is and how good a job he did for me." I got that extra $2,500. . . (Pretest, Indianapolis, May 31, 1975).

Our attorney is complaining about the unethical behavior of his fellow lawyer, his dishonesty for the purpose of self-promotion. Both the speaker and his fellow lawyers in the group where the story was related considered the behavior to be "unprofessional." Although that is the kind of situation with which neither the Code nor courses on professional responsibility deal, it is precisely that kind of encounter that, when discovered, diminishes esteem for the profession.[26]

The respondents also indicated a belief that professional responsibility extends beyond the obligation to client. Like the late Karl Llewellyn they recognize that the obligation to society as officer of the court and that which derives from representation of the client are in many ways self-contradictory:

> Duty to client reads in terms of taking advantage of each technicality the law may show, however senseless. It reads in terms of distortion of evidence and argument to the utter bounds of the permissible. Duty to court reads in terms of shaping every piece of the machinery that can be made to give, toward better functioning. It reads in terms of trying issues of fact to reach the probable truth (1933, pp. 181–82).

Despite the inconsistent directives, the lawyer is provided few if any clear guidelines for making the choices that inevitably arise in practice. According to Llewellyn, the tension has been resolved in favor of the client. His conclusion is supported by the absence of any further references to the obligation to society (or, more particularly, to what that might mean in terms of the actual practice of law), beyond the Preamble and selected general headings of the Code of Professional Responsibility. While the "vanishing tradition . . . of the lawyer as an officer of the judicial institution" of which Llewellyn speaks may always have been more image than substance, the tradition itself is strongly reflected in the following suggestions by practitioners as to the role that law schools ought to play in the development of professional responsibility among its students (Q. 2, p. 18):

26. It is also the kind of issue that is not likely to be considered in the disciplinary process, with its dependence on client complaints—in this case because the client is unaware of the chain of events.

the school should attempt to instill in each student the concept that without law—fairly administered—society fails

sense of social responsibility

analysis of [the] role lawyers play in society and government as [a] basis
for high standards of conduct

teach [the] obligation to assist society to understand how to govern itself
for its own best interest

Such opinions emerged despite the fact that more than 60 percent of the
respondents who received some instruction in law school had exposure
only to the Canons of Professional Ethics, the Code of Professional Responsibility, and/or documented cases of violations.

Thus, there is still substantial support for the view that "the function
of a law school [is] to train the students to think and to be sensitive to
the broader issues of justice, not just [to] produce trade specialists in
legal services."[27] Indeed, the tradition to which Llewellyn refers must be
considered to constitute one dimension of the concept we call professional responsibility.[28] It is this socioprofessional role of the lawyer, in
particular, that is neglected in law school. Only 25.6 percent of the
respondents said that their law schools ever raised any question of a
lawyer's special responsibility to comment on attempts to use the law for
social goals, and 66.2 percent of those perceived the issue to have been
raised exclusively in one course or in connection with the consideration
of particular topics (Q. 4, p. 20):

Exposure in law school to a lawyer's special responsibility to con-
template changes in the law is directly related to lawyers' perceptions of
that responsibility: 84.2 percent ($N = 542$) of practicing lawyers are inclined to "think that lawyers, *as legal professionals*, have a special obligation to take a stand and/or speak out on issues where legal changes
are contemplated as a mechanism to affect the society," with most (69.4
percent) responding that they *definitely* have such a responsibility.[29]
Even with such a large proportion of the bar in agreement on their
special responsibility, lawyers are significantly more likely to indicate

27. Judge Malcolm Wilkey, of the U.S. Court of Appeals, D.C. Circuit, in remarks
made during his participation in a panel sponsored by the Section on Legal Education and
Admissions to the Bar at the 1977 Annual Meeting of the American Bar Association, Chicago, Illinois, August 8, 1977.

28. Actually resolution of the tension between duty to client and duty to the court has
evolved into a merging of the two, such that fulfilling one obligation is taken to be
equivalent to fulfilling the other. Lawyers' contributions to the social justice of the legal
system have been assumed to follow naturally from the adversary system and the behavior
it requires, most particularly the obligation to the individual client. See Morgan (1977) for
a discussion of the Code's bias toward protection of the profession rather than the client
and Rosenthal (1974) for a study revealing the fundamental economic conflict of interest
between lawyer and client in personal injury claims.

29. See questionnaire (pt. V, Q. 3, p. 19). Responses were given on a 4-point scale according to the following categories: "definitely," "somewhat," "not more than any responsible citizen," and "not at all." The 84.2 percent represents those who selected one
of the first two categories; the 69.6 percent selected the strongest positive response.

support of this obligation if the matter was covered in their own law school experiences ($\chi^2 = 9.81$, $p < 0.05$). The perceived obligation to speak out on issues affecting the society is also not uniformly distributed among graduates of different types of law schools, with those from national law schools significantly less likely to perceive that obligation ($\chi^2 = 14.13$, $p < 0.005$) than those from non-national law schools.[30] Again the graduates of the national law schools present a narrower, more technically based value-free perception of professionalism.

There is a similar pattern with respect to our inquiry into curricular consideration of the potential social impact of the law. Almost 60 percent of the bar (59.8 percent of 537 lawyers) believe the potential social impact of the law was touched on in law school. Yet again, most (61.9 percent of 289 lawyers) indicate that such consideration was given in the context of selected courses, particularly constitutional law (54.9 percent) and criminal law (31.0 percent), two areas of law that have the most obvious public impact. While such consideration is surely appropriate, its restrictive nature implies that the rest of the law, indeed the areas in which most lawyers practice, do not have the same potential to affect society, that the role played by lawyers who practice in other areas is relevant only to those persons directly involved in a given controversy. That view, however, simply does not comport with the reality of the role of law in the American polity.

In a common law system where considerable law is judge made, lawyers have long contributed to and focused the development of the law that is to guide behavior (Hurst, 1950). The very nature of law dictates that the rules articulated in a judicial decision are applicable well beyond the parties to the controversy. The bulk of law work does not take place in courtrooms and is not focused on the development of new legal principles. Indeed the sociopolitical impact of lawyers extends well beyond their role in contributing to judge-made law. It is in the day-to-day mobilization of the law, the invocation of legal norms to regulate behavior,[31] that lawyers exert enormous distributive impact. Although the single legal matter handled by an attorney only rarely has a substantial distributive effect, it is in the aggregation of the multitude of individual issues that lawyers' behavior has its broadest impact.[32] It is this perva-

30. There is no relationship between an attorney's age and response to this question. In contrast to what might be expected, there is not even a trend for younger attorneys, particularly the 1960s cohort, to have a greater sense of obligation to speak out.

31. This definition of legal mobilization is taken from Lempert's essay, "Mobilizing Private Law," in *Law and Society Review* (1976); see footnote 1, p. 173, for an elaboration of that definition, and footnote 2 for a discussion over Black's widely cited definition of legal mobilization as "the process by which a legal system acquires its cases," with law defined as "governmental social control" (1973, p. 126).

32. See, for example, studies of insurance claims adjustment in H. Laurence Ross, *Settled Out of Court: The Social Process of Insurance Claims Adjustment* (Chicago: Aldine Publishing Co., 1970) and consumer protection laws in Stewart Macaulay, "Lawyers and Consumer Protection Laws: An Empirical Study," Working Paper 1979-1 Disputes Processing Research Program (Madison, Wisconsin: University of Wisconsin Law School, 1979).

sive social role of law and its practitioners to which legal education gives little attention. Given the highly technical, client-specific conceptualization of the practice of law which underlies both legal education and the Code of Professional Responsibility, it would be somewhat surprising were it otherwise.

The Potential for Law School Instruction in Professional Responsibility

Discussions of the teaching of professional responsibility in law school are grounded upon anticipation of having some effect, presumably a positive one, on the practice of law. Yet even having documented the limited role law schools currently assume in promoting professional responsibility, and considering the urgings of practitioners that they do more, it is not necessarily immediately obvious just what law schools can or should do.[33]

As currently constituted with its emphasis upon the analysis of appellate opinions, legal education is particularly appropriate for inculcating a morality of duty by means of instruction in the limits set by the Code. In 1933 Llewellyn noted that the case method, the traditional teaching technique, was a peculiar way to teach ethics:

> so far as ethical training is concerned, the study of authoritative rulings tends rather to a training in unethics, being a careful delineation of precisely how far the lawyer can go *without* disbarment, with copious suggestions as to how to do most of the things lawyers ought not to be doing (p. 185).

While such information may be necessary for practicing lawyers, it is not sufficient given their multidimensional and aspirational conceptualizations of professional responsibility. Even Llewellyn, so cognizant of its limited potential, did not completely dismiss instruction in legal ethics. He acknowledged that "to spread instances before the future lawyer will inform him of some of the problems he must face" (p. 185). Yet the instruction offered often misses this mark.

Now that instruction in professional responsibility is necessary for ABA accreditation, law schools offer and require students to take instruction deemed to meet the ABA standard. Typically it is a course with "professional responsibility" in the title, but sometimes it is a more general course on "the legal profession" with at least some consideration of the responsibilities of the profession.[34] While the ultimate goal of such

33. It is worth recalling the data presented in chapter 3 with respect to the values and orientations toward the practice of law which new students bring with them to law school. The data indicate that the perceptions of the lawyer's role by future lawyers do not reveal much recognition of some of the facets of professional responsibility elaborated above. Neither working with people nor being helpful to individuals or to society is given much weight in the selection of careers in the law.

34. Law schools are not alone in the flurry of attention being accorded to ethical concerns. Half of the medical schools in the United States have either departments or regular programs in ethics, with virtually all schools offering at least one course on medical ethics. For a review of the issues involved and a survey of programs see Robert M. Veatch, Willard Gaylin, and Councilman Morgan, eds., *The Teaching of Medical Ethics* (Hastings-

courses may be to convey an understanding of the broad social role of the profession, the presentation is often abstract or couched in hypotheticals that the student has not experienced and cannot easily imagine.

Given the continuing socialization perceived by the practitioners, what, we may ask, is the peculiar role, if any, of formal instruction in professional responsibility in law school, and to what extent is legal education as currently constituted appropriate to the task? As noted in a recent text on professional responsibility, "ethical issues always arise in a context and abstract discussion of them without reference to that context is unproductive" (Morgan & Rotunda, 1976, p. xvii). If abstract discussion of ethical issues is unproductive, what is the desirable approach?

Growing recognition of the need to deal with ethical issues in context is reflected in the expansion of clinical education as a forum for instruction in professional responsibility. The Council on Legal Education for Professional Responsibility, Inc. (CLEPR) has funded such programs, presumably on the assumption that they contribute to the development of professionally responsible behavior. Indeed, in a commentary on a major study financed by CLEPR (Gee & Jackson, 1977), Barnhizer argues that "the most unique capabilities of the clinical method lie within the goal category of professional responsibility." He presents "a specifically adapted model of the clinical method designed to teach an affirmative system of professional responsibility" and offers this model "as the best available method by which an affirmative, coherent, and personalized system of professional values and responsibility can be created for most law students" (1977, pp. 1034–35). Certainly active clinic participation provides experience with real cases which traditional approaches do not. Instead of abstract legal doctrine, law students are faced with real persons and their very human problems. With proper guidance the pervasive relevance of interpersonal behavior and skills to the practice of law can be conveyed. Such programs, however, are severely circumscribed by the limited applicability of the bulk of the cases encountered to the practice that most law students will pursue. As Barnhizer observes, among "the issues and problems clinical students can experience as they function as lawyers" are "racism; dissimilar treatment of poor people; abuses against certain classes of people by judges, prosecutors, other lawyers, and police" (1977, p. 1040). While such experience is worthwhile for every future lawyer, it is likely to have only limited direct transferability to their own practices. To the extent that clinical legal

---

on-Hudson, N.Y.: The Hastings Center, 1973) and Robert M. Veatch and Sharmon Sollitto, "Medical Ethics Teaching: Report of a National Medical School Survey," 235 *JAMA: Journal of the American Medical Association* 1030 (1976). A similar phenomenon is found in other professional schools and in preprofessional courses. For example, Cornell Law School established a Center for Law, Ethics and Religion in 1976, designed, according to its director, John Lee Smith, to "provide occasions where students can see moral issues hidden in legal jargon and technicality" (Fiske, 1978, p. B8).

education is meant to provide the "practical" experience missing in the traditional curriculum, the typical experiences do not meet this need.[35]

There is, however, quite another aspect of professional responsibility which is conveyed by these experiences precisely because of the skew in types of cases encountered in law school clinics: it is here that some of the less attractive realities of the law and its roles in society may become glaringly apparent.[36] Still, the clinic experience as a whole provides a very limited and skewed picture of the breadth of issues involved in professional responsibility, given the practice settings in which most law students will later find themselves, at least under current market demands for legal services.

While there is surely a content to professional responsibility—indeed we have discussed just how extensive and complex it is—it is not substantive in the sense that it can be conceptualized as an area of law; it is, rather, a way of doing lawyering, an approach, and probably to some extent a state of mind. It is also a cognitive capacity of valuation. Like "thinking like a lawyer," it pervades the practice of law; unlike "thinking like a lawyer," it does not pervade the curriculum. Rather, we have seen that in most cases and for the various dimensions of professional responsibility considered in law school, it is set apart. No one would suggest such an arrangement for teaching the analytic skills considered basic to the lawyering process; indeed, the typical law school curriculum is designed to teach the method of the law and the skills for using it. That curricular design does not change whether the particular course is torts, contracts, constitutional law, or property. It is anticipated that when delving into a new area of the law the lawyer will be able to perform proficiently because of the equal applicability of the same analytic skills. It is in this respect that lawyers are still trained as generalists capable, with some experience, of practicing in a number of unrelated substantive areas of the law.

There has been some recognition that a more pervasive approach to instruction in professional responsibility would be more appropriate to the task, that to segregate professional responsibility as a separate course takes it out of the context in which it will be relevant in practice. This is not a new idea. One of the resolutions adopted at the 1968 National Conference on Education in the Professional Responsibilities of the Lawyer was: *"Be it Resolved* that this Conference encourages casebook authors to include more materials on professional responsibility in their books and encourages the publication of additional pervasive ap-

---

35. This limitation, it should be cautioned, is not necessarily inherent in the clinical model but rather emerges from the programs as currently oriented toward the legal needs of the poor.

36. In addition, given what we have shown in chapter 4 about the stability of law practice, both substantively and contextually, such experience may have the effect of influencing some law students to pursue careers in the law more oriented toward the people and problems encountered in clinical practice than the careers they would otherwise have entered.

proach materials'' (Weckstein, 1970, p. 356). In practice, however, the response to this resolution has been limited and typically restricted to selected areas of the law and the law school curriculum which are deemed appropriate for consideration of the attorney's professional responsibility.[37] Yet it is precisely in those areas where the ethical questions are less obvious that law school may be able to play an important role in sensitizing lawyers to the continuous and universal relevance of professional responsibility to the lawyer's role.

The very nature of the case method with its reliance upon appellate opinions may itself preclude consideration of some dimensions of professional responsibility. Certainly the lawyer's interpersonal relationship with the client remains totally outside the educative process if the materials of instruction are, exclusively, selected written opinions of appellate courts with the ''facts'' filtered through a judge's reading of a lower court hearing and no mention or recognition of the circumstances of a controversy which have not been admitted into evidence. Yet much of a lawyer's exercise of professional responsibility occurs in the office when a client seeks assistance with a problem. This is the level of interaction to which Cahn and Cahn (1970) refer when they criticize law schools for rewarding ''removal from the chaotic world of emotion, events, passions and people to the rarefied stratosphere of metaphysical debate'' (p. 1027).[38]

The importance of this fuller view of the lawyer-client relationship is not limited to the interpersonal dimension of professional responsibility.

37. The presentation of a relatively broader view of professional responsibility has been attempted within the context of particular substantive courses, as is reported in chapter 4, ''The Pervasive Approach,'' in the published proceedings of the 1968 conference (Weckstein, 1970, pp. 113-78). Monroe Freedman, for example, has included issues of professional responsibility beyond the Code in his contracts course (Freedman, 1970), and A. Leo Levin, in the teaching of advocacy and civil procedure (Levin, 1970). To use the pervasive approach, Levin says, is ''to pause while studying a substantive problem in order to probe in depth the related demands of the profession upon the lawyer'' (p. 135). As an example, he cites a discussion of discovery rules, which would include consideration of tactical use and abuse of the procedures, the ethics of utilizing ''discovery to harass, to increase the likelihood of settlement because you are hurting the other side'' (p. 136). The preparation of witnesses provides another area ''rich in ethical problems'' which Levin discusses at some length and with an appreciation for the complexities and subtleties of the issues involved (pp. 143-44). One example of a school-wide program designed to teach professional responsibility by the pervasive method is the ''planned pervasive'' approach instituted in January 1974 at Brigham Young University. This program, however, is limited by its strong orientation toward the Code as reflecting the core issues in professional responsibility. (See Memorandum, ''Report on 1974-75 Experience,'' Ed Kimball, Coordinator for Professional Responsibility Training, to Law Faculty, May 1, 1975, J. Reuben Clark Law School, Brigham Young University.)

38. It should be noted that there has been a flurry of activity in the development of new materials and approaches to the teaching of professional responsibility in recent years. Examples of newer tests include Redlich's *Professional Responsibility* (1976) and Kaufman's *Problems in Professional Responsibility* (1976). Although the practitioners who provided the data for this analysis were not exposed to the most recent changes, new law students who have been do not rate their law school instruction in professional responsibility any differently (Pipkin, 1979).

Indeed the fulfillment of the lawyer's more traditional obligation to zealously represent the client's interests not infrequently depends upon a choice of which legal argument to make, the selection of statutory or case law that most closely supports the client's side. Informed decision making, in turn, directly depends upon the fullest possible understanding of all the circumstances surrounding a controversy. Again we find that professional responsibility is similar to skill development in its importance to practice and in its neglect by law schools. In chapter 6 we discussed the poor marks lawyers give to law schools for training in the nuances of negotiating or the details of fact gathering, both considered to be extremely important to the practice of law by the practitioners themselves. There as here we allude to the limits of strict reliance on appellate opinions if such skills are to be recognized and developed during law school training.

Although it is certainly the norm, not all legal education is based exclusively upon consideration of appellate court opinions. Some recently published texts reflect conscious efforts to avoid upper court opinions as the sole basis of analysis by their inclusion of actual court transcripts. These encourage students to consider the development of an entire case with attention given to the extensive nonadversarial role of the American lawyer.[39] While such approaches open the way for consideration of professional responsibility in the context within which the lawyer must face it, they need substantial expansion if they are to cover the more socially oriented dimensions of professional responsibility. These include questions about and discussion of things like the costs of litigation, including contigent fees and their effects on the distribution of legal services; the filing of spurious law suits, as in some medical malpractice and automobile accident cases; excessive procrastination of cases that may "wear down" the other side and use up scarce court resources; and litigiousness that keeps disputes alive to the detriment of both the client and the larger society. These are examples of very real issues in professional responsibility which the practicing attorney faces but for which law schools provide very little assistance.

One representative view of the limits of law school training in professional responsibility is UCLA law professor Murray Schwartz's observation that "the orientation of most law faculty members is that of skepticism; moreover, liberal ideology and notions of academic restraint tend to preclude deliberate efforts to affect the moral standards or values of the students" (1974, p. 20). While this view appears to raise a difficult problem of principle, it may in fact be something of a cop-out by legal academics on two different counts. First, failure to even raise the ethical questions implies support for the extant arrangement, that there are only technical and few if any normative matters involved in the lawyering

---

39. See as examples of these modes Lempert and Saltzburg's *A Modern Approach to Evidence* (1977) and Brown and Dauer's *Planning by Lawyers: Materials on a Nonadversarial Legal Process* (1978).

role. This is, indeed, part of what Cornell Law School dean Roger C. Cramton characterizes as the "ordinary religion of the law school classroom," a "short-hand expression" for "the unarticulated value system" of law schools (1978, p. 248). Since, as the argument goes, lawyers are merely skilled technicians engaged in the implementation of clients' values, they need not themselves be directly concerned with values. As Cramton goes on to point out, however, "the process of socialization by which a law student becomes a lawyer involves the . . . acceptance of these accepted truths about law and lawyering" (p. 248). Second, to acknowledge the value choices inherent in the work of the lawyer is not to actually make value choices for the student. As former University of Michigan Law School dean Theodore J. St. Antoine observed in 1975, "it is one thing for a conscientious teacher to refrain from making a student's ultimate value choice for him, and quite another to refuse so totally to come to grips with these fundamental issues that the student is left to infer that value judgments are no significant part of a lawyer's function" (p. 50). Actually that message is not left to student inference, for a strong message regarding the place of values pervades the curriculum and the academy's approach to the law: it is a message, at best, of the low priority of values or, at worst, of their total irrelevance.[40]

Conclusion

Any attempt to promote desirable behavior patterns can be approached as a morality of duty or a morality of aspiration. In situations where the behavior is considered critical to the organization of the society or to the particular role involved, minimal standards are typically established. Such standards can be clearly delineated and operationalized to provide for the determination of violations. That is the nature of the positive law. It is also the essence of the bulk of the Code of Professional Responsibility to which lawyers are obligated to conform. In addition, it is the orientation taken by legal education toward the law in general and toward professional responsibility in particular. The role of the practicing lawyer to use legal skills so as to minimize the requirements of the law for clients is consistent with that approach.

When it comes to the teaching of professional responsibility, the focus is similarly on the "rule." This translates to instruction in the Code of Professional Responsibility and actual cases and opinions of bar association grievance proceedings. This orientation gives the impression that the topic can be researched much like any legal question.

As we have noted, Llewellyn (1933) referred to this focus on the Code as "training in unethics," that is, learning what *not* to do rather than what one *ought* to do to merit the appellation "professional." If being a

---

40. There is no doubt that the time spent on the ethical dimension is time, however limited, not spent on more traditional materials. The decision to concentrate on legal doctrine and analytic techniques to the exclusion of the ethical issues is, of course, in itself a reflection of the priorities of legal education.

professional entails the kind of social responsibility and contribution to the public good that the legislative granting of powers of self-regulation presumes, then a more aspirational orientation needs to be adopted. There is, to be sure, nothing in such an orientation that prohibits inculcation of the minimal standards below which one is expected not to fall and for which some negative sanction may follow. For as Fuller points out, the two moralities represent different ends of a single scale "starting at the bottom with the conditions obviously essential to social life and ending at the top with the loftiest strivings toward human excellence. The lower rungs of this scale represent the morality of duty; its higher reaches, the morality of aspiration" (1969, p. 27).

A similar scale exists within the Code itself, divided as it is between the duties of the Disciplinary Rules and the aspirations of the Ethical Considerations. Being a morality of duty, only the Disciplinary Rules are subject to enforcement; yet it is the Ethical Considerations, a morality of aspiration, that actually embody the norms of professionalism. As a morality of aspiration, these norms are not subject to the direct enforcement appropriate to the Disciplinary Rules. That does not, however, necessarily dictate that formal training in professional responsibility be confined to those aspects that are similar in kind to positive law and therefore more amenable to the traditional mode of law school instruction.

The duality of moralities in the enterprise of promoting professionally responsible attorneys is inherent in most socialization processes from child rearing through formal education and beyond. Education generally, whether formal or informal, encompasses inculcating minimal standards of acceptable conduct or achievement as well as aspirations toward higher goals. Thus, parents do not limit themselves to "the rules" but encourage their children to reach toward those values and achievements they deem important. In formal education the process is much the same. Students are required to attain a minimal level of competence, but that is hardly the ultimate goal of the educational process. The difference between education and training is not in the minimal level of competence required. Rather, it is in the morality of aspiration, inherent only in education, which encourages and promotes continual striving toward goals of excellence. Although the role of law school in promoting professionally responsible behavior is much more restricted than the influence of parents and other agents of early socialization, the analogy holds with respect to the duality between minimal standards and aspirational goals and to the absence of any inherent conflict between them. Indeed, the minimal standards should be the first step toward the aspirational goals. Yet in practice the morality of duty in the Code is often taken to represent the totality of professionalism—a stance that sharply narrows and may distort the very concept of professional responsibility.

Any evaluation of law schools' potential to encourage professionally responsible behavior needs to take into account the multidimensional nature of the concept as reflected in the responses of the practitioners.

In addition to some of the principles of obligation to client embodied in the Code, practicing lawyers put substantial emphasis on both the interpersonal and social dimensions of professional responsibility and the interweaving of various strands of this highly complex concept. They also implicitly endorse a developmental-interactive view of the socialization process (Tapp & Levine, 1974). Although they are influences separated by a substantial time period, the lawyers in our sample pointed to "general upbringing" and "lawyers in their own offices" as the most important influences on their professional responsibility. It is instructive that this view does not narrowly limit ethical development either to childhood or to the role-specific environment of law practice. There is, furthermore, general agreement on the poor record of legal education in contributing substantially to professional responsibility however it is conceptualized.[41]

It is the difference in the conceptualization of just what constitutes legal ethics and professional responsibility that accounts for much of the controversy over the appropriate role for law schools to play and for varying evaluations of that role to date in contributing to professionally responsible behavior by law school graduates. According to one commentator:

> Legal ethics, like politeness on subways, kindness to children, or fidelity in marriage, cannot to great effect be taught in school or enforced by third parties.
> The observed ethical standards are largely a consequence of the social and professional environment (Schnapper, 1978, p. 205).

While at first glance that summary statement of the limited influence that law schools and enforcement have on the ethical standards of the bar seems apt, some elaboration is needed if it is not to be taken to prove much more than it actually does.

First, we do not know what effects active enforcement of the Code might have, for the actual threat of sanction is extremely small. There is strong evidence (Carlin, 1966; Steele & Nimmer, 1976) that only a minute proportion of complaints against lawyers for unprofessional conduct results in any unfavorable action against them.[42] In addition, there

---

41. It would be interesting to follow young lawyers through their careers and periodically evaluate their conceptions of professional responsibility and related behavior, and the changes that do or do not occur. Although we do not have the data to do such an analysis, we think that the multidimensional conceptualization of professional responsibility which has become apparent to us provides a necessary framework.

42. Carlin's *Lawyers' Ethics* reveals that from 1951 to 1962 an average of only 4 percent of the complaints in New York City were ever brought to a formal hearing, with many fewer resulting in any sanction (1966, p. 151). In 1970 the ABA Special Committee on Evaluation of Disciplinary Enforcement reported "a scandalous situation" (Clark Report, p. 1). See also Bonomi for some of the figures from the Clark Committee's survey of discipline (1970, p. 339). In a later study of self-regulation by the bar, Steele and Nimmer (1976) compared official reports of complaint disposition in California, Illinois, Michigan, and New York City and found the same pattern in all jurisdictions; in each more than 90 percent of the complaints were dismissed without investigation, with fewer than 3 percent resulting in any sanction (Steele & Nimmer, 1976, p. 982).

is a severe skew in complaints toward attorneys' conduct that is perceived to be injurious to the client (Steele & Nimmer, 1976, p. 949). The facts of disciplinary enforcement send a strong message: one is most likely to get into trouble because of clients' dissatisfaction with the services provided by their attorneys. Consequently, concern with professional responsibility is directed away from the dimensions related to the social good and toward those dimensions that are most closely client related.[43]

Further, the reliance of disciplinary enforcement upon the complaints of clients constitutes official recognition of the interpersonal dimension of professional responsibility. Although Steele and Nimmer note that such complaints are often settled informally, the very intervention by a bar disciplinary committee lends legitimacy to that dimension of professional responsibility and reflects recognition that the truly responsible attorney would seek to avoid such circumstances. Nevertheless, the enforcement practices of the bar have been seen by the public as grossly insufficient. The perceived failure of the bar to mind its own house has surely contributed to the legal malpractice explosion, which itself carries a message about lawyer behavior that is not lost on the bar, lawyers-in-training, or the public at large.

Inherent in the view that ethical standards are determined by the social and professional environment is recognition that professional behavior is in part a matter of role modeling. The difficulty that this conclusion presents for inculcating high standards of professional responsibility in law students was succinctly stated by one practitioner: law students "say 'you know, the Canons of Ethics say you shall not do A, B, and C.' But they see very prominent, well-known, and reputable attorneys doing these types of things day in and day out" (Pretest, Indianapolis, 5/30/75). This aspect of the socialization process is not the exclusive preserve of professionals. Indeed the scenario sounds peculiarly like the old "do as I say, not as I do" that parents often express in their actions and words. Just as children learn by watching and are acutely aware of discrepancies between stated rules and the behavior of their exponents, so too lawyers learn from observation. This applies to the record of bar disciplinary committees, malpractice litigation, and some particularly prominent cases of flagrant lawyer misconduct.[44]

43. The marked increase in the frequency and value of legal malpractice claims in recent years is an additional part of the client-related professional environment that affects lawyers' behavior. See *St. Paul Fire and Marine Insurance Company* (1976) (leaflet put out periodically by the St. Paul Fire and Marine Insurance Company, St. Paul, Minnesota) and the ABA Special Committee on Lawyers' Professional Liability, *Informational Report* (Chicago: American Bar Association, February 1977) for national figures from the major legal malpractice insurers (p. 4). Although malpractice is not the same as professional responsibility, the litigation threat it presents may prove beneficial to the professional responsibility of lawyers, at least as a morality of duty.

44. The *National Student Marketing* case provides a good example of the kind of case that receives wide media coverage and can affect the image of the profession held by both the general public and professionals in training. The crux of the SEC complaint against the prominent Wall Street law firm of White & Case and its partner, Marion Jay Epley, III

Finally, and we think importantly, law school training is part of the very social and professional environment to which the extant professional standards are attributed. That is not to say that law school is the only or even the most important influence on the development of standards of professional responsibility of the bar; the data directly contradict such a conclusion. What is learned in law school is itself limited by the lessons of practice, by observed enforcement (or lack thereof), and by the observed intrabar and social status of known violators. That is to say that perceptions of both the positive and negative sanctions associated with ethical or unethical, responsible or irresponsible, professional behavior provide a continuing source of socialization in professional responsibility.

Yet law school does provide the future lawyer's introduction to the professional role and the behavior appropriate to it. Just as legal education presents an image of what constitutes the core tasks of the practice of law, so too does it project its own conception and evaluation of the importance of professional responsibility to the practice of law. It is a lesson that is not lost on its students.[45]

(among the 19 codefendants), was the failure to make full and truthful disclosure of the financial state of the National Student Marketing Corporation to its merger partners. That case was settled with White & Case's agreement that "it will not engage, directly or indirectly, in acts and practices which will not be in compliance with, or would constitute aiding and abetting violations of [sections of the Securities laws]" (see *Securities and Exchange Commission v. National Student Marketing Corp.*, [Commerce Clearing House 1977–78 Transfer Binder] *Federal Securities Law Reporter*, May 11, 1977, p. 91, 598, ¶96,027). Such a stipulation sounds curiously like promising to do better next time. This is no small case. Its magnitude is reflected in a recent settlement of $1.3 million for stockholders by Lord, Bissell & Brook, a Chicago law firm among the codefendants in the original SEC suit (reported in the *Wall Street Journal* by Crock, 1980). Yet despite the consent decree, and continuing stockholder litigation, there is no evidence of any bar disciplinary proceedings against any of the lawyers involved in the case. There is, further, no indication that their status within the bar has suffered at all. To our law student quoted above and his cohort, the message is loud and clear.

45. Our conclusions are necessarily tentative, for our understanding of the complex nature of professional responsibility has emerged in the process of the data analysis. The findings call for further study designed to elicit data oriented specifically to the complexity of professional responsibility and the interactive contributions of the multiple socializing contexts.

Chapter 8
CONCLUSION

As the primary gatekeepers to the administration of justice, the legal profession has long enjoyed both substantial public power and high social status. The well-documented dominance of lawyers as public office holders and advisors in American society represents but a part of the political role of this public profession. Its more substantial and more pervasive public power emanates from the role of lawyers in applying and interpreting the law, in advising on and settling legal matters for private clients, in setting the policy agenda of the public courts by filing cases for litigation, and in influencing judicial decisions and the development of the common law through the formulation of relevant issues in legal argument. The locus of so much power over the distribution of justice has generated substantial public criticism of the bar. With its virtual monopoly over access to the profession, legal education has been the particular focus of recommendations for reform. Whether concerned with competence at trial advocacy, skills relevant to office practice, or the social role and professional responsibility of the bar, suggestions have been proffered without evidence of the actual or potential contribution of law schools or other socializing contexts to the nature and structure of the legal profession.[1]

Law school graduation has become the almost universal prerequisite of admission to the bar. Yet law school may contribute both more and less to a lawyer's career and the nature and structure of the profession than may seem obvious on first consideration. As a credential for both

1. A number of studies have attempted to attribute changes in the values and attitudes of law students to their experiences in law school. Most of the findings have been either negative or inconclusive. By and large they have been severely limited by their reliance upon cross-sectional rather than time-series data. See for example Erlanger and Klegon (1978), Hedegard (1979), Katz and Denbeaux (1976), Kay (1978), Rathjen (1976), and Thielens (1965, 1969).

initial recruitment and subsequent job opportunities, law schools are centrally important. As preparation for practice, law school curricula contribute but a part, albeit a well-defined one, to the skills and areas of knowledge important to the lawyer's actual role in representing the legal status of others.

Since lawyers are virtually indistinguishable with respect to the amount of schooling so important to occupational mobility, the source of schooling provides the credential for the distribution of lawyers within the legal profession. With respect to intergenerational mobility, it is important to note that the effects of law school are independent of both family background and academic achievement. While the impact of the law school credential is most obvious at the time of placement in the first job, its effects permeate the entire career span of the lawyer. In part this pervasive impact is due to the extreme stability in the practice of law. Although there is some movement among different practice contexts (even less among different specialties) it conforms to a pattern that is itself predictable along the law school dimension. Yet stability alone is insufficient as an explanation, for in the legal profession, unlike other occupations and even other professions, the source of one's formal education is a mantle worn for life (as is participation on a law review or selection for the Order of the Coif, a law school honor society).

Although law schools can be categorized according to the careers of their graduates, law school reputations (with perhaps half a dozen or so exceptions) are largely specific to particular geographic areas.[2] Within those regions, there is further discrimination among individual schools which may be equally important to the graduate seeking a law job. Law schools contribute directly to the distributional process by influencing the perceptions of particular work settings as appropriate and attractive and by participating heavily in recruitment campaigns. The national law schools in particular provide law school space and time for representatives of law firms to visit the schools and interview prospective employees, both for summer jobs during law school and for permanent jobs after graduation. The larger firms have a decided advantage. For the students they seek to attract there is little need of "pounding the pavement." Although the students may go so far as to don their suits and ties or best dresses, they need only saunter a few yards from their classes for interviews with prospective employers. Combined with the sense of incomplete training felt by many law school graduates and the belief by both students and practitioners that larger firms provide further training, the structure of legal education contributes to the elaboration of legal practice within the particular organizational context of the large law firm.

The recruitment role and credentialing effects of law school are essen-

2. As discussed in chapter 3, the reputations of even the most prestigious schools are somewhat localized, with their greatest influence on careers occurring in the same general geographic area in which they are located.

tially context oriented. That is to say, attendance at particular law schools predicts the context within which graduates practice, particularly distinguishing along the size dimension within private practice. To cite the extremes, graduation from some law schools virtually excludes the possibility of practicing within a large law firm, while graduation from others severely reduces the likelihood of solo practice. This context-based credentialing process presents a curious paradox with respect to the perceived contribution of law school education to the practice of law, for the actual tasks considered important to the lawyer's role vary significantly by the specialty of practice, which, given the selective attention of law school curricula, in turn influences the evaluation of law schools' contributions to lawyers' competencies.

While context and specialty are related, that relationship is rather broad and cannot be distinguished along the dimension of tasks relevant to the practice of law. For example, recruitment of lawyers to a large law firm is highly predictive of the nature of the clientele (business) and the general areas of law relevant to their interests, but these range among such diverse specialties as antitrust, tax, and real estate. Yet it is the specific specialty that significantly affects the tasks that will occupy the lawyer's time and the skills and knowledge that will be requisite to the appropriate representation of the client's interests, even within the overly broad specialty categories traditionally employed. The data indicate that with few exceptions (tax and patent law being the clearest examples) there is no predictable pattern to the determination of the legal specialty, and therefore the competencies, that will define the lawyer's career. There is, rather, a substantial amount of drift in the process, with the momentary needs of the clientele upon the lawyer's entry to practice a central factor in the distribution of lawyers among practice specialties.

There is a substantial disjuncture between the intent attributed to law schools and the message received by their students. Thus, for example, a former law school dean's comprehensive definition of what most law schools attempt to accomplish is closer to practitioners' views of what law schools *should do* than it is to their perceptions of what they *actually do*. These goals of legal education were characterized in 1973 by Kenneth Pye as follows (emphasis added):

> (1) a number of *intellectual competencies*—analysis; reasoning by analogy, snythesis; capacity for precise written expression, a sense of relevance (legal and factual); an ability to construct solutions to controversies which will be acceptable to all concerned; an *understanding of interpersonal relationships*; a capacity for judgment to choose wisely from among different alternatives; (2) certain habits and attitudes—an appreciation of the importance of ascertaining facts; respect of disciplined thought; accuracy; skepticism of overgeneralities; self-discipline; effective use of time; *moral integrity*; *empathy*; a willingness to explore value judgments; (3) *an understanding of the legal system*, including both knowledge of law and the nature of legal institutions; the impact of history upon what we do to-

day; a functional grasp of how the legal process really functions (Pye, as quoted in McKay, 1979, pp. 139–40).[3]

Practicing lawyers, by contrast, and irrespective of age or law school attended, perceive law schools' contributions much more narrowly. Rather than taking a broad approach to the lawyer's role in and contribution to the social order on the macro level, legal education is perceived to be oriented to the micro level of providing the technical requisites of practice. More specifically, law schools are seen as emphasizing a cluster of more purely analytic skills to the virtual exclusion of the more interpersonal skills that are equally central to the practice of law in the aggregate. Since the analytic skills are not equally important throughout the profession, law schools provide better preparation for some specialties than for others. Further, this curricular orientation confers greater legitimacy on those areas of practice in which these competencies are most relevant. The curricular message is that students ought to aspire to careers that will emphasize the same set of analytic skills. A similar theme is repeated with respect to professional responsibility with curricular attention devoted almost exclusively to a morality of duty subject to the same analysis and interpretation as the positive law.

One of the curiosities of recent criticisms and reform efforts has been the lack of concern with the issues and areas for which practitioners fault legal education; instead the emphasis has been on the need for trial skills training in law school.[4] It is important to note that the actual data used as evidence of the insufficiency of competency in advocacy skills among the trial bar indicate quite clearly that the major single failure is one of professional responsibility. The Federal Judicial Center study *The Quality of Advocacy in the Federal Courts*, commissioned by the Devitt Committee,[5] reports that the majority of lawyers and judges agree that one of the two most frequent causes of inadequate trial performance is "failure by lawyers to prepare cases to the best of their ability" (the other was "lack of specialized trial skills or knowledge," but it received less emphasis in actual courtroom evaluations) (1978, p. 6).

3. McKay is quoting from Pye's "On Teaching the Teachers: Some Preliminary Reflections on Clinical Education as Methodology," in *Clinical Education for the Law Student* (CLEPR Conference Proceedings, Buck Hill Falls, June 1973) (New York: Council on Legal Education for Professional Responsibility, 1973), p. 21.

4. See, for example, the Devitt Committee's suggestion that trial practice experience be required prior to admission to practice in the federal courts (*Report and Tentative Recommendations*, 1978, p. 9) and our discussion of this recommendation in chapter 1, note 16. Although the recommendations of the committee were accepted by the Judicial Conference of the United States only for pilot programs, some states are implementing similar reforms. South Carolina, for example, in addition to required law school courses, now requires 11 trial experiences under supervision before a lawyer can independently represent a client in court.

Although clinical programs often include training in these neglected competencies within their goals, in practice the crisis- and litigation-oriented cases brought by the bulk of their clientele limit its realization.

5. See chapter 1, note 16, for a description of the formation of the Devitt Committee and its recommendations.

Another survey of state and federal judges in trial courts of general jurisdiction asked respondents to list, in order of importance, "the factors they considered most important in determining the competence of a trial advocate" (Maddi, 1978, p. 124). A full 85 percent mentioned "preparation," with 54 percent listing it as the most important factor. A further inquiry into the specific type of incompetence exhibited by attorneys rated as partially or predominantly incompetent yielded similar results. "Inadequate preparation" was adjudged the single greatest failure, with 60 percent of the judges estimating that more than 60 percent of the incompetent advocates exhibit this particular form of incompetence (p. 126).[6]

By all evaluations, then, performance is only one part competence and one part preparation; it is one part ability and one part responsibility. Despite these findings, the law school image of the requirements for competent, not to say stellar, performance in the practice of law centers on intellective skills. This view was recently expressed quite succinctly by the dean of one of this country's most prestigious law schools: "Brain power is and always has been the central, if not the only, factor important in lawyers' performances."[7] The practicing bar holds quite another view.

While important, perhaps even critical, intellective skills are not sufficient to good lawyering.[8] It may seem curious, then, that the bar relies

6. Clients' complaints about lawyers also echo concerns that are matters of professional responsibility rather than of competence or ability. Although a national survey indicated that the extent of lawyer use alone has little impact on overall attitudes toward lawyers, some of the differences in views of specific components of competence and responsibility are instructive. Multiple users are more negative with respect to the following items:

Lawyers are (not) prompt about getting things done

Lawyers will take a case . . . (even) if they (do not) feel sure they know enough about that area of the law to handle the case well

Lawyers (do not) usually try to be frank and open with their clients

Lawyers are generally not very good at keeping their clients informed of progress on their cases

(Curran, 1977, table 6.8, pp. 235-36; omissions and additions in parentheses are as shown in the table, indicating reversal of statements as originally asked for purposes of uniformity in the presentation).

7. This comment, made at a meeting for which the papers in *Perspectives on Legal Education* (Redlich, 1979) were prepared, cannot be universally attributed to legal educators. Dean Norman Redlich of New York University School of Law, for example, sees a relationship between the mode of instruction and neglect of preparation in practice:

The case method, with its emphasis on principles of law rather than facts, leads to a teaching environment in which theoretical constructs are considered far more important than facts. Cases are selected for casebooks because they illustrate new legal principles, and rarely because they demonstrate how changing facts will affect the application of those principles. In such an environment, law teachers will inevitably project themselves as being far more concerned with legal principles rather than operative facts. It is then but a short, and devasting, step to the conclusion that sharp thinking is far more important than careful preparation (Redlich, 1979, p. 217).

8. By "good lawyering" we mean the practice of law as it has been defined herein to indicate the representation of the legal rights of others. Lawyers of course, often by virtue of their law degree as a credential, fulfill many roles that do not involve representation of a client. Indeed it appears that with the increasing number of law graduates more and more lawyers enter occupations where the analytic skills are less important than those in the interpersonal cluster. Arbitration is one example.

so heavily, in some cases almost exclusively, on law school grades for hiring, recognizing full well that they reflect only the intellective skills tested in examinations and leave problematic the ability "of turning rules into sensible action" (Llewellyn, 1935, p. 658). The limits of the grade criterion in evaluating the potential of future lawyers is circumvented, to some extent, particularly by the larger firms, through elaborate summer job programs. These provide opportunities to evaluate students' abilities to apply their analytic skills in a practice context. Other competencies considered essential to good performance but untested, indeed frequently not even addressed in the law school environment, can also be evaluated in such programs.

Despite the view that legal education is biased toward the more purely analytic skills to the neglect of the more interpersonal, lawyers by and large express satisfaction with their experiences in law school. To claim, as some critics have, that formal legal education as currently constituted is irrelevant to practice is patently absurd. The difference between what the law schools offer and what its consumers want speaks neither to the quality of the instruction nor to the relevance of the competencies on which legal education focuses. Rather, it addresses the parameters of the appropriate mission of legal education. Law schools' self-defined mission is tied to the analytic skills that constitute the core image, the ideal type of the work of the profession. (Accordingly, it is the most prestigious schools that are considered the most narrowly focused.) It is these skills that most particularly set the legal profession apart and give it the substantial social prestige it enjoys. In accordance with this mission law schools pay much less, if any, attention to the interpersonal skills and general ethics that may be central but are in no way peculiar to the practice of law.

While wishing that it had done more, practicing lawyers recognize their formal training as but a part of the requisite socialization to their professional role. As previously observed, lawyers support a developmental-interactive model of socialization. As for critical competencies given short shrift in law school and the multiple dimensions of professional responsibility, practicing lawyers attribute much of their education to their experiences prior and subsequent to law school. In particular, general upbringing is directly, and overwhelmingly, credited as the source of lawyers' professional responsibility, In addition, by implication, skills such as effective oral expression, for which law school is given only very limited credit but which new lawyers are expected to bring with them to their first job, are developed prior to law school in other socializing contexts. In addition, and again consistent with a developmental view of the socialization process, except for the competencies unique to the practice of law (such as ability to understand and interpret opinions, regulations, and statutes or knowledge of the substantive law), lawyers credit their own experience as the greatest source of learning. In particular, practice in a firm context is perceived to provide an important part of the legal education for practitioners with that experience. In fact there is a recognizable complementarity between the perceived contributions of law school on the one hand and of law practice on the other in the inculcation of competencies and standards important to the responsible practice of law. Many of the very skills for which law school receives least credit (e.g., fact gathering, negotiation, drafting legal documents) but which are considered very important to the practice of law are precisely the competencies that attorneys with experience in a firm attribute to that practice. The same is true for professional responsibility. That is, those who have had the opportunity to learn from other attorneys in their own offices are less likely to credit law school with assisting them in resolving problems of professional responsibility than are those who have practiced alone. As with the skills important to the practice of law, the larger the firm context of practice, the more likely are lawyers to credit their associates with developing their own sense of professional responsibility. Despite substantial variance in the reputations of law schools and in the credentialing value of their degrees, the nature of their contributions to law practice remains relatively constant. Since the failure of law schools to provide a full complement of preparation is substantially less problematic for lawyers who enter large-firm practice than for those without similar institutional support, law school education is more compatible with large-firm practice than with other practice contexts.

For those skills and dimensions of professional responsibility which are peculiar to the lawyer's role and for the application of the more general skills and dimensions of responsibility applied within the context of law practice, later socialization in law school and law practice is necessarily filtered through the more basic skills and conceptions of responsibility developed earlier by each individual. Law school is the first opportunity to consider directly how these basic norms and skills are manifest within the lawyer's role.

Given the extensive variability in the nature of practice, there are of course substantial limits on the level of specificity to which legal education can aim its consideration of tasks and professional responsibility in practice. But uniformity in legal education belies the diversity in practice and further is perceived as oriented toward preparation for a firm practice where training can continue and toward specialties more likely to require analytic skills. Recognizing that socialization is a developmental process, with each step influenced by its predecessors, law schools could set the stage for continuing socialization throughout a career in the law, but they are limited by virtue of their assumption of and dependence upon the availability of subsequent opportunity for further training that is in fact not evenly distributed in legal practice. With early learning providing a foundation for the development of skills and norms and for their application within the context of the practice of law, our model of socialization highlights the importance of access to the profession, and more narrowly access to legal education, if the profession is to be sensitive to the variability in demands for legal services.

Since Langdell's day, law as a science has been the modus operandi of legal education. Like science, the training was to be highly technical and supposedly value free. Legal education would provide the proper tools and the lawyer would use them to defend and promote clients' interests. Lawyers then need not be concerned with social issues and values. But the lawyer is constantly called upon to make policy judgments; as Reisman has observed:

> Even as technicians, the means they use to carry out their clients' policies shape the ends which are achieved. In human affairs, there are no machine tools. The lawyer as technician plays a part in bringing about the future even when he may not wish to, even when he may be unconscious of his role (1941, p. 639).

Yet legal education promotes the technical view of the lawyer's role. With Langdell's reforms "thinking like a lawyer" became the ultimate in legal skills and the most frequently cited contribution of law school training to professional socialization. It became the equivalent of the scientific method to the scientist. "Thinking like a lawyer" has many parts. It includes the ability to distinguish a legal issue and to see any and every problem from many sides. Although not synonymous with formal reasoning and logic, it is closely tied to them. Promotion of these skills encourages abstracting legal issues out of their social context to see issues narrowly and with precision. These skills are perfectly consistent with the adjudicative model where issues and evidence are narrowed for purposes of decision making. But the adjudicative process itself has come under criticism for its irrelevance to the real-world situations out of which controversies evolve. There has been increasing recognition that the end of a court case is often only one step in a continuing conflict rather than a final settlement. It is these same lawyers' skills that have been criticized as promoting litigiousness over minutiae to the neglect of broader goals, even of lawyers' own clients. That is the essential complaint of the business person who fears that lawyers will translate a good working business relationship into a fight over a narrow legal point.

Were a value-free science of the law possible, then lawyers would not need to be concerned with social and professional responsibility. It would be a science of technical expertise. But there is no such thing as a value-free human enterprise, and most certainly not in the law, the very embodiment of authoritative values. To point to the limits of technical expertise is not to diminish its value. We concur with Llewellyn that

> a lawyer's first job is to be a *lawyer*. . . . that we must teach him, first of all, to make a legal table or chair that will stand up without a wobble. Ideals without technique are a mess.
>
> But technique without ideals is a menace. The boy must be hard-headed, with trained hands and brain . . . . not merely as to "law," but as to

"fact," and "policy." Peculiarly as to those *socially* vital facts which practice as such, in civil cases, so quietly and insidiously drops beneath the table (1935, pp. 662–63).

Training that concentrates on the technical mode of analysis, without taking specific cognizance of the appropriate social role of the law and the lawyer *in the context of practice*, seems sorely deficient. The law deals directly with social and human norms; it is society's official statement of social values and the conduct and procedures by which they are to be promoted. Yet law school gives these scant attention. The impression left by concentration on technical training in learning to "think like a lawyer" was neatly articulated by Harvard Law Professor Duncan Kennedy while a student at Yale Law School:

> The impression grows that the law is without what could properly be called theoretical or philosophical problems. There are only "conflicting principles," factors to be "balanced," and problems to be "left" to this, that or the other institution, and the process by which that institution reaches its decision is somehow irrelevant to an understanding of the law (1970, p. 84).

The question "why?" is rarely raised, with barely a mention of how any of what the lawyer does positively affects the society or promotes its most cherished norms or perhaps even contributes to justice, however defined.

One critic of the legal system and legal education has argued that "a distinctive approach to problem solving is imparted in law school, and that this approach influences the way lawyers think about societal issues more generally. A world view . . . implicit in legal analysis . . . tends to come along as a kind of silent partner in legal education" (Scheingold, 1974, p. 152). Surely that is the case. Indeed law schools pride themselves on this unique analytic training that enables one to "think like a lawyer," to manipulate legal doctrine so as to best represent the interests of the client. The norms and realities of human behavior and politics which underlie the law, however, are given short shrift in legal education.[9]

We are not suggesting that the fundamental orientation of law schools can or even should be transformed into a presentation of either a behavioral or a philosophical approach to the law.[10] The function of the law school is after all technical training to fill a social role for which there is substantial demand. Yet that training need not exclude consideration of

9. Given the passivity and allegedly value-free role to which lawyers are socialized, it is rather paradoxical that lawyers are the ones so frequently called on to make extremely value-laden decisions for the polity. For many policy-making jobs that demand highly normative decision making, the technical expertise reflected in the law school credential is a virtual prerequisite. It is perhaps their alleged value-free expertise that makes lawyers attractive appointees to politically sensitive roles.

10. We might, however, be willing to argue that liberal education in general should consider law from just those perspectives, particularly in a society where public law has become so pervasive.

the broader issues and the part that the legal profession ultimately plays in the society. Perhaps it is the increased questioning about the legitimacy of the law itself which is generating renewed criticisms of the legal profession and legal education. But surely if that is the case, then it is all the more important that those who will use the law be required to consider its role in society and the broad implications of their behavior as lawyers. The day has passed when even the "pure" sciences can hide behind a veil of "science" without consideration of the impact their work has on the larger society.[11] Surely the same must be true for those who largely control the distribution of justice.

The need for further inquiry into this topic is demanded by the passing of the day when the technical expert can simply declare service and presume acceptance. Self-regulation granted to the profession assumes the service component in the lawyer's work. Yet it is left unclear just exactly how it is that the lawyer benefits the society. For the legitimacy of the law and the lawyer's role ultimately depend on the society's evaluation of the contributions to the social order, and it is precisely those contributions that have been increasingly questioned in recent years. The documented decline in support for public institutions is particularly critical in a democratic society. For the power of public institutions ultimately relies upon the citizenry's belief in their legitimacy. If law is central to our society, then it seems obvious that the institutions that are producing its practitioners have an obligation to make that point quite explicitly. The notion that the law is a purely technical enterprise is simply inconsistent with the complex intertwining of law and social norms in any society, and most assuredly in a democratic one. To imply otherwise, even if it is only through inferences drawn from the law schools' failure to deal with these issues in a straightfoward fashion, is a disservice.

11. Science, once viewed as value free, no longer has that luxury. A recent example of the impossibility of a value-free stance, and one that has been instrumental in generating a flurry of government regulations of scientific research, is the Tuskegee Syphilis Study, which entailed observation of the progression of the disease without the consent of subjects, including the failure to inform them of the possibility of treatment even after penicillin became available. (See *Final Report of the Tuskegee Syphilis Study Ad Hoc Advisory Panel*, 1973). As noted in the "Introduction" to a recent issue of *Daedalus* (Spring 1978) devoted to the "Limits of Scientific Inquiry," there has been a shift in emphasis away from internal self-regulation and toward external government controls (p. viii). The U.S. Department of Health, Education, and Welfare developed standards to protect human subjects in research applicable to all government research grants (*Code of Federal Regulations*, title 45, revised as of October 1, 1979, pt. 46 "Protection of Human Subjects," pp. 113–27); these standards are still in force. Research institutions, including particularly universities that receive government research funds, have also begun to require the same standards of all research done by those affiliated with it. For a further discussion of some of the relevant issues, see chapter 13, "Deceptive Social Science Research," of Bok's *Lying: Moral Choice in Public and Private Life* (1978).

Appendix 1
THE QUESTIONNAIRE

LEGAL EDUCATION AND THE PROFESSIONAL DEVELOPMENT OF LAWYERS

Introduction

Legal education has been praised and criticized from a number of quarters. Our goal in the questionnaire that follows is to enable you to express your views on legal education and the practice of law. You will find that many of the questions ask you to choose among selected responses. This format has been developed to facilitate comparisons and help us formulate a composite picture of the views of the practicing bar. At the same time, you will have the opportunity to add to our categories as well as answer a number of questions for which no response choices have been provided. This will allow you to contribute to the depth and breadth of the questionnaire and the project.

It is important for the validity of the study and its potential impact on legal education that your responses be as complete as possible with all questions answered. Since we are interested in the views of the practicing bar in the aggregate, we have no need or reason to identify individual participants. Thus, you are not identified on this questionnaire, and the anonymity of your responses is assured.

The questionnaire has been divided into the following six sections to adequately cover the relationship between legal education and the practice of law:

     I.   Law School Experience

    II.   Career Development

   III.   Knowledge and Skills Important to
          the Practice of Law

    IV.   Legal Ethics and Professional Responsibility

    V.   Socio-legal Issues

   VI.   Background Information

Instructions for completing the questions appear throughout the questionnaire and should be clear. You will find that several questions include numbers to the right of the response choices. Where this occurs you need only circle the appropriate number. As an example:

Did you attend law school?

Yes..①

No....2

We appreciate your participation in the study and hope that it both stimulates your thoughts and provides you with an opportunity to express your views on legal education and the practice of law.

-2-

PART I: Law School Experience

First we'd like to know something about your decision to go to law school
and your experiences there.

`01` `1 - 2`

`3 - 5`

1. Below is a list of possible reasons one might have for going to law
    school. On the first line, please enter an X next to each factor that
    was at all influential in your decision to go to law school. Check as
    many as are applicable.

	Influential Factors	Rank of Importance	
a. prestige of the profession	___	___	`6 - 7`
b. interest in the subject matter	___	___	`8 - 9`
c. influence of family	___	___	`10-11`
d. influence of friend or teacher	___	___	`12-13`
e. wanted to practice law	___	___	`14-15`
f. good background for other occupational goals (*if you check this category, please indicate which of the occupations listed below you had in mind*)	___	___	`16-17`
			`18-19`
			`20-21`
			`22-23`
g. uncertainty about future plans	___	___	`24-25`

         politics.........1
         business.........2
         judiciary........3
         government work...4
         legal education...5

	Influential Factors	Rank of Importance
h. stable secure future expected	___	___
i. wanted to postpone military service	___	___
j. opportunity to work with people rather than things	___	___
k. opportunity to have an influence on the settlement of legal questions	___	___
l. opportunity to be helpful to others and/or useful to society in general	___	___
m. relative freedom from supervision by others	___	___
n. prospects of above average income	___	___
o. like to argue and debate	___	___
p. other:_____ (*specify*)	___	___

2. Looking at only those factors which you noted above as having had an
    influence on your decision to attend law school, please rank them in
    order of their importance to that decision. Begin with number 1 as
    the most important and insert the numbers in the second column above.

-3-

3. Which law school(s) did you attend?_____

26-27

                      full-time...1

28-29

                      part-time...2

30
31

4. Here is a list of some factors that are often taken into consideration when one selects a law school. Please rank these in the order in which they influenced your decision to attend the law school that you did. Beginning with number 1 as the most important, please insert the ranking you assign to each factor on the appropriate line to the right. Rank only those that had a significant influence.

32-33

  a. prestige   _____

34-35

  b. opportunity for financial aid   _____

36-37

  c. liked the community   _____

38-39

  d. wanted to practice law in that community or state   _____

40-41

  e. quality of the school   _____

42-43

  f. special professors· or area of specialization   _____

44-45

  g. relative or friend who attended   _____

46-47

  h. cost   _____

48-49

  i. classes scheduled to allow opportunity to work full or part-time while attending law school   _____

50-51

  j. only school at which accepted

  k. graduates had good record passing local bar exam   _____

  l. diploma privilege (diploma from law school sufficient for admission to state bar)   _____

5. In addition to generally educating students to become lawyers, what were the major goals of the law school you attended?

52-53

  a. prepare students for practice in the following particular specialty:_____   _____

54

  b. instill high level of respect for the judicial process   _____

55

  c. prepare graduates to pass the bar examination   _____

56

  d. provide theoretical basis of the law   _____

57

  e. provide good basis for the practice of law   _____

58

  f. combine theoretical and practical approaches to the law   _____

59

  g. teach students to think analytically   _____

60-61

  h. other:_____   _____
             (specify)

6. Do you wish that the goals had been different?   yes...1

                                 no....2

62

               (If yes) In what ways?

63-64

-4-

7. Certain law school courses are often cited as being particularly helpful to one's career. Among the possible reasons to explain the merit of particular courses are 1) professor quality, 2) useful to practice of my specialty and 3) underlies most legal issues. Using these and any other reasons you might think relevant please note those courses (up to 3 in number) which have been most helpful to your career and why.

_____ 65-66

_____ 67-68

_____ 69-70

           Course   Reason

_____ 71-72

a. _____   _____

_____ 73-74

b. _____   _____

_____ 75-76

c. _____   _____

8. Given the courses you took in law school are there any areas of the curriculum which you would eliminate or drastically shorten?

                                     yes...1

     (If yes) Which courses and why?   no....2

                77
                ____ 78-79

02 ____ 1 - 2

      ____ 3 - 5

      ____ 6 - 7

      ____ 8 - 9

      ____ 10-11

      ____ 12-13

9. Did your law school experience influence you in any way to select a field(s) of specialization?

                       ____ 14-15

                     yes...1

                     no....2   16

     (If yes) How? (e.g. courses, faculty and fellow students.)

                       ____ 17-18

10. There are some who contend that law school need not take three years, that the first two years and the material covered therein are sufficient for the law school curriculum. Do you think law schools should maintain their three year program or change to a two year curriculum? Beneath your response please indicate the one or two most important reasons for your choice.

        3 years   2 years

law is very complex
  needs much time.................1   2 yrs. covers the basic...........1

law school is evolutionary   3rd yr. filled with courses
process requiring 3 yrs.   too narrow to be relevant
  (or more).......................2   to most attorneys' practice......2

3rd yr. gives chance for   ____ 19-20
  specialization..................3   3rd year redundant................3

3rd yr. affords opportunities   benefits received do not
  for contact with faculty........4   justify cost.....................4

need a full year just
  to get started..................5   other:_____.....5

other:_____.....6   (specify)
     (specify)

-5-

11. Were you involved in any of the following law school activities outside of the classroom? Please put an X next to each of the activities in which you **actively** participated.

law school student bar association	_____	21
organized sports	_____	22
student government	_____	23
law clinic	_____	24
law school fraternity/sorority	_____	25
law school committees	_____	26
moot court	_____	27
law review	_____	28
other publications:_____ (specify)	_____	29-3
other activities:_____ (specify)	_____	31-3
no law school activities	_____	33

12. Have you maintained a relationship with your law school in any of the following ways? Put an X next to each of those which apply to you.

alumni association	_____	34
financial contributions	_____	35
recommend it to potential students	_____	36
recommend its graduates for legal positions or seek to hire them yourself	_____	37
continuing legal education programs	_____	38
read its publications	_____	39
other:_____ (specify)	_____	40-41
no relationship	_____	42

13. Given the same circumstances, would you attend the same law school that you did?

yes...1

no....2

43

(If no) To what law school would you have gone instead and why?

44-45

46-47

-6-

14. Would you encourage your child or grandchild to study law? Beneath your
response please indicate the one or two most important reasons for
your choice.

<u>Yes</u>	<u>No</u>
independence....................1	constantly forced into controversy...1
intellectual challenge.........2	there are better ways to be useful to society.................2
security.......................3	
	financial return insufficient for the time demanded by practice..3
opportunity to contribute to society....................4	
	declining prestige of the profession.........................4
law is useful in many occupations..................5	
	increasing numbers of attorneys decreases probability of secure future.....................5
enjoyable career...............6	
other:_____....7 　　(specify)	unenjoyable career..................6
	law study not useful outside law practice......................7
	other:_____.......8 　　　(specify)

48-49.

PART II: Career Development

Now we would like to ask you some questions about your legal career and the
kind or kinds of practice in which you have been involved.

1. Before or during law school did you hold any jobs, full or part-time,
which contributed sigificantly to your career?

　　　　　　　　　　　　　yes...1

　　　　　　　　　　　　　no....2

50

51-52

(If yes) List those jobs in chronological order, noting the way in which
they contributed to your career, including any skills pertinent to your
practice that you think were developed. Choose among the following categories to indicate when you held each job: 1) before college, 2) during
college, 3) after college, but before law school, or 4) during law school;
insert the appropriate number in the space provided.

53

54-55

56-57

58

59-60

Job	When held	Contribution to career/ skills developed

61-62

63

64-65

66-67

68

69-70

71-72

73

74-75

-7-

2. **After graduation from law school, what was your first law-related employment?**_____

_____76-77_

3. **Which one of the following was most important in the selection of that employment?**

geographical considerations...........1	
offered independence..................2	
opportunity to learn practice from other attorneys................3	_____78-79_
no other job offers...................4	
chance to learn a specialty...........5	
most promising practice available.....6	
other:_____ 7	

4. **Here is a list of different substantive areas of the law. Please indicate by putting an X on the first line to the right of each category, those areas of the law in which you did a _significant_ amount of work in your first employment as a lawyer.**

Areas in which worked		Rank order
1. corporate	_____	_____
2. criminal		
3. administrative	_____	_____
4. family law		
5. personal injury	_____	_____
6. tax law		
7. poverty law	_____	_____
8. trusts & estates		
9. bankruptcy	_____	_____
10. labor law		
11. insurance	_____	_____
12. patent law		
13. antitrust	_____	_____
14. real estate law		
15. other:_____	_____	_____
(specify)		

Coding column:
03 1 - 2
 3 - 5
6 - 7
8 - 9
10 - 11
12-13
14-15
16-17
18-19
20-21

5. **Looking at those substantive areas in which you did a significant amount of work, please rank them in order of the amount of your time contributed to each. Begin with number 1 next to the area in which you spent most of your time in your first employment.**

-8-

6. Considering the same substantive areas of the law, please indicate by putting an X on the first line to the right of each category, those areas of the law in which you do a significant amount of work in your current practice.

Areas in which worked		Rank order	
1. corporate			**22-23**
2. criminal			
3. administrative			24-25
4. family law			
5. personal injury			26-27
6. tax law			
7. poverty law			28-29
8. trusts & estates			
9. bankruptcy			30-31
10. labor law			
11. insurance			32-33
12. patent law			
13. antitrust			34-35
14. real estate law			
15. other:			36-37

(specify)

7. Looking at those substantive areas in which you do a significant amount of work, please rank them in order of the amount of time you contribute to each. Begin with number 1 next to the area in which you spend most of your time in your current practice.

8. Which of the following categories best describes the nature of your current practice?

solo practitioner........1   large firm......................5

2 person office..........2   number in firm_____   38-39

small firm...............3   government lawyer...............6

number in firm:_____   _____   40-41
                                       (specify kind)
medium sized firm........4
                                   legal staff of a business firm...7
number in firm:_____
                                   other:_____...8
                                          (specify)

-9-

9. Among the decisions every attorney must make is which cases and/or clients
to accept. (If this is not applicable to your practice because cases are
assigned to you, please skip to question 11). Please indicate (by putting
an X in the first line to the right of each category) which of the
following factors you consider when deciding which cases and/or clients
to take.

	Factors Considered	Rank of Importance	
Novel questions at law and legal precedent	_____	_____	
Expected duration of litigation	_____	_____	_____42-43
Subject matter	_____	_____	_____44-45
Jurisdiction of the case	_____	_____	_____46-47
Ability of client to pay	_____	_____	_____48-49
Other attorney asked you to	_____	_____	
Personal friend or relative	_____	_____	_____50-51
Opportunity to influence social policy	_____	_____	_____52-53
Belief in the justness of the cause	_____	_____	_____54-55
Potential size of the fee	_____	_____	
Consistent with work you are doing	_____	_____	_____56-57
Take almost all cases that come to me	_____	_____	_____58-59
Legal merit of the case	_____	_____	
Time available to handle properly	_____	_____	_____60-61
Other:_____ (specify)	_____	_____	

10. Looking only at those factors which you have noted above as influencing your
decisions to accept cases and/or clients, please rank them in order of their
importance to those decisions. Begin with number one (1) as the most
important and insert the numbers in the second column above.

11. Do you think that you have achieved your maximum level of earnings from the
practice of law?

                                    yes...1
                                                                    62
                                    no....2

         (If no) At what age do you expect to reach it?_____   _____63-64

12. Do you feel you have reached your full potential as an effective attorney?

                                    yes...1
                                                                    65
                                    no....2

         (If no) At what age do you expect to reach it?_____   _____66-67

13. By what criteria do you measure an attorney's effectiveness?

                                                                    _____68-69

-10-

14. Please complete the following:

Compared to other Chicago attorneys in my specialty with approximately the same time at the bar, I would rate my success as equal
to or greater than____% of those attorneys.

____70-71

15. Please complete the following:

Compared to other Chicago attorneys in my specialty with approximately the same time at the bar, I would rate my legal skills as
equal to or better than____% of those attorneys.

____72-73

16. What do you see yourself doing professionally in the <u>next five years</u>?
Do you expect to be similarly employed (i.e., in the same or a similar
firm or office) and doing basically the same kind of work?

    a. same or similar employment....1

        different employment..........2   (If different) What?

74

____75-76

    b. same work.....................1

        different work................2   (If different) What?

77

____78-79

17. What do you see yourself doing professionally in the long run?
Do you expect to be similarly employed (i.e., in the same or a similar
firm or office) and doing basically the same kind of work?

04 1 ⌣ 2

    a. same or similar employment....1

        different employment...........2   (If different) What?

____3 - 5

6

____7 - 8

    b. same work.....................1

        different work................2   (If different) What?

9

____10-11

18. Have you ever seriously contemplated leaving the practice of law?

                               yes...1

                               no....2

12

(If yes) What alternative(s) were you considering and why?

____13-14

____15-16

____17-18

-11-

PART III: Knowledge and Skills Important to the Practice of Law

The following questions deal with the knowledge and skills that you think are important in your practice.

1. Below you will find a list of categories of knowledge and skills that might be important to your practice. For each of these skills please indicate by circling the appropriate number the degree to which you think it is important or unimportant to your practice.

	Extremely Important	Important	Somewhat Important	Not Very Important	Not Important At All	
Legal research	1	2	3	4	5	19
Fact gathering	1	2	3	4	5	20
Knowledge of the substantive law	1	2	3	4	5	21
Negotiating	1	2	3	4	5	22
Drafting legal documents	1	2	3	4	5	23
Instilling others' confidence in you	1	2	3	4	5	24
Ability to understand and interpret opinions, regulations, and statutes	1	2	3	4	5	25
Accounting skills	1	2	3	4	5	26
Knowledge of procedural law	1	2	3	4	5	27
Effective oral expression	1	2	3	4	5	28
Writing briefs	1	2	3	4	5	29
Getting along with other lawyers	1	2	3	4	5	30
Ability to synthesize law	1	2	3	4	5	31
Financial sense	1	2	3	4	5	32
Knowledge of theory underlying law	1	2	3	4	5	33
Interviewing	1	2	3	4	5	34
Letter writing	1	2	3	4	5	35
Understanding the viewpoint of others to deal more effectively with them	1	2	3	4	5	36
Capacity to marshall facts and order them so that concepts can be applied	1	2	3	4	5	37
Knowledge of political science, psychology, economics, sociology	1	2	3	4	5	38
Opinion writing	1	2	3	4	5	39

-12-

2. The previous question dealt with areas of knowledge and skills that may be important
to the practice of law. Each of these may be learned from a variety of sources
(some of which are listed from left to right below). For <u>each</u> area of knowledge
and skills (e.g., legal research) consider which of the sources listed (e.g., general
law school curriculum) made a substantial contribution to your development of that
knowledge or skill. Then <u>rank</u> only the sources you think were significant (beginning
with 1 as the most important) in the order in which they contributed to your
developing directly or indirectly each knowledge or skill.

	General law school curriculum	Law school attention to training in the specific area	Clinical training/ moot court
Legal research			
Fact gathering			
Knowledge of the substantive law			
Negotiating			
Drafting legal documents			
Instilling others' confidence in you			
Ability to understand and interpret opinions, regulations, and statutes			
Accounting skills			
Knowledge of procedural law			
Effective oral expression			
Writing briefs			
Getting along with other lawyers			
Ability to synthesize law			
Financial sense			
Knowledge of theory underlying law			
Interviewing			
Letter writing			
Understanding the viewpoint of others to deal more effectively with them			
Capacity to marshall facts and order them so that concepts can be applied			
Knowledge of political science, psychology, economics, sociology			
Opinion writing			

-13-

Law review experience	Observation of or advice from other lawyers in your law office	Observation of or advice from other lawyers not in your law office	Your own repeated experience	Your own study of the area	
———	———	———	———	———	40–47
———	———	———	———	———	48–55
———	———	———	———	———	56–63
———	———	———	———	———	64–71
———	———	———	———	———	72–79 ⎰ 05 1–3
———	———	———	———	———	6 –13 ⎱ ___3–5
———	———	———	———	———	14–21
———	———	———	———	———	22–29
———	———	———	———	———	30–37
———	———	———	———	———	38–45
———	———	———	———	———	46–53
———	———	———	———	———	54–61
———	———	———	———	———	62–69
———	———	———	———	———	70–77 ⎰ 06 1–2
———	———	———	———	———	6 –13 ⎱ ___3–5
———	———	———	———	———	14–21
———	———	———	———	———	22–29
———	———	———	———	———	30–37
———	———	———	———	———	38–45
———	———	———	———	———	46–53
———	———	———	———	———	54–61

-14-

3. Regarding the development of skills and knowledge necessary to the practice
    of law, there are various views as to the actual contribution of law school
    and what that contribution ought to be. Please indicate your view by
    circling a yes or no response for each of the skills and knowledge listed.

	Did law school training indicate the potential value of this to the practice of law?		Was sufficient attention given to this in the law school curriculum?	
	Yes	No	Yes	No
Legal research	1	2	1	2
Fact gathering	1	2	1	2
Knowledge of the substantive law	1	2	1	2
Negotiating	1	2	1	2
Drafting legal documents	1	2	1	2
Instilling others' confidence in you	1	2	1	2
Ability to understand and interpret opinions, regulations, and statutes	1	2	1	2
Accounting skills	1	2	1	2
Knowledge of procedural law	1	2	1	2
Effective oral expression	1	2	1	2
Writing briefs	1	2	1	2
Getting along with other lawyers	1	2	1	2
Ability to synthesize law	1	2	1	2
Financial sense	1	2	1	2
Knowledge of theory underlying law	1	2	1	2
Interviewing	1	2	1	2
Letter writing	1	2	1	2
Understanding the viewpoint of others to deal more effectively with them	1	2	1	2
Capacity to marshall facts and order them so that concepts can be applied	1	2	1	2
Knowledge of political science, psychology, economics, sociology	1	2	1	2
Opinion writing	1	2	1	2

-15-

Was too much attention given to this in law school?		Can this be taught effectively in law school?		Did you learn this essentially in law school?		
Yes	No	Yes	No	Yes	No	
1	2	1	2	1	2	62-66
1	2	1	2	1	2	67-71
1	2	1	2	1	2	72-76 07 1-2
1	2	1	2	1	2	6-10 3-5
1	2	1	2	1	2	11-15
1	2	1	2	1	2	16-20
1	2	1	2	1	2	21-25
1	2	1	2	1	2	26-30
1	2	1	2	1	2	31-35
1	2	1	2	1	2	36-40
1	2	1	2	1	2	41-45
1	2	1	2	1	2	46-50
1	2	1	2	1	2	51-55
1	2	1	2	1	2	56-60
1	2	1	2	1	2	61-65
1	2	1	2	1	2	66-70
1	2	1	2	1	2	71-75
1	2	1	2	1	2	76-80 08 1-2
1	2	1	2	1	2	6-10 3-5
1	2	1	2	1	2	11-15
1	2	1	2	1	2	16-20

16

FOR CODING
USE ONLY

4. Have you had the opportunity during your legal career to evaluate a lawyer as a prospective associate or employee?

yes...1 (If yes, continue to question (a) below)

no....2 (If no, please skip to part IV, page /F)

21

a. For how many years?_____

22-23

b. Are you currently doing such evaluation? yes...1

no....2

24

c. When you are evaluating a prospective associate or employee do you consider any particular law school courses as essential prerequisites?

yes...1 (If yes) Which courses? _____

no....2 _____

25

26-27
28-29
30-31

d. In hiring, do you give extra weight to a prospective associate or employee with experience in any of the following:

1) clinical education   yes...1

no....2

32

2) moot court work   yes...1

no....2

33

e. Focusing on new lawyers, how realistic a notion of what the practice of law actually entails do you think they have?

excellent...1

very good...2

good........3

fair........4

poor........5

34

f. Do you think that it is the job of law schools to prepare their students for the practical aspects of legal practice?

yes...1

no....2

(If yes) How and in what ways?

35

36-37

g. Do you think that law schools do a good job of teaching the realities of law practice?

yes...1

no....2

38

h. For each of the categories listed below please indicate by circling
the appropriate number whether you expect new lawyers (1) largely to
bring these abilities with them or (2) largely to develop them on the
job. In addition, if you have been evaluating lawyers as prospective
associates or employees for a number of years, please rate recent law
school graduates in relation to their predecessors as to whether you
think they are 1) much better, 2) somewhat better, 3) about the same,
4) somewhat worse or 5) much worse in terms of their preparation in each
of the categories listed.

	Expect new lawyers to bring or develop skill (circle number)		Recent law school graduates compared to predecessors (circle 1,2,3,4,5)						
	Bring	Develop							
Legal research	1	2	1	2	3	4	5	39	40
Fact gathering	1	2	1	2	3	4	5	41	42
Knowledge of the substantive law	1	2	1	2	3	4	5	43	44
Negotiating	1	2	1	2	3	4	5	45	46
Drafting legal documents	1	2	1	2	3	4	5	47	48
Instilling others' confidence in you	1	2	1	2	3	4	5	49	50
Ability to understand and interpret opinions, regulations, and statutes	1	2	1	2	3	4	5	51	52
Accounting skills	1	2	1	2	3	4	5	53	54
Knowledge of procedural law	1	2	1	2	3	4	5	55	56
Effective oral expression	1	2	1	2	3	4	5	57	58
Writing briefs	1	2	1	2	3	4	5	59	60
Getting along with other lawyers	1	2	1	2	3	4	5	61	62
Ability to synthesize law	1	2	1	2	3	4	5	63	64
Financial sense	1	2	1	2	3	4	5	65	66
Knowledge of theory underlying law	1	2	1	2	3	4	5	67	68
Interviewing	1	2	1	2	3	4	5	69	70
Letter writing	1	2	1	2	3	4	5	71	72
Understanding the viewpoint of others to deal more effectively with them	1	2	1	2	3	4	5	73	74
Capacity to marshall facts and order them so that concepts can be applied	1	2	1	2	3	4	5	75	76
Knowledge of political science, psychology, economics, sociology	1	2	1	2	3	4	5	77	78
Opinion writing	1	2	1	2	3	4	5	79	80

-18-

PART IV: Legal Ethics and Professional Responsibility

1. Were legal ethics and/or professional responsibility considered in your law school?

        yes...1   *(If yes, continue to question a)*

        no....2   *(If no, skip to question 2)*

    (If yes) (a) Did your school have a separate course in legal ethics and/or 'professional responsibility?

                          yes...1

                          no....2

        (if no) How and in what ways were legal ethics and professional responsibility taught?

        (if yes) Did you take the   yes...1

                    course?   no....2

    (b) How much emphasis were legal ethics and professional responsibility given in your law school?

                      great deal......1

                      some...........2

                      not very much...3

    (c) What was actually taught concerning legal ethics and professional responsibility?

    (d) Most attorneys at some time in their practice encounter questions of legal ethics and/or professional responsibility. At such times in your career, were you materially aided in the resolution of these problems by the consideration given legal ethics and/or professional responsibility in law school?

                      yes................1

                      no.................2

                      such problems have

                            never occurred...3

    (If yes) How?   *(If no)* Why not?

2. Do you think law schools should teach legal ethics and/or professional responsibility?

                      yes...1

       Why/why not?   no....2

    (If you answered yes to question 2) Should law school consideration of these matters extend beyond the Canon of Ethics & The Code of Professional responsibility?

                      yes...1

                      no....2

        (If yes) What else would you include?

Coding column values:

Item	Code
1 - 2	09
3 - 5	
6	
7	
8 - 9	
10	
11	
12-13	
14	
15-16	
17	
18-19	
20	
21-22	

3. **Following is a list of possible sources from which one may develop their sense of legal ethics and/or professional responsibility. Please rank them (beginning with #1) in the order of their importance for you in resolving questions of legal ethics and/or professional responsibility that have arisen in your practice.**

Observation of or advice from other attorneys <u>in your</u> law office	_____
Observation of or advice from other attorneys <u>not in your</u> law office	_____
Advice from persons other than attorneys	_____
Law school consideration of these topics	_____
General upbringing	_____
Other:_____ (specify)	_____

PART V: Socio-Legal Issues

1. **During your years in law school was the question of the potential social impact of the law raised within the curriculum?**

                                          yes...1

                                          no....2

     (If yes) Did it pervade the curriculum or was this done in the
              context of particular courses?

                              pervasive...........1

                              particular courses...2

                  Which ones?

2. **Did you get the impression from your law school experience that the law is quite distinct from other social forces?**

                                          yes...1

                                          no....2

3. **Do you think that lawyers, <u>as legal professionals</u>, have a special obligation to take a stand and/or speak out on issues where legal changes are contemplated as a mechanism to affect the society?**

                              definitely.............1

                              somewhat...............2

                              not more than any
                                responsible citizen...3

                              not at all.............4

-20-

4. Was the question of any special responsibility that a lawyer might have to comment on attempts to use the law for social goals ever raised in your law school?

yes...1

no....2

36

(If yes) How, and in what context?

37-38

5. There are a number of current public issues where the law is either changing or under some pressure to change. For each of the following issues, please circle the degree to which you have considered each issue from the perspective of an attorney.

		Great Deal of Con- sider- ation	Some Con- sider- ation	Not Much Con- sider- ation	No Con- sider- ation	
a.	Capital punishment	1	2	3	4	39
b.	Individual's right to participate in private consensual homosexual acts	1	2	3	4	40
c.	Due process rights for student suspension from public schools for disciplinary reasons	1	2	3	4	41
d.	Divorce as an essentially administrative matter like marriage	1	2	3	4	42
e.	An individual's right to own guns	1	2	3	4	43
f.	"No fault" or "basic protection" automobile accident insurance	1	2	3	4	44
g.	Government funding of legal aid programs	1	2	3	4	45
h.	Use of pro se adjudication for the settlement of small claims	1	2	3	4	46
i.	Application of the exclusionary rule in criminal trials	1	2	3	4	47
j.	Prepaid legal services plans for the public	1	2	3	4	48

-21-

6. Looking at statements about these same issues below, please circle the degree to which you agree or disagree with each of them.

Issues	Strongly agree	Mildly agree	Mildly disagree	Strongly disagree	
a. Capital punishment should be legalized.	1	2	3	4	49
b. Individual should have the right to participate in private consensual homosexual acts.	1	2	3	4	50
c. Students suspended from public schools for disciplinary reasons should not be guaranteed due process.	1	2	3	4	51
d. Divorce should be changed to an essentially administrative matter like marriage.	1	2	3	4	52
e. An individual's right to own guns should be maintained.	1	2	3	4	53
f. "No fault" or "basic protection" automobile accident insurance should be expanded.	1	2	3	4	54
g. Government funding of legal aid programs should be restricted.	1	2	3	4	55
h. Use of pro se adjudication for the settlement of small claims should be increased.	1	2	3	4	56
i. The application of the exclusionary rule in criminal trials should be limited.	1	2	3	4	57
j. Prepaid legal services plans for the public should be expanded.	1	2	3	4	58

-22-

PART VI: Background Information

Finally, we'd like to know a little about you and your personal background.

1. When were you born, and where?

Year_____   _____59-60

Place_____   _____61-62
(city, state)
_____63-64

2. Sex: Male......1
Female....2   65

3. Race: White.....1
Black.....2
Chicano...3
Oriental..4   66

4. Where did you live most of the time until you were 18?   _____67-68
(city, state)

5. Where did you receive your undergraduate degree?   _____69-70

_____ _____   _____71-72

6. What was your undergraduate major?_____   _____73-74

7. Did you receive any advanced degrees before entering law school?

yes...1   75
no....2   _____76

(If yes) What degree and from which institution?_____   _____77-78

8. In what year did you graduate from law school? 19____

_____79-80

9. If you received any graduate law degrees, please indicate the degree,
when received and at what school? (If no graduate law degrees, please   10   1 - 2
continue to question #10.)   _____3 - 5

degree_____   _____6
year_____   _____7 - 8
school_____   _____9-10

10. Do you now or have you participated in any continuing legal education
programs outside of those provided by your own law school?

yes...1
no....2   11

(If yes) How frequently?

more then 4 times a year...1
2-4 times a year..........2   12
once a year...............3
less than once a year......4

11. How many other lawyers are or were there in your family?_____   _____13

FOR CODING
USE ONLY

12. If your father is not or was not a lawyer, what is or was his occupation? (Please be as specific as possible.)

_____

_____14-15

13. If your mother is not or was not a lawyer, what is or was her occupation? (Please be as specific as possible.)

_____

_____16-17

14. When you graduated from law school what was your class standing?

Top 1-10%........1
11-20%........2
21-40%........3
41-60%........4
61-80%........5
81-100%.......6

18

15. When did you first pass a state bar examination successfully?

before law school graduation......................1
within six months after law school graduation.....2
more than six months, but within 1 year
    after law school graduation.....................3
more than 1 year, but within 2 years
    after law school graduation.....................4

19

      Thank you very much for the time and thought you have devoted to completing the questionnaire. As noted in the introduction, to achieve the goals of this study we do not need to identify any of the participants--our concern is with the views of the practicing bar in the aggregate. At the same time, however, to insure a representative sample of opinions, the participation of all of the randomly selected attorneys is essential. Since the names of individual respondents are not requested on the questionnaire, we need some mechanism to indicate who has not yet replied. Those attorneys can then be contacted and encouraged to participate. The attached postcard is for your convenience in letting us know that you have completed and returned the questionnaire. This postcard is to be mailed separately so that the anonymity of your responses will be maintained. Please detach the postcard and forward it to us at the appropriate time.

      Thank you again for your cooperation in contributing to our understanding of legal education.

RATING LAW SCHOOLS

There is much debate about the relevant criteria by which law schools should be measured and how they actually differ. Efforts to rate law schools have, in fact, become a particular focus of controversy, with the Association of American Law Schools and their representatives sensitive to the impact that ratings may have on the reputation and perhaps well-being of various law schools.

Elite, prestige, national, regional, and *local* are the terms most frequently used to classify law schools. Out of that set of terms an interesting, if somewhat strange, ranking from "best" to "worst" law schools has evolved. Although a meaningful ranking should be based upon a single dimension, law school rankings have reflected both reputation and location. As selected schools won appellations like "elite" or "prestige," others were being categorized according to the geographical area from which they drew most of their students and in which most of their graduates practiced (not mutually exclusive phenomena). Our findings reveal two patterns that help us evaluate the merits of the location criterion. First, law schools in major metropolitan areas draw most of their students from the local area. Their graduates, in turn, tend to remain there to practice law. Thus the two parts of the location criterion are intimately related. Second, the localism of law school graduates is not nearly as skewed by law school as we might have imagined. Graduates of even the "elite" schools are likely to stay in the same general area after graduation.[1]

Gradually over time the qualitative and geographic criteria merged, probably because the so-called elite schools did in fact draw their student body from a wider geographical area, and their graduates often, although we have learned not usually, practiced in areas far removed from the law school. We think the common four-category ranking—*elite, prestige, regional,* and *local*—evolved as a result. Although developing from two quite different traditions, they merged into one rank order.

The inappropriateness of such a ranking became very clear to us when we

1. See chapter 3, under the section on geographic considerations in law school selection, for a discussion of practicing lawyers in Chicago, Boston, and New York.

began to evaluate just what graduation from a law school in one category as opposed to another would mean to the graduate in terms of job options. The most curious examples came as we tried to justify classifying "local" Chicago law schools (Loyola, DePaul, Kent, John Marshall) while following the typical rule of categorizing the law school of any major state university as "regional." The implication that a law school graduate from, let us say, the University of Colorado would have a better chance in the job market we were investigating in Chicago than a graduate of Loyola University of Chicago simply made no sense. This might even be true for a graudate of the University of Texas, which according to the latest attempt to classify law schools, ranks tenth in faculty quality nationally ("The Cartter Report," 1977, p. 46).

In fact, we have found that much of the job market is localized, and that any distinction between "regional" and "local" has more to do with the availability of law schools in the general area and the extent of the geographical area from which the bulk of students are drawn than with job options. This is not to say that there are not well-recognized "national" law schools whose reputations are, as the classification implies, national in scope. Their students are drawn from a wider area and their graduates can more easily market their degrees throughout the country than those from schools that do not have national reputations. In this way the merging of the reputational and location criteria makes some limited sense. Still there remained the question of the basis on which to divide law schools according to such criteria.

Three well-known efforts have been made to rate law schools, and each has raised many questions and generated many criticisms. The earliest and most widely distributed rating was done by Blau and Margulies, first appearing in an article in 1973 and then in a replication published in 1974-75.[2] The reported top-ranked law schools were drawn from a survey of law school deans, who were asked to name the five "most distinguished law schools." The schools that were selected by at least 10 percent of the deans made the top list. Although nine schools met the requirement, the large gap between the votes received by the sixth and seventh schools (45 and 19, respectively) led to the decision to classify the top six as "elite."[3]

In an attempt to "objectify" law school ratings, Charles Kelso (1975) developed a rating on the basis of law school resources. While he stressed that "it is *not* a quality rating of the law schools" (emphasis his, p. 39), a rating of resources is implicitly worth doing precisely because of the built-in assumption that resources relate to quality.[4] The Kelso ratings are based on scores for num-

2. The top six law schools, in order of the number of times mentioned (from 101 to 45) in the Blau and Margulies survey as among the five most distinguished, were Harvard, Yale, Michigan, Columbia, Chicago, and Stanford.

3. This elite categorization has been relied on by other researchers. See, for example, Heinz et al. (1976, p. 726).

4. In order of their resource scores the schools are ranked as follows: Columbia, Northwestern, and Yale; Michigan and Pennsylvania; University of Washington; Berkeley and Chicago; Harvard, Illinois, Iowa, Minnesota, Ohio State, and Stanford (Kelso, 1975, pp. 41, 51). It is therefore necessary to proceed substantially down the list to include Blau and Margulies's elite schools. The limits of the relationship between resources and educational quality are not peculiar to law schools. Jencks (1972), for example, examined this same relationship for high schools and found it wanting.

High schools with ample resources have slightly fewer dropouts and send slightly more students to college than high schools with scanty resources. But this is because high schools with ample resources enroll students with slightly more successful parents, higher test scores, and higher ini-

bers of students, size of the faculty, and volumes in the library, and ratios among them. The question of whether more is better is not addressed, but schools with more of each get higher ratings.

The most recently published rating of law schools, "The Cartter Report" (1977), in part challenges the Blau-Margulies approach. In contrast to the Blau and Margulies study, this research, part of a study commissioned by the California Board of Regents, solicited the opinions of practicing scholars representing appropriate subfields and faculty ranks.[5] Nevertheless, despite a response rate of only 51.9 percent, it upholds many of the Blau and Margulies ratings.[6] Although "The Cartter Report" concludes that its findings are quite different from those of Blau and Margulies, we disagree. The differences cited in the report are based on the composite ranking of "faculty quality" and "educational attractiveness," the latter including "reputation and accessibility of faculty, curricula, innovative programs, library resources, other educational facilities, quality of students, prominence of the alumni, and other factors which contribute to an effective and professional environment" (p. 45). However, if we compare Blau and Margulies's results with only the ranking of "faculty quality," the findings are quite similar.[7] We think this comparison is justified, since Blau and Margulies's query about the "five most distinguished law schools" was likely to be interpreted by the responding deans as directly related to faculty quality.

The various limitations of attempts to rank law schools convinced us of the need to find a new measure. Since prestige is a matter of reputation, and since this study is based on the opinions of practicing lawyers, it was decided that it would be most appropriate to build a scale out of the opinions of the respondents. The final prestige ranking of law schools and how it was determined are described in the text in chapter 3.

---

tial aspirations than the average high school. If students are alike in these respects, they end up with the same amount of schooling, regardless of how much their high school spends (p. 149).

In the sample Jencks studied, teacher salaries and class size were not associated with college entrance rates once ninth graders' characteristics were taken into account.

5. For a more complete description of the research design, see "Methodological Note" ("The Cartter Report," 1977, p. 45).

6. The reported role of the dean of a major law school in leading a movement through the Association of American Law Schools (AALS) to discourage cooperation with the study is some testament to the strong negative feelings generated by law school ratings. ("The Cartter Report," 1977, p. 45).

7. The top schools cited in order of faculty quality are Harvard, Yale, Stanford (tied with) Michigan, Chicago, and Columbia ("The Cartter Report," 1977, p. 46).

REFERENCES

Allen, Francis A. "Resolving the Tension Between Professors and Practitioners." 2 *Learning and the Law* 50 (Winter 1976).

Annotated Code of Professional Responsibility. Chicago: American Bar Foundation, 1979.

Approval of Law Schools: American Bar Association Standards and Rules of Procedure, as amended 1977. By the American Bar Association Section of Legal Education and Admissions to the Bar. [Chicago:] American Bar Association, 1977.

Arthurs, H. W., J. Willms, and L. Taman. "The Toronto Legal Profession: An Exploratory Survey." 21 *University of Toronto Law Journal* 498 (1971).

Auerbach, Jerold S. *Unequal Justice: Lawyers and Social Change in Modern America.* New York: Oxford University Press, 1976.

Barber, Bernard. *Social Stratification: A Comparative Analysis of Structure and Process.* New York: Harcourt Brace, 1957.

Barnhizer, David R. "Clinical Education at the Crossroads: The Need for Direction." 1977 *Brigham Young University Law Review* 1025.

Becker, Howard S. "The Nature of a Profession." In *Education for the Professions: The Sixty-first Yearbook of the National Society for the Study of Education,* edited by Nelson B. Henry. Chicago: National Society for the Study of Education, 1962.

———, Blanche Beer, Everett C. Hughes, and Anselm L. Strauss. *Boys in White: Student Culture in Medical School.* Chicago: University of Chicago Press, 1961.

"Behaving Responsibly: What Does It Mean for a Lawyer?" A symposium in 2 *Learning and the Law* 41 (Spring 1975)

Bellow, Gary, and Bea Moulton. *The Lawyering Process: Materials for Clinical Instruction in Advocacy.* Mineola, N.Y.: Foundation Press, 1978.

Bendix, Reinhard, and Seymour Martin Lipset, eds. *Class, Status, and Power: Social Stratification in Comparative Perspective.* 2d ed. New York: Free Press, 1966.

Benthall-Nietzel, Deedra. "An Empirical Investigation of the Relationship Between Lawyering Skills and Legal Education." 63 *Kentucky Law Journal* 373 (1975).

Bingaman, Charles C. "Some Wise Words About Continuing Legal Education." 2 *Learning and the Law* 22 (Winter 1976).

Black, Donald J. "The Mobilization of Law." 2 *Journal of Legal Studies* 125 (1973).

Blau, Peter M., and Otis Dudley Duncan. *The American Occupational Structure.* New York: John Wiley & Sons, 1967.

Blau, Peter M., and Rebecca Zames Margulies. "The Pecking Order of the Elite: America's Leading Professional Schools." 5 *Change* 211 (Nov. 1973).

————— . "A Research Replication: The Reputations of American Professional Schools." 6 *Change* 42 (Winter 1974–75).

Boden, Robert F. "Is Legal Education Deserting the Bar?" 3 *John Marshall Journal of Practice and Procedure* 179 (1970).

Bok, Sissela. *Lying: Moral Choice in Public and Private Life.* New York: Random House, Pantheon Books, 1978.

Bonomi, John G. "The 'Clark Committee' on Evaluation of Disciplinary Enforcement." In *Education in the Professional Responsibilities of the Lawyer,* edited by Donald T. Weckstein. Charlottesville: University Press of Virginia, 1970.

Boyer, Barry B., and Roger C. Cramton. "American Legal Education: An Agenda for Research and Reform." 59 *Cornell Law Review* 221 (1974). Reprinted in *Research Contributions of the American Bar Foundation,* 1974, no. 1.

Brim, Orville, and Stanton Wheeler. *Socialization After Childhood: Two Essays.* New York: John Wiley & Sons, 1966.

Brown, Louis M., and Edward A. Dauer. *Planning by Lawyers: Materials on a Nonadversarial Legal Process.* Mineola, N.Y.: Foundation Press, 1978.

Buchwald, Art. "'The First Thing We Do, Let's Save the Bad Lawyers.'" *Washington Post,* February 21, 1978, p. B1.

Burger, Warren E. "The Special Skills of Advocacy: Are Specialized Training and Certification of Advocates Essential to Our System of Justice?" 42 *Fordham Law Review* 227 (1973).

Cahn, Edgar S., and Jean Camper Cahn. "Power to the People or the Profession?—the Public Interest in Public Interest Law." 79 *Yale Law Journal* 1005 (1970).

————— . "What Price Justice: The Civilian Perspective Revisited." 41 *Notre Dame Lawyer* 927 (1966).

Carlin, Jerome. *Current Research in the Sociology of the Legal Profession.* New York: Columbia University Bureau of Applied Social Research, August 1962. (a)

————— . *Lawyers' Ethics: A Survey of the New York City Bar.* New York: Russell Sage Foundation, 1966.

_____ . *Lawyers on Their Own: A Study of Individual Practitioners in Chicago.* New Brunswick, N.J.: Rutgers University Press, 1962. (b)

Carlson, Alfred B., and Charles E. Werts. *Relationships Among Law School Predictors, Law School Performance, and Bar Examination Results.* Princeton, N.J.: Educational Testing Service, September 1976.

"The Cartter Report on the Leading Schools of Education, Law, and Business." 9 *Change Magazine* 44 (February 1977).

Cavers, David F. "Legal Education in Forward-Looking Perspective." In *Law in a Changing America,* edited by Geoffrey C. Hazard, Jr. Englewood Cliffs, N.J.: Prentice-Hall, 1968.

Christensen, Barlow F. *Lawyers for People of Moderate Means: Some Problems of Availability of Legal Services.* Chicago: American Bar Foundation, 1970.

_____ . *Specialization.* Tentative Draft. Chicago: American Bar Foundation, 1967.

Chroust, Anton-Hermann. "The Legal Profession in Colonial America." 3 pts. 33 *Notre Dame Lawyer* 51 (1957), 350 (1958); 34 *Notre Dame Lawyer* 44 (1958).

Church, Virginia Anne. "Bridging the Academic Practitioner War over Legal Education: Some New Proposals for Competency Training as Alternative Education." Mimeographed. N.p.: 1975.

Clare, Robert L. "Minimum Qualifications for Admission to the Federal Second Circuit." 6 *ALI-ABA CLE Review,* March 21, 1975, p. 3.

Clare Committee report. See *Final Report on Proposed Rules for Admission to Practice* (1975).

Clark Report. See *Problems and Recommendations in Disciplinary Enforcement.*

Code of Professional Responsibility and Code of Judicial Conduct, as amended August 1978. By the American Bar Association Committee on Ethics and Professional Responsibility. [Chicago:] American Bar Association, 1978.

Cowger, Nancy. "Do Lawyers Really Need a Detailed Code of Ethics?" 64 *American Bar Association Journal* 522 (1978).

Cox, Michael P. "Part-Time Legal Education: The Kelso Report and More." 27 *Journal of Legal Education* 473 (1975).

Cramton, Roger C. "The Ordinary Religion of the Law School Classroom." 29 *Journal of Legal Education* 247 (1978).

Crock, Stan. "SEC Agrees to Settle a Landmark Case Involving National Student Marketing." *Wall Street Journal,* January 21, 1980, p. 10.

Curran, Barbara A. *The Legal Needs of the Public: The Final Report of a National Survey.* Chicago: American Bar Foundation, 1977.

Dahrendorf, Ralf. "On the Origin of Inequality Among Men." In *Essays in the Theory of Society.* Stanford, Cal.: Stanford University Press, 1968.

Davis, James A. *Great Aspirations: The Graduate School Plans of America's College Seniors.* Chicago: Aldine Publishing Co., 1964.

_____ . *Undergraduate Career Decisions: Correlates of Occupational Choice.* Chicago: Aldine Publishing Co., 1965.

DeCotiis, Thomas A., and Walter W. Steele, Jr. "The Skills of the Lawyering Process: A Critique Based on Observation." 40 *Texas Bar Foundation* 483 (1977).

Deitch, Lillian, and David Weinstein. *Prepaid Legal Sources: Socioeconomic Impacts.* Lexington, Mass.: D.C. Heath & Co., Lexington Books, 1976.

Devitt Committee report. See *Report and Tentative Recommendations of the Committee to Consider Standards for Admission to Practice in the Federal Courts to the Judicial Conference of the United States.*

Dickerson, David. "Graduation from Non-ABA Approved Law School. Its Effect on Ability to Practice Outside California." *Los Angeles Daily Journal,* April 23, 1976, p. 2.

"Dreaming the Impossible Dream." Editorial in *Wall Street Journal,* February 10, 1976.

Dunn, Richard E. "Legal Education and the Attitudes of Practicing Attorneys." 22 *Journal of Legal Education* 220 (1970).

Easton, David, and Jack Dennis with the assistance of Sylvia Easton. *Children in the Political System: Origins of Political Legitimacy.* New York: McGraw-Hill Book Co., 1969.

"Economics of Legal Services in Illinois—a 1975 Special Bar Survey." 64 *Illinois Bar Journal* 73 (October 1975).

Ehrlich, Thomas, and Geoffrey C. Hazard, Jr., eds. *Going to Law School? Readings on a Legal Career.* Boston: Little, Brown & Co., 1975.

Elkin, Frederick. *The Child and Society: The Process of Socialization.* New York: Random House, 1960.

Erlanger, Howard S. "The Allocation of Status Within Occupations: The Case of the Legal Profession." 58 *Social Forces* 882 (1980).

_____ . "Social Reform Organizations and Subsequent Careers of Participants: A Follow-Up Study of Early Participants in the OEO Legal Services Program." 42 *American Sociological Review* 233 (1977).

_____ , and Douglas A. Klegon. "Socialization Effects of Professional School: The Law School Experience and Student Orientations to Public Interest Concerns." 13 *Law and Society Review* 11 (1978). Reprinted as Research Contribution of the American Bar Foundation 1979, no. 2.

Federal Judicial Center study. See Partridge and Bermant (1978).

"Final Report of the Tuskegee Syphilis Study Ad Hoc Advisory Panel." N.p.: U.S. Department of Health, Education, and Welfare, Public Health Service, April 28, 1973.

Final Report on Proposed Rules for Admission to Practice. By the Advisory Committee to the Judicial Council on Qualifications to Practice Before the United States Courts in the Second Circuit. New York: n.p., March 1975. [Clare Committee report.] Reprinted without appendixes as "Final Report of the Advisory Committee on Proposed Rules for Admission to Practice," in 67 Federal Rules Decisions 161. St. Paul, Minn.: West Publishing Co., 1976.

Fiske, Edward B. "Ethics Courses Now Attracting More U.S. College Students." *New York Times,* February 20, 1978, pp. 1A and B8.

Fossum, Donna. "Law School Accreditation Standards and the Structure of American Legal Education." 1978 *American Bar Foundation Research Journal* 515.

Frank, Jerome. *Courts on Trial: Myth and Reality in American Justice.* Princeton, N.J.: Princeton University Press, 1950.

_____ . "A Plea for Lawyer-Schools." 56 *Yale Law Journal* 1303 (1947).

_____ . "Why Not a Clinical Lawyer School?" 81 *University of Pennsylvania Law Review* 907 (1933).

Freedman, Monroe H. "Professional Responsibility of the Civil Practitioner: Teaching Legal Ethics in the Contracts Course." In *Education in the Professional Responsibilities of the Lawyer,* edited by Donald T. Weckstein. Charlottesville: University Press of Virginia, 1970.

Freund, Paul A. On Understanding the Supreme Court. Boston: Little, Brown & Co., 1949.

Friedman, Lawrence M. *A History of American Law.* New York: Simon & Schuster, 1973.

_____ . *Law and Society: An Introduction.* Englewood Cliffs, N.J.: Prentice-Hall, 1977.

Fromson, David. "Let's Be Realistic About Specialization." 63 *American Bar Association Journal* 74 (1977).

Fuller, Lon L. *The Morality of Law.* Rev. ed. New Haven, Conn.: Yale University Press, 1969.

Gee, E. Gordon, and Donald W. Jackson. "Bridging the Gap: Legal Education and Lawyer Competency." 1977 *Brigham Young University Law Review* 695.

Goldberg, Stuart C. "National Survey on Current Methods of Teaching Professional Responsibility in American Law Schools." In *Pre-Conference Materials 1977 National Conference on Teaching Professional Responsibility,* edited by Patrick A. Kennan. Detroit: University of Detroit Press, 1979.

Green, Wayne E. "Lawyers' Competence at Courtroom Work Stirs Growing Debate." *Wall Street Journal,* February 24, 1975, p. 1.

Greenwood, Glenn, and Robert F. Frederickson. *Specialization in the Medical and Legal Professions.* Mundelein, Ill.: Callaghan & Co., 1964.

Grossman, George S. "Clinical Legal Education: History and Diagnosis." 26 *Journal of Legal Education* 162 (1974).

Hall, Richard H. *Occupations and the Social Structure.* Englewood Cliffs, N.J.: Prentice-Hall, 1969.

Handler, Joel F. *The Lawyer and His Community: The Practicing Bar in a Middle-Sized City.* Madison: University of Wisconsin Press, 1967.

_____ , Ellen Jane Hollingsworth, and Howard S. Erlanger. *Lawyers and the Pursuit of Legal Rights.* New York: Academic Press, 1978.

Harno, Albert J. *Legal Education in the United States.* San Francisco: Bancroft-Whitney Co., 1953.

Harris, Louis. "Confidence in America Is Rising." Survey in *Chicago Tribune,* January 5, 1978, sec. 3, p. 4.

Hedegard, James M. "The Impact of Legal Education: An In-Depth Examination of Career-relevant Interests, Attitudes, and Personality Traits Among First-Year Law Students." 1979 *American Bar Foundation Research Journal* 791.

Heinz, John P., Edward O. Laumann, Charles L. Cappell, Terence C. Halliday, and Michael H. Schaalman. "Diversity, Representation, and Leadership in an Urban Bar: A First Report on a Survey of the Chicago Bar." 1976 *American Bar Foundation Research Journal* 717.

Hochberg, Jerome A. "The Drive to Specialization." In *Verdicts on Lawyers,* edited by Ralph Nader and Mark Green. New York: Thomas Y. Crowell, 1976.

Hodge, Robert W., Paul M. Siegel, and Peter H. Rossi. "Occupational Prestige in the United States: 1925–1963." In *Class, Status, and Power: Social Stratification in Comparative Perspective,* edited by Reinhard Bendix and Seymour Martin Lipset. 2d ed. New York: Free Press, 1966.

Hughes, Everett C., Barrie Thorne, Agostino M. DeBaggis, Arnold Gurin, and David Williams. *Education for the Professions of Medicine, Law, Theology and Social Welfare.* A Report Prepared for the Carnegie Commission on Higher Education. New York: McGraw Hill Book Co., 1973.

‗‗‗‗‗‗ . *Men and Their Work.* Glencoe, Ill.: Free Press, 1958.

Hurst, James Willard. *The Growth of American Law: The Law Makers.* Boston: Little, Brown & Co., 1950.

International Encyclopedia of the Social Sciences, edited by David L. Sills. New York: Crowell Collier and MacMillan, Inc., 1968. Essay on "Socialization" in vol. 14.

Jacob, Herbert. *Justice in America: Courts, Lawyers, and the Judicial Process.* 2d ed. Boston: Little, Brown & Co., 1978.

Jencks, Christopher. *Inequality: A Reassessment of the Effect of Family and Schooling in America.* New York: Basic Books, 1972.

Jennings, M. Kent, and Richard G. Niemi, "Patterns of Political Learning." 38 *Harvard Educational Review* 443 (1968).

‗‗‗‗‗‗ . *The Political Character of Adolescence: The Influence of Families and Schools.* Princeton N.J.: Princeton University Press, 1974.

Johnstone, Quintin, and Dan Hopson, Jr. *Lawyers and Their Work: An Analysis of the Legal Profession in the United States and England.* Indianapolis: Bobbs-Merrill Co., 1967.

"Judicial Conference Joins Push for Trial Skills Training." 65 *American Bar Association Journal* 1466 (1979).

Katz, Alan N., and Mark P. Denbeaux. "Trust, Cynicism, and Machiavellianism Among First-Year Law Students." 53 *Journal of Urban Law* 397 (1976).

Kaufman, Andrew L. *Problems in Professional Responsibility.* Boston: Little, Brown & Co., 1976.

Kay, Susan Ann. "Socializing the Future Elite: The Nonimpact of a Law School." 59 *Social Science Quarterly* 347 (1978).

Kelso, Charles D. "The AALS Study of Part-Time Legal Education: Final Report." In *Association of American Law Schools 1972 Annual Meeting Proceedings,* pt. 1, sec. II. Washington, D.C.: Association of American Law Schools, 1972.

_____ . "Adding Up the Law Schools: A Tabulation and Rating of Their Resources." 2 *Learning and the Law* 38 (Summer 1975).

Kennedy, Duncan. "How the Law School Fails: A Polemic." 1 *Yale Review of Law and Social Action* 71 (no. 1, 1970).

Kilmer, James. "The Fifth Annual Salary Survey." 8 *Student Lawyer* 21 (November 1979).

Kimball, Spencer L. *Historical Introduction to the Legal System: Cases and Materials.* Ann Arbor, Mich.: Overbeck Co., 1961.

Kitch, Edmund W., ed. *Clinical Education and the Law School of the Future: Law Students in Court.* University of Chicago Law School Conference Series, no. 20. Resource papers of the conference held October 31 and November 1, 1969. Chicago: University of Chicago Law School, 1970.

Klein, Fannie J., Steven H. Leleiko, and Jane H. Mavity, comps. *Bar Admission Rules and Student Practice Rules: A Report.* Report prepared for the Council on Legal Education for Professional Responsibility, Inc., by the Institute of Judicial Administration. Cambridge, Mass.: Ballinger Publishing Co., 1978.

Ladinsky, Jack. "Careers of Lawyers, Law Practice, and Legal Institutions." 28 *American Sociological Review* 47 (1963). (a)

_____ . "The Impact of Social Backgrounds of Lawyers on Law Practice and the Law." 16 *Journal of Legal Education* 127 (1963). (b)

Lasswell, Harold D., and Myres S. McDougal. "Legal Education and Public Policy: Professional Training in the Public Interest." 52 *Yale Law Journal* 203 (1943).

Laumann, Edward O., and John P. Heinz. "Specialization and Prestige in the Legal Profession: The Structure of Deference." 1977 *American Bar Foundation Research Journal* 155.

Lawyer Competency: The Role of the Law Schools. Report and Recommendations of the Task Force on Lawyer Competency. [American Bar Association Section of Legal Education and Admissions to the Bar, June 1979.] Chicago: American Bar Association, 1979.

Lawyer Statistical Reports. See *The 1971 Lawyer Statistical Report.*

Lempert, Richard O. "Mobilizing Private Law: An Introductory Essay." 11 *Law and Society Review* 173 (1976).

_____ , and Stephen A. Saltzburg. *A Modern Approach to Evidence: Text, Problems, Transcripts, and Cases.* St. Paul, Minn.: West Publishing Co., 1977.

Levin, A. Leo. "The Lawyer's Professional Responsibilities in Trial Advocacy and Civil Procedure." In *Education in the Professional Responsibilities of the Lawyer,* edited by Donald T. Weckstein. Charlottesville: University Press of Virginia, 1970.

Levine, Felice J., Howard S. Erlanger, and Kenneth H. Barry. *Socialization into the Legal Profession: A Comparative Study.* (In preparation.)

Lieberman, Jethro K. *Crisis at the Bar: Lawyer's Unethical Ethics and What to Do About It.* New York: Norton, 1978. (a)

_____ . "How High Is Your Calling?" 8 *Juris Doctor* 32 (April 1978). (b)

"Limits of Scientific Inquiry." Spring issue of 107 *Daedalus* (1978).

Llewellyn, Karl. "The Bar Specializes—with What Results?" 169 *Annals of the American Academy of Political and Social Science* 177 (1933).

_____. "On What Is Wrong with So-called Legal Education." 35 *Columbia Law Review* 651 (1935).

Lortie, Dan C. "Laymen to Lawmen: Law School, Careers, and Professional Socialization." 29 *Harvard Educational Review* 352 (1959).

Maddi, Dorothy Linder. "Trial Advocacy Competence: The Judicial Perspective." 1978 *American Bar Foundation Research Journal* 105.

Martindale-Hubbell Law Directory. Summit, N.J.: Martindale-Hubbell, published annually.

Maru, Olavi, comp. *Parallel Tables Between the ABA Canons of Professional Ethics and the ABA Code of Professional Responsibility.* Chicago: American Bar Foundation, 1970.

_____. *Research on the Legal Profession: A Review of Work Done.* Chicago: American Bar Foundation, 1972.

Mayer, Martin. *The Lawyers.* New York: Harper & Row, 1967.

McKay, Robert B. "Legal Education and Legal Services." In *Perspectives on Legal Education,* edited by Norman Redlich. Papers Prepared for the Council on Legal Education for Professional Responsibility. Working draft. October 10, 1979.

Miller, Delbert C., and William H. Form. *Industrial Sociology: An Introduction to the Sociology of Work Relations.* New York: Harper & Bros., 1951.

Miller, Perry, ed. *The Legal Mind in America from Independence to the Civil War.* Ithaca, N.Y.: Cornell University Press, 1962.

Model Rules of Professional Conduct. A Discussion Draft. By the American Bar Association Commission on Evaluation of Professional Standards. [Chicago:] American Bar Association, January 30, 1980.

Morgan, Thomas D. "The Evolving Concept of Professional Responsibility." 90 *Harvard Law Review* 702 (1977).

_____, and Ronald D. Rotunda. *Problems and Materials on Professional Responsibility.* Mineola, N.Y.: Foundation Press, 1976.

Morison, Robert S. "Introduction" to spring issue "Limits of Scientific Inquiry." 107 *Daedalus* vii (1978).

Nader, Ralph. "Law Schools and Law Firms." 54 *Minnesota Law Review* 493 (1970). Also in 3 *Beverly Hills Bar Journal* 8 (December 1969), and *New Republic,* October 11, 1969, p. 20 (under title of "Crumbling of the Old Order: Law Schools and Law Firms").

Nash, Gary B. "The Philadelphia Bench and Bar, 1800–1861." 7 *Comparative Studies in Society and History* 203 (1965).

Nash, Gerard. "Clinical Education in Australia—the Monash Experience." 12 *Council on Legal Education for Professional Responsibility, Inc.* [newsletter] (October 1979).

"Nationally Recognized Accrediting Agencies and Associations." U.S. Department of Health, Education, and Welfare, Office of Education, 1976.

The 1971 Lawyer Statistical Report. Edited by Bette H. Sikes, Clara N. Carson, and Patricia Gorai. Most recent in series published irregularly by the American Bar Foundation. Chicago: American Bar Foundation, 1972.

Occupational Profile of State Legislatures. New York: Insurance Information Institute, 1979.

Oldham, James C. "Contracts, Capability, and the Classroom." 77 *Michigan Law Review* 949 (1978–79).

Packer, Herbert L., and Thomas Ehrlich with the assistance of Stephen Pepper. *New Directions in Legal Education.* A Report Prepared for the Carnegie Commission on Higher Education. New York: McGraw-Hill Book Co., 1972.

Partridge, Anthony, and Gordon Bermant. *The Quality of Advocacy in the Federal Courts: A Report to the Committee of the Judicial Conference of the United States to Consider Standards for Admission to Practice in the Federal Courts.* [Commissioned by the Devitt Committee.] Washington, D.C.: Federal Judicial Center, August 1978.

Pashigian, B. Peter. "The Market for Lawyers: The Determinants of the Demand for and Supply of Lawyers." 20 *Journal of Law and Economics* 53 (1977).

Pavalko, Ronald M. *Sociology of Occupations and Professions.* Itasca, Ill.: F. E. Peacock Publishers, 1971.

Pipkin, Ronald M. "Law School Instruction in Professional Responsibility: A Curricular Paradox." 1979 *American Bar Foundation Research Journal* 247.

_____ . *Student Responses to Law School Curricula.* Paper presented to the Section on Legal Education and Admissions to the Bar at the Annual Meeting of the American Bar Association, Chicago, 1977.

Pound, Roscoe. *The Lawyer from Antiquity to Modern Times with Particular Reference to the Development of Bar Associations in the United States.* St. Paul, Minn.: West Publishing Co., 1953.

Problems and Recommendations in Disciplinary Enforcement. By the American Bar Association Special Committee on Evaluation of Disciplinary Enforcement. Final Draft, June 1970. [Clark Report.] Chicago: American Bar Foundation, 1970.

Professional Responsibility and the Lawyer: Avoiding Unintentional Grievances. By the American Bar Association Standing Committee on Professional Discipline and the Center for Professional Discipline. Chicago: ABA, 1975.

Quarantelli, Enrico L., Margaret Helfrich, and Daniel Yutsy. "Faculty and Student Perceptions in a Professional School." 49 *Sociology and Social Research* 32 (1964).

Rathjen, Gregory J. "The Impact of Legal Education on the Beliefs, Attitudes and Values of Law Students." 44 *Tennessee Law Review* 85 (1976).

Redlich, Norman. *Professional Responsibility: A Problem Approach.* Boston: Little, Brown & Co., 1976.

_____ . "Professional Responsibility of Law Teachers." In *Perspectives on Legal Education,* edited by Norman Redlich. Papers Prepared for the Council on Legal Education for Professional Responsibility. Working draft. October 10, 1979.

Reed, Alfred Z. *Training for the Public Profession of the Law.* New York: Charles Scribner's Sons, 1921.

Reisman, David, Jr. "Law and Social Science: A Report on Michael and Wechsler's Classbook on Criminal Law and Administration." 50 *Yale Law Journal* 636 (1941).

Reiss, Albert J., Jr., with Otis Dudley Duncan, Paul K. Hatt, and Cecil C. North. *Occupations and Social Status.* New York: Free Press of Glencoe, 1961.

Report and Tentative Recommendations of the Committee to Consider Standards for Admission to Practice in the Federal Courts to the Judicial Conference of the United States. Washington, D.C.: Judicial Conference of the United States, September 21, 22, 1978. [Devitt Committee report.] Reprinted as "Final Report of the Committee to Consider Standards for Admission to Practice in the Federal Courts to the Judicial Conference of the United States, September 19, 20, 1979," in 83 *Federal Rules Decisions* 215. St. Paul, Minn.: West Publishing Co., 1980.

"Report of the Special Committee to the Section of Legal Education and Admissions to the Bar of the American Bar Association." In 46 *Reports of American Bar Association* 679 (1921).

Review of Legal Education: Law Schools and Bar Admission Requirements in the United States. Chicago: American Bar Association Section of Legal Education and Admissions to the Bar, 1958, 1961, 1966, 1969, 1976.

Rosenthal, Douglas E. *Lawyer and Client: Who's in Charge?* New York: Russell Sage Foundation, 1974.

Rueschemeyer, Dietrich. *Lawyers and Their Society: A Comparative Study of the Legal Profession in Germany and in the United States.* Cambridge, Mass.: Harvard University Press, 1973.

St. Antoine, Theodore J. "Behaving Responsibly: The Role of the Law School." 2 *Learning and the Law* 50 (Spring 1975).

Savoy, Paul N. "Toward a New Politics of Legal Education." 79 *Yale Law Journal* 444 (1970).

Scheingold, Stuart A. *The Politics of Rights: Lawyers, Public Policy, and Political Change.* New Haven, Conn.: Yale University Press, 1974.

Schlesinger, Joseph A. "Lawyers and American Politics: A Clarified View." 1 *Midwest Journal of Political Science* 26 (1957).

Schnapper, Eric. "The Myth of Legal Ethics." 64 *American Bar Association Journal* 202 (1978).

Schudson, Michael. "Public, Private, and Professional Lives: The Correspondence of David Dudley Field and Samuel Bowles." 21 *American Journal of Legal History* 191 (1977).

Schultz, James M. Law Schools and the Differentiation of Recruits to Firm, Solo, and Government and Business Careers. Ph.D. dissertation, University of Chicago, 1969.

Schwartz, Murray L. "Law Schools and Ethics." *Chronicle of Higher Education,* December 9, 1974, p. 20.

Schwartz, Robert A. D. "The Relative Importance of Skills Used by Attorneys." 3 *Golden Gate Law Review* 321 (1973).

Securities and Exchange Commission v. National Student Marketing Corpora-

tion. 1977–78 [Transfer Binder] *Federal Securities Law Reports* (CCH) ¶ 96,027 (D.D.C. 1977); 457 *Federal Supplement* 682 (D.D.C. 1978).

Siegel, Paul M. Prestige in the American Occupational Structure. Ph.D. dissertation, University of Chicago, 1971.

Simon, Rita J., Frank Koziol, and Nancy Joslyn. "Have There Been Significant Changes in Career Aspirations and Occupational Choices of Law School Graduates in the 1960's?" 8 *Law and Society Review* 95 (1973).

Sims, Joe. "The Future of Self-Regulation in the Legal Profession." Remarks before the American Bar Association National Workshop on Disciplinary Law and Procedure, Chicago, Illinois, June 2, 1978.

Slonim, Scott. "Bar Exam Experiment Could Blaze New Path." 66 *American Bar Association Journal* 139 (1980).

Smigel, Erwin O. *The Wall Street Lawyer: Professional Organization Man?* (New York: Free Press of Glencoe, 1964).

Smith, Peter S. "Developments in Clinical Legal Education in England." 11 *Council on Legal Education for Professional Responsibility, Inc.* [newsletter] (June 1979).

Somers, Robert H. "A New Asymmetric Measure of Association for Ordinal Variables." 27 *American Sociological Review* 799 (1962).

Sovern, Michael. "The 4th Revolution in Legal Education." 1 *Learning and the Law* 26 (Winter 1975).

Steele, Eric H., and Raymond T. Nimmer. "Lawyers, Clients, and Professional Regulation." 1976 *American Bar Foundation Research Journal* 919.

Stern, Bernard. "Retrospection: What Recent Law School Graduates Think of Their Education: The University of Toledo Experience." 17 *Student Lawyer* 27 (June 1972).

Stevens, Robert. "Law Schools and Law Students." 59 *Virginia Law Review* 551 (1973).

Stewart, Russell. *Curriculum Development for the Practical Legal Training Course.* St. Leonards, Australia: The College of Law, 1979.

Stone, Alan A. "Legal Education on the Couch." 85 *Harvard Law Review* 392 (1971).

Sullivan's Law Directory for the State of Illinois. Chicago: Chicago Title and Trust Co., published annually.

"The Super-Billers." *Newsweek,* October 9, 1978, p. 96.

Survey and Directory of Clinical Legal Education 1978–1979. New York: Council on Legal Education for Professional Responsibility, Inc., 1979.

Tapp, June Louin, and Felice J. Levine. "Legal Socialization: Strategies for an Ethical Legality." 27 *Stanford Law Review* 1 (1974).

Thielens, Wagner P., Jr. "The Influence of the Law School Experience on the Professional Ethics of Law Students." 21 *Journal of Legal Education* 587 (1969).

———. The Socialization of Law Students. Ph.D. dissertation, Columbia University, 1965.

_____ . "Some Comparisons of Entrants to Medical and Law School." In *The Student-Physician: Introductory Studies in the Sociology of Medical Education*, edited by Robert K. Merton, George G. Reader, and Patricia L. Kendall. Cambridge, Mass.: Harvard University Press, 1957. Reprinted in substantially the same form in 11 *Journal of Legal Education* 153 (1958).

Thorne, Barrie. "Professional Education in Law." In *Education for the Professions of Medicine, Law, Theology, and Social Welfare*. A Report Prepared for the Carnegie Commission on Higher Education. New York: McGraw-Hill Book Co., 1973.

Tocqueville, Alexis de. *Democracy in America*. The Henry Reeve Text as revised by Francis Bowen, further corrected and edited by Phillips Bradley. 2 vols. New York: Alfred A. Knopf, 1963.

Twiss, Benjamin R. *Lawyers and the Constitution: How Laissez Faire Came to the Supreme Court*. Princeton, N.J.: Princeton University Press, 1942.

Vose, Clement E. "Litigation as a Form of Pressure Group Activity." 319 *Annals of the American Academy of Political and Social Science* 20 (September 1958).

Vukowich, William T. "The Lack of Practical Training in Law Schools: Criticisms, Causes and Programs for Change." 23 *Case Western Reserve Law Review* 140 (1971).

Warkov, Seymour. "Allocation to American Law Schools." 73 *School Review* 144 (1965).

_____ , and Joseph Zelan. *Lawyers in the Making*. Chicago: Aldine Publishing Co., 1965.

_____ . *Lawyers in the Making: The 1961 Entrants to American Law Schools*. Report no. 96, December 1963. Chicago: National Opinion Research Center, 1963.

Warren, Charles. *A History of the American Bar*. New York: Howard Fertig, Inc., Edition, [1911, 1939] 1966.

Wasserstein, Bruce, and Mark J. Green, eds. *With Justice for Some: An Indictment of the Law by Young Advocates*. Boston: Beacon Press, 1970.

Wasserstrom, Richard. "Lawyers as Professionals: Some Moral Issues." 5 *Human Rights* 1 (1975).

Watson, Andrew S. "Some Psychological Aspects of Teaching Professional Responsibility." 16 *Journal of Legal Education* 1 (1963).

Weckstein, Donald T., ed. *Education in the Professional Responsibilities of the Lawyer*. Proceedings of the National Conference on Education in the Professional Responsibilities of the Lawyer, University of Colorado, Boulder, June 10–13, 1968. Charlottesville: University Press of Virginia, 1970.

White, James P. "Law School Enrollment Up Slightly but Leveling." 65 *American Bar Association Journal* 577 (1979).

Wilson, John P. "Profile of the Alumni." 19 *Harvard Law School Bulletin* 5 (May 1968).

York, John C., and Rosemary D. Hale. "Too Many Lawyers? The Legal Services Industry: Its Structure and Outlook." 26 *Journal of Legal Education* 1 (1973). Reprinted in *Going to Law School? Readings on a Legal Career,* edited by Thomas Ehrlich and Geoffrey C. Hazard, Jr. Boston: Little, Brown & Co., 1975.

Zehnle, Richard. *Specialization in the Legal Profession: An Analysis of Current Proposals.* Chicago: American Bar Foundation, 1975.

Zelan, Joseph. "Social Origins and the Recruitment of American Lawyers." 18 *British Journal of Sociology* 45 (1967).